THE ROYAL HORTICULTURAL SOCIETY

PLANT ❧ GUIDES

ROCK
PLANTS

THE ROYAL HORTICULTURAL SOCIETY

PLANT ❧ GUIDES

ROCK
PLANTS

DORLING KINDERSLEY
www.dk.com

A DORLING KINDERSLEY BOOK
www.dk.com

Produced for Dorling Kindersley by PAGE*One*
Cairn House, Elgiva Lane, Chesham,
Buckinghamshire HP5 2JD

PROJECT DIRECTORS Bob Gordon and Helen Parker
EDITOR Charlotte Stock
DESIGNER Matthew Cook

MANAGING EDITOR Francis Ritter
MANAGING ART EDITOR Derek Coombes
PRODUCTION Martin Croshaw
PICTURE RESEARCH Joanne Beardwell

First published in Great Britain in 1997
by Dorling Kindersley Limited
9 Henrietta Street, London WC2E 8PS

2 4 6 8 10 9 7 5 3

A CIP catalogue record for this book
is available from the British Library

ISBN 0-7513-0306-2

Colour reproduction by Colourscan, Singapore
Printed and bound by Star Standard Industries, Singapore

CONTENTS

LARGE

SMALL

CONTRIBUTORS

CHRISTOPHER GREY-WILSON
Consultant

LINDEN HAWTHORNE
Writer

HOW TO USE THIS BOOK

THIS BOOK PROVIDES the ideal quick reference guide to selecting and identifying rock plants for the garden.

The ROCK PLANTS IN THE GARDEN section is a helpful introduction to rock plants and gives advice on choosing a suitable plant for a particular site or purpose, such as for a border, container, or simply as a specimen.

To choose or identify a rock plant, turn to the CATALOGUE OF ROCK PLANTS, where photographs are accompanied by concise plant descriptions and useful tips on cultivation and propagation. The entries are grouped by size, season of interest, as well as by colour (see the colour wheel below) to make selection easier.

For additional information on rock plant cultivation, routine care, and propagation, turn to the GUIDE TO ROCK PLANT CARE, where general advice on all aspects of caring for your rock plants can be found.

At the end of the book is a useful two-page glossary, which explains key terms. An index of every rock plant, its synonyms, and common names, together with a brief genus description, allows quick and easy access to the book by plant name.

The colour wheel

All the rock plants in the book are grouped according to the colour of their main feature of interest. They are always arranged in the same order, indicated by the colour wheel below. Variegated plants are categorized by the colour of their variegation.

THE SYMBOLS

The symbols below are used throughout the CATALOGUE OF ROCK PLANTS to indicate a plant's preferred growing conditions and hardiness. However, both the climate and soil conditions of your particular site should also be taken into account, as they may affect a plant's growth.

☼ Prefers full sun   ◊ Prefers well-drained soil

☀ Prefers partial shade   ◖ Prefers moist soil

☀ Tolerates full shade   ◕ Prefers wet soil

pH Needs acid soil

❋   Half-hardy – can withstand temperatures down to 0°C (32°F)

❋ ❋   Frost hardy – can withstand temperatures down to -5°C (23°F)

❋ ❋ ❋ Fully hardy – can withstand temperatures down to -15°C (5°F)

🏆   RHS Award of Garden Merit. The symbol indicates those rock plants deemed by the Royal Horticultural Society to be of exceptional quality and reliability. They must be of good constitution and not susceptible to any pest or disease, as well as not requiring any highly specialized care.

Rock plant size categories

The rock plants featured in the CATALOGUE OF ROCK PLANTS are divided according to the average height they attain. However, heights may vary from the ones given, according to site, growing conditions, climate, and age.

The categories are as follows:

LARGE
Over 15cm (6in)

SMALL
Up to 15cm (6in)

HOW TO USE THE CATALOGUE OF ROCK PLANTS

HEADINGS
Each chapter is subdivided into sections, according to the average size of the plants and their main season of interest.

The plant's *family name* appears here.

The plant's *common name(s)* appear here.

The plant's *botanical name* appears here.

PLANT PORTRAITS
The colour photographs show each plant's main features and colour (see the colour wheel on previous page).

ENTRIES
A brief plant description giving details of growing habit, flowers, fruits, and leaves, followed by information on native habitat, tips on cultivation and propagation, and a list of other botanical names.

FEATURE PAGES
Plant groups or genera of special interest to the gardener are presented on separate feature pages. A brief introduction giving general information on appearance, use, cultivation, and propagation, is followed by concise plant entries.

---

72 • SMALL/Spring

Ranunculaceae	RUE ANEMONE

ANEMONELLA THALICTROIDES
Habit Clump-forming, tuberous, herbaceous, perennial. **Flowers** Cup-shaped, to 2cm (¾in) across, borne in sprays of 2–4, from spring to early summer. White or pale pink. **Leaves** Finely divided, delicate, and fern-like. Dark bluish-green.
• NATIVE HABITAT Woodland, eastern N. America.
• CULTIVATION Grow as a pot plant in an alpine house. Outdoors, prefers moist but well-drained, fertile soil. The tubers will rot in over-wet soils.
• PROPAGATION Sow seed as soon as ripe in a cold frame, or divide young plants in early spring.

HEIGHT
10cm (4in)

SPREAD
30cm (12in)

Portulacaceae	

LEWISIA TWEEDYI
Habit Rosette-forming, evergreen, perennial. **Flowers** Open funnel-shaped, to 6cm (2½in) across, borne singly or in clusters of up to 4, from spring to early summer. White to pink, or apricot. **Leaves** Lance-shaped to oval, fleshy. Mid-green.
• NATIVE HABITAT Rock crevices. northwest USA.
• CULTIVATION Grows best as a pot plant in an alpine house. Needs neutral to acid soil that is rich in organic matter, and a dry summer dormancy.
• PROPAGATION By seed in autumn, or by offsets in early summer.

HEIGHT
20cm (8in)

SPREAD
30cm (12in)

Diapensiaceae	

SHORTIA UNIFLORA 'Grandiflora'
Habit Vigorous, mat-forming, evergreen, perennial. **Flowers** Solitary, half-nodding flared bells to 5cm (2in) across, with toothed petals, borne in spring. White or pale pink. **Leaves** Leathery, rounded, toothed, heart-shaped base. Deep green.
• NATIVE HABITAT Woodlands, Japan.
• CULTIVATION Suits a rock garden, peat bed, or open woodland glades, with leaf-rich, moist, well-drained soil. Dislikes dry climates and bright sun.
• PROPAGATION By seed as soon as ripe in a cold frame. Separate rooted runners carefully in spring.

HEIGHT
15cm (6in)

SPREAD
25cm (10in)

Liliaceae/Trilliaceae	

TRILLIUM RIVALE
Habit Compact, erect, rhizomatous, herbaceous, perennial. **Flowers** Semi-upright, to 2.5cm (1in) across, borne in spring. White or pale pink, with purple-spotted base and green sepals. **Leaves** Oval and pointed, borne in threes. Mid blue-green.
• NATIVE HABITAT Mountain woods, western USA.
• CULTIVATION Grows best in pockets in a peat garden. Needs moist but well-drained, neutral to slightly alkaline soil, enriched with organic matter.
• PROPAGATION By ripe seed but it may take 5–7 years to flower. Divide large, established clumps.

HEIGHT
12cm (5in)

SPREAD
15cm (6in)

---

134 • ANEMONE

ANEMONE

The genus *Anemone* comprises about 120 species of perennials, most of which suit growing in flower borders. For ease of reference, their cultivation requirements may be grouped as follows.
Group 1 Moist but well-drained soil, enriched with organic matter, in partial shade. Tolerate drier conditions when dormant in summer.

Group 2 Well-drained soil that is enriched with organic matter, in sun or partial shade.
Group 3 Light, sandy soil in full sun. Sow seed of species when fresh in containers in a cold frame. Divide rhizomatous species in spring or after the leaves have faded. Separate tubers when dormant in summer.

A. NEMOROSA 'Bracteata Pleniflora'
Habit Rhizomatous, patch-forming, herbaceous, perennial. **Flowers** Star-shaped, semi-double, borne in late spring. White, often with a green ruff. **Leaves** Deeply divided. Mid-green.
• CULTIVATION 1 or 2.
• HEIGHT 12cm (5in).
• SPREAD 30cm (12in).

A. nemorosa 'Bracteata Pleniflora'

A. BLANDA 'White Splendour'
Habit Tuberous, herbaceous, perennial. **Flowers** Solitary, star-shaped, 5cm (2in) across, borne during spring. White, with a pink tint on the outside. **Leaves** Deeply divided. Dark green.
• CULTIVATION 1 or 2.
• HEIGHT 15cm (6in).
• SPREAD 15cm (6in).

A. blanda 'White Splendour'

A. MULTIFIDA
Habit Vigorous, clump-forming, semi-evergreen, perennial. **Flowers** Cupped, 2.5cm (1in) wide, borne in spires of 2–3 in summer. Creamy-yellow. **Leaves** Rounded, lobed. Shiny, deep green.
• OTHER NAMES *A. globosa, A. magellanica.*
• HEIGHT 30cm (12in).
• SPREAD 15cm (6in).

A. multifida

A. LIPSIENSIS
Habit Rhizomatous, herbaceous, perennial. **Flowers** Solitary, flat, to 2cm (¾in) across, borne in spring. Soft yellow. **Leaves** Rounded and deeply lobed. Mid-green.
• OTHER NAMES *A. x seemannii.*
• HEIGHT 5–15cm (2–6in).
• SPREAD to 45cm (18in).

A. x lipsiensis

A. BLANDA 'Radar'
Habit Tuberous, herbaceous, perennial. **Flowers** Solitary, flattened star-shaped, 4cm (1½in) across, borne in spring. Rich magenta, with white centre. **Leaves** Deeply divided. Dark green.
• CULTIVATION 1 or 2.
• HEIGHT 15cm (6in).
• SPREAD 15cm (6in).

A. blanda 'Radar'

A. HORTENSIS
Habit Tuberous, herbaceous, perennial. **Flowers** Solitary, single, 3.5–4.5cm across, borne in spring. Deep rosey-pink, with paler underside. **Leaves** Deeply divided. Mid-green.
• HEIGHT to 30cm (12in).
• SPREAD 12–15cm (5–6in).

A. hortensis

SYMBOLS
The symbols indicate the sun, soil, and temperature requirements (see THE SYMBOLS on previous page). Minimum temperatures are given for plants that cannot survive below 0°C (32°F).

FEATURE PLANT DESCRIPTIONS
As with the main Catalogue entries, a brief plant description is followed by useful tips on cultivation and propagation where these are not already given in the general introduction.

SIZES
The average height and spread of the plants are given, although these may vary according to site, growing conditions, climate, and age.

ROCK PLANTS IN THE GARDEN

THE diverse habitats of the world's mountain ranges are home to some of the most attractive plants ever introduced to gardens. True alpines occur at high altitudes above the tree-line, often in specialized habitats, such as rockface crevices, scree slopes, or in sparse, high-alpine turf. They make characteristic adaptations to survive the extremes of climate at high altitudes. A low, creeping habit reduces wind resistance and helps alpines to resist the crushing weight of snow in winter.

A well-constructed rock garden
On a sloping site, a construction that mimics natural rock strata provides perfect drainage and diverse planting niches, from vertical rock crevices to broader terrace.

An extensive root system provides strong anchorage, while searching deeply for water and nutrients in the often poor, sharply drained alpine soils. A reduced leaf size, fleshy leaves, or leathery or hairy leaf surfaces, and a dense, mat- or cushion-forming habit all help the plants to conserve moisture in the face of strong, cold winds and protect them from the burning effects of brilliant sun. Equally, a perennial, woody, or bulbous habit with an underground food-store, permits rapid growth in spring so as to draw the most benefit from the short summer season.

In the wild, alpines are adapted to extremes of temperature but, in winter, high-growing species are insulated with a deep covering of snow, and remain dormant at around 0°C (32°F). Few of them can withstand the constant wetness at their roots that is often experienced in gardens at lower altitudes in winter. Alpines demand very sharp drainage and protection from winter wet, and they also dislike warm, humid summers. In the wild, alpines experience fresh, constantly moving air, and often brilliant sunshine during their growing period. While many alpines are quite amenable and undemanding in cultivation, the high-growing alpines have precise requirements. However, they include many beautiful species, with disproportionately large flowers in unrivalled, jewel-bright colours, that will richly reward the extra attention paid to fulfilling these needs.

Rock plants

The term rock plants is used to describe relatively slow-growing plants that are suitable in scale for the rock garden, although they may not necessarily be of alpine origin. These species are usually easier to grow than true alpines and possess several other advantages in the

A blaze of summer colour
The brilliant red flowers of Helianthemum *and* Sedum *cascade down a rockface, providing both focus and counterpoint to the grey leaves of* Dianthus *in the background.*

garden. Most true alpines bloom very early in the year, so that they can flower and set seed before the onset of winter snows. Many rock plants, however, bloom well into summer, thus extending the period of interest. For example, helianthemums, which often occur on sunny hills around the Mediterranean, share the need for sharp drainage and bloom from spring into summer. The smaller veronicas, sedums, and phloxes, as well as *Armeria maritima*, a coastal native, also bloom later in the season. Dwarf trees and shrubs, like *Salix, Genista,* and *Daphne* are useful as framework plantings. Native woodlanders, like *Cornus canadensis, Sanguinaria,* or *Hepatica* species, which prefer moister, shadier conditions, are ideal for niches in a rock garden, where sun-loving rock plants and alpines would fail to thrive.

Planting in the open garden
A free-flowering shrub in bloom, (here, Daphne x burkwoodii *'Somerset'), provides a focal point in a mixed border and acts as a framework for other plantings during the rest of the year.*

Open gardens

Nearly all rock plants and alpines are characterized by a restricted size or neat habit and so are particularly well suited to the confines of a smaller, modern garden. Those that need relatively little cultivation can easily be grown in the open garden, in scree, or in the crevices of paving and patios.

A sunny, south- or southwest-facing slope that is situated away from any shade cast by large trees or buildings is ideal for a rock garden. In hotter and drier climates, a north-facing slope can be equally effective. A rock garden should try to emulate natural rock formations as closely as possible and provide a diversity of niches to replicate the natural habitats of alpine plants. To achieve this effect and for the greatest visual impact, the rock garden should be constructed on as generous a scale as the site allows.

The arrangement of different-size rocks in natural-looking layers, with terraces and pockets of deeper soil between them, will provide niches that suit a range of plants from various habitats. If sited properly, large rocks provide a deep, moist, and cool root run beneath them, as well as insulating the roots from the worst of the winter cold. Wherever it is positioned, a rock garden will provide different aspects for a wide range of alpines. A series of rocky outcrops with crevices and gullies between them provide ideal conditions for rock-crevice dwellers like the cushion-forming saxifrages or, if given a more northerly aspect, for the shade-loving lewisias. Deep pockets of gritty soil at the base of rocks provide niches for many of the gentians, while wider terraces suit mat-formers like phloxes or *Persicaria affine* 'Donald Lowndes'.

A scree garden is, essentially, a gently sloping bed of loose rock fragments mixed with low-fertility gritty compost. It is a less-expensive alternative to a rock garden, and can either be created separately or integrated between or below large rocks to provide a home for natural scree-dwellers, such as *Edrainthus serpyllifolius*.

The most natural rock gardens are constructed of local stone, which not only harmonizes better with the surrounding landscape, but also has economic advantages in terms of purchase and transport costs. Equally, important conservation issues need to be considered where rock has been extracted from ecologically precious limestone pavements (see p. 157). Where space or expense prohibits the creation of a rock garden, several alternative ways of growing alpines can be considered.

Raised beds and walls

One of the most notable features that make a raised bed suitable for small gardens is its highly economical use of space. Since drainage is entirely independent of the surrounding soil, a raised bed makes a good option for gardens with heavy, poorly drained clay soils that alpine plants dislike intensely. In addition, dimensions can be planned so that the entire bed can be protected in winter with a frame light. This is ideal for plants that need unrestricted air movement and protection from winter wet. A raised bed should be created as an integral part of the overall garden design. A square or rectangular bed offers both sunny and shady sides, and can also be constructed so that the walls incorporate planting niches for crevice-dwelling plants. Larger beds can be designed to provide separate areas with different compost types to suit specific cultivation needs. They may even be "landscaped" by bedding rocks into the surface to provide vertical or shaded niches for plants that need

A tapestry of colour
The dark foliage of these evergreen shrubs and dwarf conifers provide an attractive backdrop that contrasts with and sets off the jewel-like colours and varied forms of the alpines.

A low raised bed
Here, a low raised bed flanks a narrow stone path and draws the eye to the open garden beyond. The alpines planted in bold and natural drifts thrive in the enhanced drainage offered by a raised bed.

those conditions. When planting up raised beds, it is important to consider successional interest as well as the final dimensions of individual species, if they are not to become visually overbearing or to swamp out smaller neighbours.

Given the right aspct, dry-stone retaining walls can be ideal sites for growing trailing, cushion-, or mat-forming plants. The crevices are almost inevitably sharply drained and roots can penetrate into the backfill beyond to seek moisture and nutrients and a cool, moist root run. If considering a brick or other type of mortared wall as a planting site, niches should be built in by leaving crevices, cracks, or spaces between the bricks or rocks.

Troughs and sinks
Old stone sinks and troughs provide one of the most attractive ways of growing a collection of alpines, although they are unfortunately both expensive and scarce. Modern facsimiles made

of hypertufa, reconstituted stone, or glazed sinks coated with hypertufa are inexpensive alternatives (see p. 163). Filled with a sharply drained, gritty compost that is adapted to suit the specific needs of individual plants, sinks and troughs make ideal sites for miniature cushion-formers like *Androsace* or *Saxifraga* species or the small and beautiful *Campanula zoysii*. They are equally effective whether landscaped as miniature gardens or devoted to a collection of a species of a single genus, with very similar cultural needs.

The alpine house
An alpine house is an unheated greenhouse, usually with raised benches for cultivating alpines under controlled conditions. It differs from an ordinary cold greenhouse mainly in the increased ventilation provided by vents along the sides and roof and, usually, offers the facility to shade plants from the hottest sun during summer. For some gardeners,

its primary function is to allow the challenging high-growing alpine plants to be grown under carefully controlled conditions. Alpines that naturally spend their winter dormancy beneath a blanket of snow are insulated from extremes of temperature and shielded from cold winds and excessive rainfall. Often these plants cannot adapt to the variable and very different conditions of low-altitude, temperate climates, although some will thrive in the open garden if given the overhead protection of an open cloche or propped pane of glass. The more demanding species, however, will need the finer control offered by an alpine house. While it is commonly associated with plants that do not suit low-altitude climates, an alpine house can also be very rewarding when used to grow to perfection otherwise robust species that flower very early in the year. It protects them from heavy rain or frost damage, and the predations of slugs, snails, and other pests (see p. 176).

An alpine house collection *(below) A variety of alpines, displayed in containers in an alpine house, make an attractive feature.*

Spilling over *(above) Part of a hollowed-out, well-drained tree trunk is used for* Sedum spathulifolium *'Cape Blanco'.*

PLANTERS' GUIDE TO ROCK PLANTS

FOR EXPOSED SITES
Antennaria dioica
Campanula portenschlagiana
Carlina acaulis
Chiastophyllum oppositifolium
Dryas octopetala
Erigeron karvinskianus
Euphorbia myrsinites
Helianthemum
Limonium bellidifolium
Pterocephalus perennis
Sempervivum

AIR POLLUTION-TOLERANT
Aubrieta
Aurinia saxatilis
   'Dudley Nevill'
Campanula garganica
Campanula poscharskyana
Erinus alpinus
Sedum some
Sempervivum

FOR MOIST SHADE
Cassiope
Daphne blagayana
Hepatica nobilis
Hepatica transsilvanica
Meconopsis cambrica
Primula many spp., cvs.
Sanguinaria canadensis
Shortia uniflora
Trillium spp.

FOR DRY SHADE
Dianthus carthusianorum
Dianthus deltoides
Genista sagittalis
Gypsophila repens
Saponaria ocymoides

SCREE GARDENS
Acantholimon glumaceum
Aethionema 'Warley Rose'
Alyssum montanum
Androsace lanuginosa
Androsace sarmentosa

Dianthus alpinus
Dianthus erinaceus
Edraianthus pumilio
Erinus alpinus
Papaver alpinum
Papaver fauriei
Sempervivum spp.
Silene acaulis

PAVING
Campanula cochleariifolia
Geranium sanguineum
Mentha requienii
Pratia pedunculata
Thymus some

WALL CREVICES
Aubrieta many cvs. 85
Aurinia saxatilis
   'Dudley Nevill' 30
Aurinia saxatilis 'Citrina'
Campanula portenschlagiana 137
Erinus alpinus 76
✿ *Globularia cordifolia* 128
Haberlea rhodopensis 99
Lewisia Cotyledon Hybrids
Lewisia tweedyi
Onosma alborosea 36
Ramonda myconi
Saxifraga longifolia
Saxifraga 96
   'Southside Seedling'
Scabiosa graminifolia

PLANTING IN TUFA
Androsace small spp., cvs.
Campanula zoysii
Physoplexis comosa
Potentilla nitida
Saxifraga

PLANTING IN TROUGHS
Anchusa caespitosa
Androsace many spp.
Arenaria purpurascens
Asperula suberosa
Dianthus alpinus

Dianthus 'Little Jock'
Dianthus 'La Bourboule'
Edraianthus pumilio
Gentiana saxosa
Omphalodes luciliae
Oxalis enneaphylla
Petrophytum hendersonii
Primula marginata
Saxifraga many
Sedum cauticola
Vitaliana primuliflora

RAISED BEDS
Aethionema 'Warley Rose'
Androsace spp.
Armeria juniperifolia
Bolax gummifera
Campanula zoysii
Daphne cneorum
Daphne petraea 'Grandiflora'
Dianthus alpine spp., cvs.
Draba rigida
Erinacea anthyllis
Globularia spp.
Haberlea rhodopensis
Iberis spp.
Leontopodium alpinum
Lewisia some spp., cvs.
Oxalis adenophylla
Oxalis enneaphylla
Papaver fauriei
Primula auricula
Primula marginata
Saxifraga some
Sempervivum
Silene acaulis
Verbascum 'Letitia'

CATALOGUE OF
ROCK
PLANTS

Compositae/Asteraceae	EDELWEISS

LEONTOPODIUM ALPINUM

Habit Clump-forming, perennial. **Flowers** Tiny, woolly, leaf-like bracts forming a star, 3–10cm (1¼–4in) across, borne in spring or early summer. White, with grey-white base. **Leaves** Linear to narrowly lance-shaped. Grey-green.
• NATIVE HABITAT Grassy and rocky areas, Europe.
• CULTIVATION Grow in a site with gritty, sharply drained soil that is neutral to alkaline, and protect plant from winter wet.
• PROPAGATION By seed when ripe or by division in spring, but can be slow to re-establish.

HEIGHT
20cm (8in)

SPREAD
10cm (4in)

Cruciferae/ Brassicaceae	

IBERIS SEMPERVIRENS

Habit Spreading, evergreen, sub-shrub. **Flowers** Tiny, uneven, cross-shaped, 5cm (2in) across, borne in dense, rounded heads in late spring or early summer. White, often flushed pink. **Leaves** Paddle- to spoon-shaped. Dark green.
• NATIVE HABITAT Mountains of southern Europe.
• CULTIVATION Needs well-drained, neutral to alkaline soil. Trim after flowering to keep compact.
• PROPAGATION By seed in autumn in a frame or by softwood or semi-ripe cuttings in mid-summer.
• OTHER NAME *I. commutata*.

HEIGHT
to 30cm
(12in)

SPREAD
60cm (24in)

Ranunculaceae	ALPINE PASQUE FLOWER

PULSATILLA ALPINA

Habit Tufted, perennial. **Flowers** Cup-shaped, fine-haired, 6cm (2½in) across, borne in spring. White, with golden stamens and a blue tint outside. **Leaves** Feathery, finely dissected, and hairy. Bright green. **Fruits** Silky-haired, rounded seedheads. Silver or grey.
• NATIVE HABITAT Central and southern Europe.
• CULTIVATION Provide moderately fertile soil and good drainage. Dislikes root disturbance.
• PROPAGATION By seed when ripe, or by root cuttings in winter.

HEIGHT
to 30cm
(12in)

SPREAD
20cm (8in)

Ericaceae	

ANDROMEDA POLIFOLIA 'Alba'

Habit Open, semi-prostrate, evergreen, shrub. **Flowers** Urn-shaped, borne in clusters to 3cm (1¼in) across, in spring and summer. Pure white. **Leaves** Narrowly linear and leathery. Dark green.
• NATIVE HABITAT Species found in peat bogs in northern Europe.
• CULTIVATION Prefers leaf-rich, acid soil that stays reliably moist. Tolerates part-shade or sun.
• PROPAGATION By softwood cuttings or by rooted layers in autumn or spring.
• OTHER NAME *A. polifolia* 'Compacta Alba'.

HEIGHT
30cm (12in)

SPREAD
30cm (12in)

Ranunculaceae

AQUILEGIA FLABELLATA var. PUMILA f. ALBA

Habit Neat, compact, clump-forming, herbaceous, perennial. **Flowers** Semi-upright to nodding, bell-shaped, measuring 3–5cm (1¼–2in) across and 2cm (¾in) in length, with 5 incurved spurs. Borne 1–3 per stem in either late spring or early summer. Creamy-white. **Leaves** Rounded, slightly fan-shaped, divided, waxy, and heavily textured. Bluish-green.

• NATIVE HABITAT Open woodland and scrub in the mountains of Japan.

• CULTIVATION Ideal for planting in a sheltered niche with partial shade in a rock garden. Grows best in gritty, moist but sharply drained soil. Prefers a site in dappled or partial shade.

• PROPAGATION By seed as soon as ripe, protected by an open frame. May take up to two years before germinating and needs at least one period of frost to induce germination. May self-seed, but is likely to hybridize unless grown in isolation.

• OTHER NAME *A. flabellata* 'Nana Alba'.

HEIGHT
to 10cm
(4in)

SPREAD
to 10cm
(4in)

Ranunculaceae	

CLEMATIS MARMORARIA

Habit Tufted, spreading, prostrate, often suckering, evergreen, dwarf, shrub. *Flowers* Unisexual, upright, saucer-shaped, spanning 2.5cm (1in) across. Borne freely, either solitary or in clusters, on long stalks in early or mid-spring. Greenish-white, becoming creamy-white at maturity. The flowers of the male plant are usually larger and whiter. *Fruits* Fluffy, seeded fruitheads. Silky-white, turning golden-brown. *Leaves* Rigid, parsley-like, finely divided, and glossy. Dark green.

• NATIVE HABITAT High mountains of South Island, New Zealand.
• CULTIVATION Best grown in a trough outdoors, protected by glass in winter. Prefers an alpine house in cold areas. Grow in a sunny site, with fertile, moist but sharply drained soil that is rich in organic matter. Under glass, grow in a mix of equal parts loam, leaf-mould, and grit. Water freely when in growth, and keep just moist in winter.
• PROPAGATION By seed as soon as ripe, in a cold frame, by softwood, or by semi-ripe cuttings.

☼ ◊
❋ ❋

HEIGHT
15cm (6in)

SPREAD
25cm (10in)

Compositae/Asteraceae	

Rhodanthemum hosmariense

Habit Bushy, spreading, evergreen, sub-shrub.
Flowers Solitary, daisy, 5cm (2in) across, borne
in spring to autumn. White, with yellow centre.
Leaves Soft-haired, lobed. Silver-green.
• NATIVE HABITAT Atlas Mountains, Morocco.
• CULTIVATION Suitable for growing in a rock
garden or raised bed. Needs well-drained soil.
• PROPAGATION By seed in spring or by taking
softwood cuttings.
• OTHER NAMES *Chrysanthemum hosmariense,
Leucanthemum hosmariense, Pyrethropsis hosmariense.*

☀ ◌
❄ ❄

Height
to 30cm
(12in)

Spread
30cm (12in)

Ranunculaceae	

Pulsatilla vulgaris f. *alba*

Habit Clumping, herbaceous, perennial. **Flowers**
Upright to nodding bells, silky-haired, 4–9cm
(1½–3½in) across, borne in spring. White. **Fruits**
Round, hairy seedheads. Silver. **Leaves** Feathery,
with linear lobes, hairy when young. Light green.
• NATIVE HABITAT Short turf and meadows in
Britain and from western France to Ukraine.
• CULTIVATION Grow in well-drained, moderately
fertile soil. Dislikes root disturbance.
• PROPAGATION By seed when ripe or by root
cuttings in winter.

☀ ◌
❄ ❄ ❄

Height
to 20cm
(8in)

Spread
20cm (8in)

Ericaceae	

Cassiope 'Muirhead' ♈

Habit Loose, bushy, upright, evergreen, shrub.
Flowers Nodding, bell-shaped, 8mm (⅜in) long,
borne on upper parts of stems in spring. White,
with red outer petals. **Leaves** Tiny, lance-shaped,
scale-like, and pressed close to stems. Dark green.
• NATIVE HABITAT Garden origin.
• CULTIVATION Suitable for a rock garden or peat
bed. Grow in moist, acid soil that is enriched with
organic matter. Prefers a site in partial shade or
sun where the soil remains reliably moist.
• PROPAGATION By semi-ripe cuttings.

☀ ◌ pH
❄ ❄ ❄

Height
20cm (8in)

Spread
20cm (8in)

Ericaceae	

Cassiope 'Edinburgh' ♈

Habit Bushy, erect, evergreen, shrub. **Flowers**
Nodding bells, 8mm (⅜in) long, borne towards the
stem tips in spring. White, with small, greenish-
brown outer petals. **Leaves** Scale-like, lance-
shaped, and pressed against stems. Dark green.
• NATIVE HABITAT Garden origin.
• CULTIVATION Suitable for growing in a rock
garden or peat bed. Needs a partially shaded
or sunny site with moist, acid soil that is rich in
organic matter and that remains reliably moist.
• PROPAGATION By semi-ripe cuttings.

☀ ◌ pH
❄ ❄ ❄

Height
25cm (10in)

Spread
25cm (10in)

Berberidaceae	RHEUMATISM ROOT, TWIN LEAF

JEFFERSONIA DIPHYLLA

Habit Tuft-forming, herbaceous, perennial.
Flowers Solitary, erect, cupped, 2.5cm (1in) across, borne in late spring and summer. White. *Leaves* Cleft into 2 kidney-shaped lobes. Grey-green.
• 'NATIVE HABITAT Damp woodlands, N. America, from Ontario to Tennessee.
• CULTIVATION Suits a shady niche in a peat bed or rock garden. Needs moist soil enriched with organic matter, and a leaf-mould mulch in summer.
• PROPAGATION By seed as soon as ripe, or by careful division of well-established plants in spring.

☀ ◊
❅ ❅ ❅

HEIGHT
15cm (6in)

SPREAD
20cm (8in)

Primulaceae	

DODECATHEON MEADIA f. ALBUM ♥

Habit Clumping, herbaceous, perennial. *Flowers* Drooping, pointed, to 2cm (¾in) long, with reflexed petals, borne in clusters from mid- to late spring. White, with yellow stamens. *Leaves* Rosette-forming, toothed and oval. Pale to mid-green.
• NATIVE HABITAT Meadows and open woods, eastern N. America.
• CULTIVATION Suits a woodland or rock garden. Needs leaf-rich, moist soil with organic matter.
• PROPAGATION By ripe seed or division in spring.
• OTHER NAME *D. pauciflorum* f. *album*.

☀ ◊
❅ ❅ ❅

HEIGHT
40cm (16in)

SPREAD
25cm (10in)

Saxifragaceae	FOAM FLOWER

TIARELLA CORDIFOLIA ♥

Habit Rhizomatous, evergreen, perennial.
Flowers Tiny, star-shaped, borne in sprays to 15cm (6in) long, in late spring. White.
Leaves Oval, with 3–5 lobes. Pale green.
• NATIVE HABITAT Woodlands, N. America.
• CULTIVATION Ideal as ground cover in a shady border or woodland garden, but is too vigorous to accompany delicate alpines. Tolerates a range of soils but prefers a cool, moist, leaf-rich site.
• PROPAGATION By seed when ripe or in late winter, or by division in spring.

☀ ◊
❅ ❅ ❅

HEIGHT
20cm (8in)

SPREAD
30cm (12in)
or more

Papaveraceae	

RUPICAPNOS AFRICANA

Habit Short-lived, evergreen, perennial.
Flowers Delicate, tubular, spurred, to 15mm (½in) long, borne in clusters in summer. Pink-purple.
Leaves Fleshy, finely divided and fern-like, forming basal clumps. Bright blue-grey.
• NATIVE HABITAT Sunny cliff faces in the Rif mountains, N. Africa.
• CULTIVATION Grow in sharply drained, gritty soil in an alpine house. Dislikes winter wet.
• PROPAGATION Collect seed when almost ripe but still green and sow immediately.

☀ ◊
❅ ❅

HEIGHT
15cm (6in)

SPREAD
20cm (8in)

Ericaceae	COMPACT BOG ROSEMARY

ANDROMEDA POLIFOLIA 'Compacta' ♑

Habit Densely twiggy, evergreen, shrub. **Flowers** Urn-shaped, borne in clusters to 3cm (1¼in) across, in spring and early summer. Pink. **Leaves** Lance-shaped. Dark green, with glaucous underside.
• NATIVE HABITAT Species found in peat bogs in northern Europe.
• CULTIVATION Suits a rock or woodland garden, or a peat bed. Needs leaf-rich, acid soil that remains reliably moist, in partial shade or sun.
• PROPAGATION By softwood cuttings, or by rooted layers, in autumn or spring.

☀ ◊ pH
❈ ❈ ❈

HEIGHT
15cm (6in)

SPREAD
20cm (8in)

Ericaceae	

PHYLLODOCE × INTERMEDIA 'Drummondii'

Habit Bushy, spreading, evergreen, dwarf shrub. **Flowers** Urn-shaped, 6mm (¼in) long, in terminal clusters on slender red stalks, borne in spring and early summer. Deep pink-purple. **Leaves** Linear and glossy. Dark green.
• NATIVE HABITAT Garden origin.
• CULTIVATION Suits a peat bed or rock garden, with moist, leaf-rich, acid soil that is rich in organic matter. Trim after flowering to keep compactness.
• PROPAGATION By semi-ripe cuttings.

☀ ◊ pH
❈ ❈ ❈

HEIGHT
23cm (9in)

SPREAD
23cm (9in)

Primulaceae	MOSQUITO BILLS, SAILOR CAPS

DODECATHEON HENDERSONII ♑

Habit Clumping, herbaceous, perennial. **Flowers** Drooping, pointed, to 2.5cm (1in) long, borne in early summer. Purple-pink, with darker centre and white base. **Leaves** Rosette-forming, narrowly oval, and fleshy. Dark green.
• NATIVE HABITAT Grassland, USA.
• CULTIVATION Suitable for a rock garden or alpine house. Keep moist during growth but provide a dry summer dormancy. Grow in leaf-rich soil.
• PROPAGATION By ripe seed or division in spring.
• OTHER NAME D. latifolium.

☀ ◊
❈ ❈ ❈

HEIGHT
40cm (16in)

SPREAD
25cm (10in)

Ericaceae	

PHYLLODOCE EMPETRIFORMIS

Habit Vigorous, evergreen, mat-forming, shrub. **Flowers** Bell-shaped, long-stalked, 6mm (¼in) long, borne in terminal clusters in spring and early summer. Pink-purple. **Leaves** Linear, toothed, glossy, with pale, downy underside. Emerald.
• NATIVE HABITAT Alpine and arctic habitats of western N. America, from Alaska to California.
• CULTIVATION Suitable for growing in a peat bed or rock garden. Needs moist, leaf-rich, acid soil.
• PROPAGATION By seed in spring, or by semi-ripe cuttings.

☀ ◊ pH
❈ ❈ ❈

HEIGHT
30cm (12in)

SPREAD
40cm (16in)

Ranunculaceae

Pulsatilla vulgaris var. *Rubra*

Habit Vigorous, clump-forming, herbaceous, perennial. ***Flowers*** Upright to nodding, bell-shaped, silky-haired, 4–9cm (1½–3½in) across, borne in spring. Red to purple-red. ***Fruits*** Spherical, silky-haired seedheads. Silver. ***Leaves*** Feathery, finely divided into linear lobes, and densely clothed in fine, silky hairs when young. Mid- to dark green with silver hairs.

• NATIVE HABITAT Short turf and meadows, from western France to Ukraine.

• CULTIVATION An easy and reliable species that thrives on a rock garden. It is ideal for growing in gravel plantings or well-drained herbaceous borders. Prefers a site with well-drained, moderately fertile soil. Dislikes root disturbance, and is best planted out when small and left undisturbed. The flowers are particularly attractive when edged with frost and they remain undamaged by short-lived frosts.

• PROPAGATION By root cuttings in winter, or by just-ripe seed. Self-sows, but may not come true.

HEIGHT
20cm (8in)
or more

SPREAD
20cm (8in)

Primulaceae	

DODECATHEON PULCHELLUM
'Red Wings'

Habit Tufted, herbaceous, perennial. ***Flowers*** Drooping, pointed, to 2cm (¾in) long, borne in strong-stemmed clusters in mid- to late spring. Magenta-pink, with prominent, deep orange-brown stamens. ***Leaves*** Rosetted, narrowly oval, forming basal clusters. Soft, pale green.
• NATIVE HABITAT Garden origin.
• CULTIVATION Suits a woodland or rock garden. Needs leaf-rich, moist soil with organic matter.
• PROPAGATION By division in spring.

HEIGHT
20cm (8in)

SPREAD
20cm (8in)

Ericaceae	MOUNTAIN HEATH

PHYLLODOCE CAERULEA

Habit Dwarf, upright, evergreen, shrub. ***Flowers*** Bell-shaped, 1cm (½in) long, borne in terminal clusters in spring and early summer. Pink-purple to rose-red. ***Leaves*** Linear, glossy, and small-toothed, with pale, downy underside. Dark green.
• NATIVE HABITAT Alpine habitats in Europe, Asia, and the USA.
• CULTIVATION Needs moist, leaf-rich, acid soil.
• PROPAGATION By seed in spring or by semi-ripe cuttings.
• OTHER NAME *P. taxifolia.*

HEIGHT
30cm (12in)

SPREAD
30cm (12in)

Leguminosae/ Papilionaceae	HEDGEHOG BROOM

ERINACEA ANTHYLLIS

Habit Dense, mound-forming, spiny, evergreen, shrub. ***Flowers*** Pea-like, to 2cm (¾in) long, borne in clusters of 2–4 in late spring and early summer. Blue-violet. ***Leaves*** Small, inconspicuous, on tough, green stems. Dark grey-green.
• NATIVE HABITAT Exposed, rocky habitats, from western Mediterranean to eastern Pyrenees.
• CULTIVATION Ideal for a raised bed, scree, or rock garden with deep, gritty, sharply drained soil.
• PROPAGATION By ripe seed or softwood cuttings.
• OTHER NAME *E. pungens.*

HEIGHT
30cm (12in)

SPREAD
80cm (32in)

Boraginaceae	

OMPHALODES CAPPADOCICA
'Cherry Ingram'

Habit Carpeting, rhizomatous, evergreen, perennial. *Flowers* Resembling forget-me-nots, 7mm (¼in) across, borne in terminal sprays in early spring. Deep azure-blue. *Leaves* Oval to heart-shaped, pointed, and fine-haired. Mid-green.
• NATIVE HABITAT Garden origin.
• CULTIVATION Good ground cover for a large border, woodland, or rock garden. Needs a partial- or dapple-shaded site with moist, leaf-rich soil.
• PROPAGATION By seed or by division in spring.

☼ ◑
❄ ❄ ❄

HEIGHT
20cm (8in)

SPREAD
60cm (24in)

Ranunculaceae	HALLEN'S PASQUE FLOWER

PULSATILLA HALLERI ♈

Habit Tufted, intensely silver-haired, herbaceous, perennial. *Flowers* Erect, goblet-shaped, to 9cm (3½in) across, borne in late spring. Lavender-blue to violet. *Leaves* Feathery, finely divided. Light green. *Fruits* Round, silky-haired seedheads.
• NATIVE HABITAT Mountain turf, from central and southeast Europe to the Crimea.
• CULTIVATION Needs moderately fertile, sharply drained soil in sun. Dislikes root disturbance.
• PROPAGATION By fresh seed or by root cuttings in winter.

☼ ◊
❄ ❄ ❄

HEIGHT
20cm (8in)

SPREAD
15cm (6in)

Ranunculaceae	PASQUE FLOWER

PULSATILLA VULGARIS ♈

Habit Clump-forming, herbaceous, perennial.[1] *Flowers* Erect to nodding bells, silky-haired, 4–9cm (2–4in) across, borne in spring. Deep to pale purple. *Leaves* Finely divided, hairy when young. Light green. *Fruits* Spherical, silky seedheads.
• NATIVE HABITAT Short turf and meadows in Britain and from western France to Ukraine.
• CULTIVATION Grow in well-drained, moderately fertile soil, and avoid disturbing the roots.
• PROPAGATION By fresh seed or by root cuttings in winter.

☼ ◊
❄ ❄ ❄

HEIGHT
40cm (16in)
or more

SPREAD
20cm (8in)

Ranunculaceae	ALPINE CLEMATIS

CLEMATIS ALPINA

Habit Deciduous, woody scrambler or leaf-twining climber. **Flowers** Solitary, nodding, open bell-shaped, to 7cm (3in) across, borne in spring and, often, again in late summer. Blue, with white centre. **Leaves** Paired, divided, oval, toothed, with twining leaf stalks. Mid-green. **Fruits** Seedheads, becoming fluffy at maturity. Silky-white.
• NATIVE HABITAT Scrub, woodland, occasionally on screes, in the mountains of Europe.
• CULTIVATION Excellent for growing in very cold, exposed sites. As a climber, it is effective in larger rock gardens if allowed to sprawl over rock faces. Choose a site away from small and less vigorous alpines. Grow in fertile, moist but well-drained soil that is rich in organic matter. Prefers a site in sun or dappled shade with its roots in shade. If necessary, prune plant after flowering, shortening shoots to allotted space.
• PROPAGATION By seed as soon as ripe, or by softwood or semi-ripe cuttings in summer.

HEIGHT
2–3m
(6–10ft)

SPREAD
1.5m (5ft)

Scrophulariaceae	

VERONICA PEDUNCULARIS

Habit Mat-forming, rhizomatous, perennial.
Flowers Saucer-shaped, 8mm (⅜in) span, borne
in erect sprays in spring and summer. Deep blue,
pink, or white. *Leaves* Lance-shaped and glossy.
Dark green, tinted purple.
• NATIVE HABITAT Grassy and rocky places in
Turkey, Caucasus, and Ukraine.
• CULTIVATION Suits a rock garden or border front
in sun with well-drained, moderately fertile soil.
• PROPAGATION By seed as soon as ripe,
or by division in autumn or late winter.

☼ ◊
❀ ❀ ❀

HEIGHT
10cm (4in)

SPREAD
60cm (24in)

Boraginaceae	CREEPING FORGET-ME-NOT, BLUE-EYED MARY

OMPHALODES VERNA

Habit Carpeting, stoloniferous, semi-evergreen,
perennial. *Flowers* Resembling forget-me-nots,
to 1cm (⅜in) across, borne in terminal sprays in
spring. Deep blue with white eye. *Leaves* Hairy,
narrowly oval, and pointed. Mid-green.
• NATIVE HABITAT Woodland in Turkey.
• CULTIVATION Good ground cover for a border,
woodland, or rock garden. Needs fertile, moist
soil with plenty of organic matter, in shady site.
• PROPAGATION By seed or by division in autumn
or late winter.

☼ ◐
❀ ❀ ❀

HEIGHT
20cm (8in)

SPREAD
30cm (12in)
or more

Boraginaceae	

OMPHALODES CAPPADOCICA ♱

Habit Clump-forming, rhizomatous, evergreen,
perennial. *Flowers* Resembling forget-me-nots,
8mm (⅜in) wide, borne in terminal sprays in early
spring. Bright, azure-blue, with white eye.
Leaves Oval, pointed, and fine-haired. Mid-green.
• NATIVE HABITAT Woodland in Turkey.
• CULTIVATION Good ground cover for a border,
woodland, or rock garden. Needs fertile, moist
soil with plenty of organic matter, in shady site.
• PROPAGATION By seed, or by division in autumn
or late winter.

☼ ◐
❀ ❀ ❀

HEIGHT
20cm (8in)

SPREAD
60cm (24in)

Ranunculaceae	ALPINE COLUMBINE

AQUILEGIA ALPINA

Habit Upright, short-lived, tufted, herbaceous, perennial. **Flowers** Nodding, lantern-shaped, to 9cm (3½in) across, with 5 straight or curved spurs measuring up to 2.5cm (1in) long. Borne in nodding heads of 2–3 in late spring. Blue, often with white tips. **Leaves** Finely divided, forming basal clumps. Bluish-green.
• NATIVE HABITAT Rocky shade, scrub, and open woodland in the·Alps and northern Apennines.
• CULTIVATION Suitable for growing in an herbaceous border, woodland, or rock garden.

Grows best in fertile, leaf-rich soil that is moist but well drained, in dappled or partial shade. Prefers climates with cool summers, where it will tolerate sun. In rock gardens, dead-head to prevent self-sowing to the point of nuisance.
• PROPAGATION By seed, as soon as ripe or in spring. Will self-seed freely, hybridizing with other aquilegias in the garden.
• OTHER NAME *A. montana.*

HEIGHT
45cm (18in)

SPREAD
30cm (12in)

Cruciferae/ Brassicaceae	

AURINIA SAXATILIS 'Dudley Nevill'

Habit Mound-forming, evergreen, perennial. **Flowers** Cross-shaped, 4-petalled, 4–6mm (⅙–¼in) across, borne in dense clusters in late spring and early summer. Soft buff-yellow. **Leaves** Oval, toothed, and hairy. Grey-green.
• NATIVE HABITAT Garden origin.
• CULTIVATION Suitable for growing in any well-drained soil in sun. Trim annually after flowering to maintain the plant's compactness.
• PROPAGATION By softwood cuttings in summer.
• OTHER NAME *Alyssum saxatile* 'Dudley Nevill'.

☼ ◊
❄ ❄ ❄

HEIGHT
20cm (8in)

SPREAD
30cm (12in)

Cruciferae/ Brassicaceae	

AURINIA SAXATILIS 'Citrina' ♈

Habit Mound-forming, evergreen, perennial. **Flowers** Cross-shaped, 4-petalled, 4–6mm (⅙–¼in) across, borne in dense clusters in late spring and summer. Soft lemon-yellow. **Leaves** Oval, toothed, and hairy. Grey-green.
• NATIVE HABITAT Garden origin.
• CULTIVATION Grow in any well-drained soil in sun. Trim annually after flowering.
• PROPAGATION By softwood cuttings in summer, or by seed in early spring.
• OTHER NAME *Alyssum saxatile* 'Citrina'.

☼ ◊
❄ ❄ ❄

HEIGHT
4m (12ft)

SPREAD
2.5m (8ft)

Crassulaceae	

CHIASTOPHYLLUM OPPOSITIFOLIUM ♈

Habit Mat-forming or tufted, rhizomatous, evergreen, perennial. **Flowers** Bell-shaped, 5mm (⅕in) long, borne in spring and early summer. Deep yellow. **Leaves** Oval, scalloped, fleshy. Pale green.
• NATIVE HABITAT Shady, rocky sites, Caucasus.
• CULTIVATION Suits rock or wall crevices. Needs moderately fertile, moist but well-drained soil.
• PROPAGATION By seed in autumn or by cuttings from sideshoots in summer.
• OTHER NAMES *C. simplicifolium*, *Cotyledon simplicifolia*.

☼ ◊
❄ ❄ ❄

HEIGHT
to 20cm
(8in)

SPREAD
15cm (6in)

Leguminosae/ Papilionaceae	

CYTISUS × BEANII ♈

Habit Deciduous, low-growing, green-stemmed, shrub. **Flowers** Pea-like, to 15mm (½in) long, in lateral clusters, borne on arching, cylindrical stems in late spring or early summer. Bright yellow. **Leaves** Small, simple, linear, hairy. Dark green.
• NATIVE HABITAT Garden origin.
• CULTIVATION Suits a rock garden or raised bed. Will cascade over a retaining wall. Tolerates any well-drained or poor soil, but needs full sun. Trim lightly after flowering, but avoid cutting old wood.
• PROPAGATION By semi-ripe or ripewood cuttings.

☼ ◊
❄ ❄ ❄

HEIGHT
60cm (24in)

SPREAD
1m (3ft)

Berberidaceae

BERBERIS × STENOPHYLLA 'Corallina Compacta'

Habit Neat and compact, evergreen, dwarf, shrub. **Flowers** Bell-shaped, to 1cm (⅜in) span, borne in profusion in late spring. Red buds, opening to bright orange. **Fruits** Rounded berries. Blue-black, with a greyish bloom. **Leaves** Linear to narrowly oval, spine-tipped, and 6–8mm (¼–⅜in) long. Dark green.
• NATIVE HABITAT Garden origin. A selection of the hybrid between *B. darwinii* and *B. empetrifolia*.
• CULTIVATION Suitable for growing on a rock garden. Associates well with heathers and dwarf conifers, adding textural and colour contrast to both. Tolerates a range of well-drained soils in either sun or dappled shade. Needs little, if any, pruning but may be trimmed lightly after flowering, if necessary.
• PROPAGATION By semi-ripe cuttings in summer, but it is difficult to propagate.

☼ ◊
❀ ❀ ❀

HEIGHT
30cm (12in)

SPREAD
30cm (12in)

PENSTEMON

The penstemons found mostly in alpine and subalpine habitats in western North America are valued for their brightly coloured, tubular, funnel- or bell-shaped flowers, which are often borne over long periods during summer and autumn. The smaller species are ideal for rock gardens or scree and raised beds, while the taller ones are excellent for growing at the front of a sunny, sheltered border in well-drained soil. The smallest penstemons, like *P. hirsutus* var. *pygmaeus*, are suitable for planting in troughs.

Most of the penstemons described are almost fully hardy to about -10°C (14°F), probably more, if given sharp drainage. However, they experience much lower temperatures in the wild, where cold weather is accompanied by a protective cover of snow or very dry conditions. This contrasts with the wet, comparatively warm winters that the plants are subjected to when grown in lowland areas with maritime climates. For the penstemons described, these less-than-ideal conditions can be improved by adding plenty of sharp grit to the soil to ensure good drainage.

Grow in gritty, well-drained soil in sun, but provide shade from the hottest mid-day sun and shelter from cold, dry winds. Trim after flowering, if necessary, to keep the plant compact. If seed is needed for propagation, leave a few flower spikes in place to allow seed to ripen. Where several species are grown together, hybridization sometimes occurs

Propagate by seed sown in late winter or early spring, in pots in a cold frame. Alternatively, take semi-ripe cuttings of non-flowering shoots in summer and root in a cold frame. Irishman's cuttings (see p. 172), which can often be found on the prostrate creeping species, can be separated and potted up in spring.

P. FRUTICOSUS var. SCOULERI ALBUS
Habit Compact, evergreen, sub-shrub.
Flowers Funnel-shaped, to 5cm (2in) long, borne freely in dense sprays in summer. White.
Leaves Narrowly lance-shaped and glossy. Mid-green.
• OTHER NAME
P. scouleri 'Albus'.
• HEIGHT 30cm (12in).
• SPREAD 30cm (12in).

P. fruticosus var. *scouleri albus*

☼ ◊ ✳✳   ♀

P. NEWBERRYI
Habit Mat-forming, downy-stemmed, evergreen, sub-shrub.
Flowers Tubular, 2.5–3cm (1–1¼in) long borne in dense sprays in summer. Dark red-pink.
Leaves Elliptic to oval, leathery, with a finely serrated margin. Dark green.
• HEIGHT 25cm (10in).
• SPREAD 30cm (12in).

P. newberryi
Mountain pride

☼ ◊ ✳✳   ♀

P. RUPICOLA
Habit Prostrate, evergreen, sub-shrub.
Flowers Funnel-shaped, to 3.5cm (1⅜in) long, borne in dense, few-flowered sprays in late spring and early summer. Dark red-pink.
Leaves Thick, elliptic to rounded, leathery. Blue-green.
• HEIGHT 10cm(4in).
• SPREAD 45cm (18in).

P. rupicola
Rock penstemon

☼ ◊ ❀❀   ♔

P. PINIFOLIUS
Habit Spreading, evergreen, sub-shrub.
Flowers Narrowly tubular, 2.5cm (1in) long, borne in loose spike-like sprays in summer. Bright scarlet.
Leaves Crowded and needle-like. Pale green.
• HEIGHT to 20cm (8in).
• SPREAD to 25cm (10in).

P. pinifolius

☼ ◊ ❀❀   ♔

P. NEWBERRYI f. HUMILIOR
Habit Evergreen, sub-shrub, compact, bushy, mat-forming, with arching, downy branches,
Flowers Tubular, 2.5cm (1in) long, borne in dense sprays in early summer. Dark red-pink.
Leaves Elliptic to oval, leathery, with a finely serrated margin. Dark green.
• HEIGHT 15cm (6in).
• SPREAD 20cm (8in).

P. newberryi f. humilior

☼ ◊ ❀❀

P. HIRSUTUS var. PYGMAEUS
Habit Mat-forming, rhizomatous, short-lived, evergreen, sub-shrub.
Flowers Tubular, 2.5cm (1in) long, borne in loose sprays in summer. Violet, with whitish tips.
Leaves Lance-shaped with a toothed margin. Dark green, with purple tint.
• HEIGHT 10cm (4in).
• SPREAD 10cm (4in).

P. hirsutus var. pygmaeus

☼ ◊ ❀❀❀

P. SERRULATUS
Habit Spreading, semi-evergreen, sub-shrub.
Flowers Narrowly bell-shaped, 2.5cm (1in) long, borne in dense, one-sided clusters in late summer. Pink-purple.
Leaves Lance-shaped, tooth-edged. Dark green.
• OTHER NAME
P. diffusus.
• HEIGHT to 50cm (20in).
• SPREAD 30cm (12in).

P. serrulatus
Cascade penstemon

☼ ◊ ❀❀❀

Parnassiaceae/ Saxifragaceae	GRASS OF PARNASSUS

PARNASSIA PALUSTRIS

Habit Tufted, semi-evergreen, perennial.
Flowers Saucer-shaped, solitary, 2.5cm (1in)
across, borne on erect stems in early summer.
White, with green veins. **Leaves** Oval and heart-
shaped, forming basal tufts. Pale green.
• NATIVE HABITAT Bogs, northern hemisphere.
• CULTIVATION Suits a bog garden or permanently
damp niche in a rock garden. Needs wet, not
stagnant, soil that is rich in organic matter, in sun.
• PROPAGATION By seed in autumn, or by division
in autumn or early spring.

☼ ♦
❀ ❀ ❀

HEIGHT
20cm (8in)

SPREAD
10cm (4in)

Plumbaginaceae	

ARMERIA PSEUDARMERIA

Habit Clumping, evergreen, perennial. **Flowers**
Small, borne in dense round heads, to 4cm (1½in)
across, in summer. White or pale pink. **Leaves**
Lance-shaped, in basal rosettes. Mid-green.
• NATIVE HABITAT Coastal areas, western Portugal.
• CULTIVATION Prefers light, sandy soil that is
moderately fertile, in an open site in full sun.
• PROPAGATION By seed in autumn or spring,
or by division in early spring.
• OTHER NAMES *A. atrosanguinea* of gardens,
A. latifolia.

☼ ◌
❀ ❀ ❀

HEIGHT
to 50cm
(20in)

SPREAD
30cm (12in)

Compositae/Asteraceae	

CELMISIA WALKERI

Habit Loose, spreading, evergreen, perennial.
Flowers Daisy-like, 4cm (1½in) across, borne
on sticky stems in early summer. White, with
yellow centre. **Leaves** Narrowly linear and
leathery. Dark green, with hairy, white underside.
• NATIVE HABITAT South Island, New Zealand.
• CULTIVATION Needs slightly acid, fertile, moist
but well-drained soil. Prefers cool climates.
• PROPAGATION By seed as soon as ripe, or
by rooting leaf-rosette cuttings in spring.
• OTHER NAME *C. webbiana.*

☼ ◌ pH
❀ ❀ ❀

HEIGHT
30cm (12in)

SPREAD
30cm (12in)

Onagraceae	

EPILOBIUM GLABELLUM

Habit Mat- or clump-forming, semi-evergreen, perennial. *Flowers* Solitary, cup-shaped, outward-facing, 2.5cm (1in) across, borne on slender stems in summer. White. *Leaves* Narrowly oval. Dark green, tinted bronze, on bristly, red-tinted stems.
• NATIVE HABITAT Riverbeds and mountain grassland, New Zealand.
• CULTIVATION Suitable ground cover for a semi-shaded border. Prefers cool, damp shade.
• PROPAGATION By seed when ripe or in spring, or by division in autumn or early spring.

☼ ◊
❀ ❀ ❀

HEIGHT
20cm (8in)

SPREAD
20cm (8in)

Leguminosae/ Papilionaceae	

CHAMAECYTISUS PURPUREUS f. *ALBUS*

Habit Dense, semi-upright, deciduous, shrub. *Flowers* Pea, 2.5cm (1in) across, borne in lateral clusters in summer. White. *Leaves* Small, with 3 oval leaflets. Dark green.
• NATIVE HABITAT Hillsides, southeast Europe.
• CULTIVATION Suits a rock garden, raised bed, or retaining wall. Tolerates most well-drained, moderately fertile soils except shallow, chalky ones. Trim after flowering, avoiding old wood.
• PROPAGATION By semi-ripe or ripewood cuttings.
• OTHER NAME *Cytisus purpureus* f. *albus*.

☼ ◊
❀ ❀ ❀

HEIGHT
45cm (18in)

SPREAD
60cm (24in)

Geraniaceae	

ERODIUM CHEILANTHIFOLIUM

Habit Compact, mound-forming, evergreen, perennial. *Flowers* Flat-faced, to 2.5cm (1in) across, borne in sprays of up to 5 in summer. White with distinct purple marks on top 2 petals. *Leaves* Oval, deep-cut, fern-like, crinkled. Grey-green.
• NATIVE HABITAT Southern Spain and N. Africa.
• CULTIVATION Suitable for a raised bed. Grow in gritty, sharply drained, neutral to alkaline soil.
• PROPAGATION By seed when ripe, or by division or basal cuttings in spring.
• OTHER NAME *E. petraeum* subsp. *crispum*.

☼ ◊
❀ ❀ ❀

HEIGHT
20cm (8in)

SPREAD
30cm (12in)

Cruciferae/ Brassicaceae	PERSIAN STONE CRESS

AETHIONEMA GRANDIFLORUM

Habit Loose, short-lived, evergreen or semi-evergreen, sub-shrub. **Flowers** Cross-shaped, 4-petalled, 6mm (¼in) across, borne in loose sprays or clusters in early summer. Pale to deep pink. **Leaves** Narrowly lance-shaped. Blue-green.
• NATIVE HABITAT Iran, Iraq, Caucasus, Turkey.
• CULTIVATION Prefers fertile, alkaline soil in sun, but will tolerate poor, slightly acid soils.
• PROPAGATION By softwood cuttings in summer, or by seed in spring. Will hybridize freely.
• OTHER NAME A. pulchellum.

☀ ○
❀ ❀ ❀

HEIGHT
20–30cm
(8–12in)

SPREAD
20–30cm
(8–12in)

Boraginaceae	

ONOSMA ALBOROSEA

Habit Low-spreading, clumping, evergreen, perennial. **Flowers** Nodding, tubular, 3cm (1¼in) long, borne in congested clusters in summer. White, turning pink, occasionally with violet-blue tips. **Leaves** Spoon- to lance-shaped, bristly, and can cause skin irritations. Grey-green.
• NATIVE HABITAT Rock crevices, southwest Asia.
• CULTIVATION Grows best in a scree bed or planted in vertical crevices of retaining walls. Needs well-drained, very gritty soil.
• PROPAGATION By seed in autumn.

☀ ○
❀ ❀

HEIGHT
25cm (10in)

SPREAD
25cm (10in)

Saxifragaceae	

ASTILBE 'Sprite'

Habit Clump-forming, rhizomatous, herbaceous, perennial. **Flowers** Tiny, star-shaped, borne in feathery, tapering clusters in summer. Shell-pink. **Leaves** Divided into oval leaflets. Mid-green.
• NATIVE HABITAT Garden origin.
• CULTIVATION Grows best in a partially shaded site with fertile, reliably moist soil that is enriched with organic matter.
• PROPAGATION By division in winter or early spring before new growth begins.
• OTHER NAME A. simplicifolia 'Sprite'.

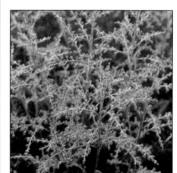

☀ ◐
❀ ❀ ❀

HEIGHT
50cm (20in)

SPREAD
to 1m (3ft)

Leguminosae/Papilionaceae	

ANTHYLLIS MONTANA

Habit Clump- or mat-forming, spreading, woody-based, perennial. **Flowers** Tiny, pea, borne in dense, clover-like heads, to 3cm (1¼in) across, with 2 lobed, leaf-like bracts beneath, in early summer. Pink, red, or purple, sometimes with white tips. **Leaves** Small, silky-haired, and finely divided into oval leaflets. Grey-green or silver.
• NATIVE HABITAT Rocky, open places in the Alps, and mountains of southern Europe.
• CULTIVATION Excellent for a scree bed, rock garden, or dry-stone retaining walls. The flowers are attractive to bees and other beneficial insects. Grow in well-drained, poor to moderately fertile soil. Tolerates dry soils, and thrives in climates with long, hot summers. Trim lightly after flowering to maintain plant's neatness.
• PROPAGATION Sow seed in autumn or winter in pots in a cold frame, or by division of established plants in autumn or spring.

☀ ◊
❄ ❄ ❄

HEIGHT
30cm (12in)

SPREAD
60cm (24in)

Ericaceae	

RHODOTHAMNUS CHAMAECISTUS

Habit Dwarf, evergreen, shrub. **Flowers** Cup-shaped, 5-petalled, 3cm (1¼in) across, solitary, or in lateral or terminal clusters, borne in early summer. Clear pink. **Leaves** Oval to lance-shaped and untoothed. Glossy, lustrous green.
• NATIVE HABITAT Pockets of fertile, acid soil among limestone rocks, eastern Alps.
• CULTIVATION Needs reliably moist but well-drained soil. Tolerates some shade in drier areas.
• PROPAGATION By seed in autumn or by semi-ripe cuttings in late summer.

HEIGHT
20cm (8in)

SPREAD
25cm (10in)

Portulacaceae	

LEWISIA 'George Henley'

Habit Clump-forming, evergreen, perennial.
Flowers Cone-shaped, 2.5cm (1in) across, silky, borne in loose clusters from late spring to late summer. Purplish-pink, with magenta veins.
Leaves Narrow, spoon-shaped, fleshy. Dark green.
• NATIVE HABITAT Garden origin.
• CULTIVATION Ideal pot-grown in an alpine house, or suits a scree bed with protection from winter wet. Needs fertile, moist but well-drained soil enriched with organic matter, in partial shade.
• PROPAGATION By root offsets in early summer.

HEIGHT
15cm (6in)
or more

SPREAD
20cm (8in)

Plumbaginaceae	MATTED SEA LAVENDER

LIMONIUM BELLIDIFOLIUM

Habit Compact, dome-forming, evergreen, perennial. **Flowers** Tiny, funnel-shaped, 5mm (⅕in) long, borne in open, wiry-stemmed spikes in early summer. Pale blue-violet. **Leaves** Spoon-shaped, leathery, in basal clumps. Dark green.
• NATIVE HABITAT Sandy salt marshes and coastal areas, eastern England, Mediterranean, Black Sea.
• CULTIVATION Suits a trough or scree garden. Grow in light, preferably sandy, well-drained soil.
• PROPAGATION By seed or by division, in spring.
• OTHER NAMES *L. reticulata, Statice bellidifolia.*

HEIGHT
15cm (6in)

SPREAD
15cm (6in)

Labiatae/Lamiaceae

ORIGANUM 'Kent Beauty'

Habit Prostrate, semi-evergreen, sub-shrub, with trailing branches and a suckering, woody rootstock. *Flowers* Small, tubular, to 15mm (⅝in) long, borne in whorls in summer. Mauve to pale pink, with large, dark rose-pink bracts. *Leaves* Aromatic, and rounded to oval. Bright green.
• NATIVE HABITAT Garden origin.
• CULTIVATION Grows best in a raised bed, on the top of a wall, or other well-drained site in a rock garden. Needs very well-drained, preferably slightly alkaline soil in a warm, sunny site.

Although almost fully cold hardy, to -10°C (15°F) or slightly lower, it will not withstand excessive winter wet combined with low temperatures. In areas with cold, wet winters, protect the crown with an open cloche or propped pane of glass.
• PROPAGATION By division in early spring, or by basal cuttings in spring and summer.

HEIGHT
10cm (4in)

SPREAD
20cm (8in)

Saxifragaceae	

ASTILBE 'Perkeo' ♥

Habit Compact, erect, clumping, herbaceous, perennial. **Flowers** Tiny, star-shaped, borne in feathery, tapering clusters in mid- to late summer. Deep salmon-pink. **Leaves** Finely cut. Dark green, with bronze tint on opening.
• NATIVE HABITAT Garden origin.
• CULTIVATION Needs fertile, reliably moist, open soil enriched with organic matter, in part shade.
• PROPAGATION By division in winter or early spring, before new growth begins.
• OTHER NAME *A. x crispa* 'Perkeo'.

☀◐ ◊
❋❋❋

HEIGHT
to 20cm
(4in)

SPREAD
to 30cm
(12in)

Primulaceae	ALPINE BELLS

CORTUSA MATTHIOLI

Habit Clumping, herbaceous, perennial. **Flowers** Bell-shaped, drooping, long-stalked, 1cm (⅜in) long, borne in one-sided clusters in late spring and early summer. Magenta to purple-violet. **Leaves** Rounded, lobed, kidney-shaped, and coarsely toothed, in basal rosettes. Dull green, rusty-haired.
• NATIVE HABITAT Mountains, western Europe.
• CULTIVATION Needs a cool site with moist but well-drained, fertile soil in partial or deep shade.
• PROPAGATION By ripe seed, or by division in early spring or immediately after flowering.

☀◐ ◊
❋❋❋

HEIGHT
20–30cm
(8–12in)

SPREAD
15cm (6in)

Crassulaceae	

CRASSULA SARCOCAULIS

Habit Bushy, evergreen or semi-evergreen, perennial, with gnarled branches. **Flowers** Star-shaped, 5mm (⅛in) wide, borne in late summer. Pink or white. **Leaves** Small, fleshy, and oval. Mid-green, with red tints.
• NATIVE HABITAT Lesotho and S. Africa.
• CULTIVATION Suits a warm, sunny rock garden. Needs sharply drained, moderately fertile soil.
• PROPAGATION By seed in spring, or by stem or leaf cuttings in early to mid-summer.
• OTHER NAME *Sedum sarcocaule*.

☀ ◊
❋❋

HEIGHT
to 30cm
(12in)

SPREAD
30cm (12in)

Labiatae/Lamiaceae	

ORIGANUM LAEVIGATUM ♥

Habit Upright, woody-based, wiry-stemmed, suckering, herbaceous, perennial. **Flowers** Tubular, 15mm (⅝in) long, borne in loose, airy, whorled clusters throughout summer. Purplish-pink. **Leaves** Aromatic and oval. Dark green.
• NATIVE HABITAT Scrub, open woods, grassland and maquis, in Turkey and Cyprus.
• CULTIVATION Suits a border front or rock garden. Attracts bees and butterflies. Grows best in well-drained, moderately fertile, preferably alkaline soil.
• PROPAGATION By seed or by division, in spring.

☀ ◊
❋❋❋

HEIGHT
to 60cm
(24in)

SPREAD
45cm (18in)

Geraniaceae	BLOODY CRANESBILL

GERANIUM SANGUINEUM

Habit Dense, rhizomatous, spreading to mound-forming, herbaceous, perennial. ***Flowers*** Upright, cup-shaped, 4cm (1½in) across, borne throughout summer. Magenta, with darker veins and pale eye. ***Leaves*** Deeply cut with lobes. Dark green.
• NATIVE HABITAT Grassy, rocky places, usually on limestone, Europe to northern Turkey.
• CULTIVATION Prefers a site in partial shade, and will tolerate a range of well-drained soils.
• PROPAGATION By seed or by division, in autumn or spring.

☀ ◊
❀ ❀ ❀

HEIGHT
20cm (8in)

SPREAD
30cm (12in)
or more

Portulacaceae	

LEWISIA Cotyledon Hybrids

Habit Tufted, evergreen, perennial. ***Flowers*** Cone-shaped, to 4cm (1½in) span, long-stalked, borne in tight clusters in early summer. Pink, or yellow. ***Leaves*** Thick, fleshy, rosetted. Mid-green.
• NATIVE HABITAT Garden origin.
• CULTIVATION Ideal pot-grown in an alpine house or suitable for a scree bed with protection from winter wet. Needs fertile, moist but well-drained soil that is rich in organic matter, in partial shade.
• PROPAGATION By offsets in early summer, or by seed in autumn or spring.

☀◑ ◊ pH
❀ ❀ ❀

HEIGHT
to 20cm
(8in)

SPREAD
15cm (6in)
or more

Scrophulariaceae	

MIMULUS 'Whitecroft Scarlet' ♈

Habit Short-lived, spreading, perennial. ***Flowers*** Trumpet-shaped, snapdragon-like, 2cm (¾in) across, borne in sprays throughout summer. Deep scarlet. ***Leaves*** Oval and toothed. Mid-green.
• NATIVE HABITAT Garden origin.
• CULTIVATION Needs reliably moist, fertile soil, enriched with organic matter, in sun or light, dappled shade.
• PROPAGATION By division in spring or by stem tip cuttings in summer.
• OTHER NAME *M. cupreus* 'Whitecroft Scarlet'.

☀ ◊
❀ ❀

HEIGHT
10cm (4in)

SPREAD
20cm (8in)

Ranunculaceae	

AQUILEGIA FORMOSA

Habit Upright, open, herbaceous, perennial, delicate-looking. **Flowers** Nodding, lantern-shaped, to 5cm (2in) across, with 5 erect spurs, to 2cm (¾in) long, borne in branched sprays in late spring and early summer. Red, with orange outer sepals and red-orange spurs. **Leaves** Finely divided, forming basal clumps. Blue-green.
• NATIVE HABITAT Damp scrub, moist woodland, from sea-level to altitudes of 3,000m (10,000ft) in western N. America, from Alaska to California, Utah, and Montana.

• CULTIVATION Suitable for planting in a rock garden, herbaceous border, or woodland. Where grown on a rock garden, dead-head the flowers to prevent self-sowing to the point of nuisance. Grows best in fertile, leaf-rich soil that contains plenty of organic matter and is moist but well drained. Provide a warm site in sun, or dappled or partial shade.
• PROPAGATION By seed, as soon as ripe or in spring. Self-seeds freely and is likely to hybridize unless grown in isolation from other aquilegias.

HEIGHT
60–90cm
(2–3ft)

SPREAD
45cm (18in)

Ranunculaceae	

DELPHINIUM NUDICAULE

Habit Slender, short-lived, erect, herbaceous, perennial. **Flowers** Hooded, funnel-shaped, 2cm (⅜in) span, borne in open sprays in mid-summer. Bright vermilion, scarlet or, sometimes, yellow. **Leaves** Fleshy, long-stalked, lobed. Mid-green.
• NATIVE HABITAT Chaparral, open woodland, and rocky places. Mountains of California.
• CULTIVATION Grow in a warm, sunny site in well-drained, moderately fertile soil.
• PROPAGATION By seed in spring. Flowers in the first season, and is sometimes grown as an annual.

HEIGHT
to 60cm
(24in)

SPREAD
20cm (8in)

Compositae/Asteraceae	ALPINE FLEABANE

ERIGERON ALPINUS

Habit Clumping, perennial. **Flowers** Slender-stemmed, daisy-like, 3.5cm (1½in) across, borne in summer. Lilac-blue to red-purple, with yellow centre. **Leaves** Oval and hairy. Mid-green.
• NATIVE HABITAT Mountains, central and southern Europe.
• CULTIVATION Suitable for planting in a rock garden. Prefers a sunny site with well-drained soil that does not dry out in summer.
• PROPAGATION By seed in early spring, or by division or basal cuttings in spring.

HEIGHT
25cm (10in)
or more

SPREAD
30cm (12in)

Scrophulariaceae	

CALCEOLARIA ARACHNOIDEA

Habit Rhizomatous, cushion- or mat-forming, evergreen, perennial. **Flowers** Pouched, 15mm (⅝in) long, borne in compact clusters from summer to autumn. Dull, deep purple. **Leaves** Lance- to spoon-shaped, and densely soft-haired. White.
• NATIVE HABITAT Chile.
• CULTIVATION Needs moist, gritty, well-drained soil. Protect from winter wet. Under glass, use a mix of equal parts loam, leaf-mould and grit.
• PROPAGATION By seed in autumn or spring, or by division in spring.

HEIGHT
to 25cm
(10in)

SPREAD
to 15cm
(6in)

Scrophulariaceae	

WULFENIA CARINTHIACA

Habit Rosette-forming, evergreen, perennial.
Flowers Small, narrowly tubular, two-lipped,
borne in one-sided, dense spikes to 10cm (4in)
long, in summer. Dark violet-blue. *Leaves* Lance-
shaped, scalloped margined, rosetted. Dark green.
• NATIVE HABITAT Southeast Alps and Albania.
• CULTIVATION Suitable for growing on a rock
garden or crevice, with gritty, most but well-
drained soil that is rich in organic matter.
• PROPAGATION Sow seed in pots in a cold frame
in autumn or spring, or divide after flowering.

☼ ◊
❄ ❄ ❄

HEIGHT
25cm (10in)

SPREAD
25cm (10in)

Ranunculaceae	FALSE COLUMBINE

SEMIAQUILEGIA ECALCARATA

Habit Slender, short-lived, upright, herbaceous,
perennial. *Flowers* Drooping, open lantern-
shaped, 2.5cm (1in) across, unspurred, borne in
clusters in early summer. Dusky pink to deep
purple-blue. *Leaves* Long-stalked and divided.
Mid-green, tinted purple underneath.
• NATIVE HABITAT Mountains of western China.
• CULTIVATION Needs a site in sun, or part-
or dappled shade with fertile, leaf-rich, well-
drained soil that remains reliably moist.
• PROPAGATION By seed in autumn or spring.

☼ ◊
❄ ❄ ❄

HEIGHT
30cm (12in)
or more

SPREAD
15cm (6in)

Labiatae/Lamiaceae	DRAGON'S MOUTH

HORMINIUM PYRENAICUM

Habit Dense, rosette-forming, rhizomatous,
evergreen, perennial. *Flowers* Tubular, 2-lipped,
2cm (⅜in) long, borne in whorls in summer. Dark
violet-blue, occasionally pink or white. *Leaves*
Leathery, toothed, oval, and glossy, forming
basal rosettes. Dark green.
• NATIVE HABITAT Pyrenees and Alps.
• CULTIVATION Good for a rock garden or border
front. Grow in well-drained, moderately fertile soil.
• PROPAGATION By seed in autumn, or by
division in early spring.

☼ ◊
❄ ❄ ❄

HEIGHT
20cm (8in)

SPREAD
50cm (20in)

Ranunculaceae

AQUILEGIA FLABELLATA

Habit Upright, herbaceous, perennial. **Flowers** Semi-erect to nodding, lantern-shaped, to 5cm (2in) across, with 5 upright, incurved spurs, to 2cm (¾in) long, borne in early summer. Soft blue-purple, with white or cream tips. **Leaves** Finely divided, forming basal clumps. Blue-green.
• NATIVE HABITAT Japan, Korea, and Sakhalin.
• CULTIVATION Suitable for growing in open woodland or rock garden. Grows best in climates with cool summers. Prefers a site in dappled or partial shade with fertile, leaf-rich soil that is moist but well-drained. Where grown in a rock garden, it is best to dead-head the flowers to prevent self-sowing to the point of nuisance.
• PROPAGATION By seed, as soon as ripe or in early spring. Self-seeds freely and is likely to hybridize unless isolated from other species of aquilegia.
• OTHER NAME *A. akitensis*.

HEIGHT
20–30cm
(8–12in)

SPREAD
to 15cm
(6in)

DAPHNE

The genus *Daphne* includes about 50 species of deciduous, evergreen, and semi-evergreen shrubs, including some smaller species that are ideal for growing in rock gardens, troughs, and raised beds. The species produce 4-lobed, tubular flowers, nearly all of which have a characteristically intense fragrance. Daphnes are valued for their flowers, attractive foliage, bright berries, and neat habit. Most of the smaller species are found in mountain habitats, often cliffs or scree. Careful handling of Daphnes is essential, as all parts of the plant, including the fruits, are highly toxic if ingested, while the sap can cause skin irritation.

Daphnes should be grown in moderately fertile soil that is enriched with leaf-mould and retains moisture but is well drained. Nearly all species prefer slightly acid to slightly alkaline soil, and a site in full sun or dappled shade. *D. arbuscula*, *D. blagayana*, and *D. genkwa* need neutral to acid soil. All daphnes resent being transplanted, so site carefully and leave undisturbed. Mulch with leaf-mould or top-dress with grit to keep the root-run cool and evenly moist. Pruning should be kept to a minimum.

Sow seed as soon as it is ripe in pots in a cold frame. Retain the seed pans for a second year, as germination can be erratic. Semi-ripe and evergreen cuttings can be taken between mid- and late summer, but many are very slow to root.

Daphnes are commonly grafted, preferably on rootstock of *D. tangutica* or *D. longilobata* rather than the more traditional *D. mezereum*. Both of these rootstocks make it easier to maintain the characteristically neat and compact habit. The prostrate species can be increased by simple layering in spring or early summer, between 4 and 8 weeks after flowering.

D. ALPINA
Habit Compact, upright, twiggy, deciduous, downy-stemmed, shrub.
Flowers Fragrant, 8–10mm (⅓–⅜in) across, borne in terminal clusters of 4–10, in late spring and early summer. White.
Fruits Oblong berries. Orange-red.
Leaves Lance-shaped and hairy. Grey-green.
• HEIGHT 60cm(2ft).
• SPREAD 60cm (2ft).

D. alpina

☀ ◊ ❀ ❀ ❀

D. BLAGAYANA
Habit Spreading, semi-evergreen or evergreen, branched, shrub.
Flowers Fragrant, 1cm (⅜in) across, borne in clusters of 20–30, in spring. Creamy-white.
Fruits Spherical. White or pink.
Leaves Oval and leathery. Dark green.
• HEIGHT to 40cm (16in).
• SPREAD 90cm (3ft).

D. blagayana

☀ ◊ pH ❀ ❀ ❀

D. JASMINEA
Habit Semi-prostrate, semi-erect, evergreen, shrub.
Flowers Fragrant, 8mm (⅓in) across, borne mostly in pairs in late spring and summer. White or cream, often flushed pink.
Leaves Oblong to oval. Blue- or grey-green.
• HEIGHT 5–30cm (2–12in).
• SPREAD 30cm (12in).

D. jasminea

☀ ◊ ❀ ❀

D. GENKWA
Habit Open, upright, deciduous, sparsely branched, shrub.
Flowers Fragrant, 2cm (⅜in) across, borne in clusters of 2–7 in spring, before the leaves. Lilac.
Fruits Small, dry, and egg-shaped. Grey-white.
Leaves Lance-shaped to oval, silky-haired when young. Mid-green.
• HEIGHT 80cm (32in).
• SPREAD 80cm (32in).

D. genkwa

☀ ◊ pH ❀ ❀

D. CNEORUM
Habit Low-growing, hummock-forming, evergreen, shrub.
Flowers Fragrant, 1cm (⅜in) across, in heads of 6–20, borne during late spring. Pale to deep pink.
Leaves Lance-shaped. Dark green.
• HEIGHT 30cm (12in).
• SPREAD to 2m (6ft).

D. cneorum
Garland flower

☼ ◊ ❋❋❋

D. PETRAEA 'Grandiflora'
Habit Compact, slow-growing, evergreen, shrub.
Flowers Fragrant, 1cm (⅜in) across, borne in terminal clusters of 3–5, in late spring. Deep rose-pink.
Leaves Narrowly spoon-shaped, leathery, and glossy. Dark green.
• HEIGHT 10cm (4in).
• SPREAD 25cm (10in).

D. petraea 'Grandiflora'

☼ ◊ ❋❋❋   ♈

D. CNEORUM 'Eximia'
Habit Vigorous, low-growing, spreading, mat-to hummock- forming, evergreen, shrub.
Flowers Fragrant, 1cm (⅜in) across, borne in terminal clusters of 6–20, in late spring. Deep pink.
Leaves Lance-shaped. Dark green.
• HEIGHT 20cm (8in).
• SPREAD to 2m (6ft).

D. cneorum 'Eximia'

☼ ◊ ❋❋❋   ♈

D. COLLINA
Habit Dome-forming. dense, evergreen, shrub.
Flowers Fragrant, 8mm (⅜in) across, silky-haired when young, borne in terminal clusters in late spring. Deep pink.
Fruits Oval. Orange-red.
Leaves Oval and glossy. Mid-green.
• OTHER NAME
D. sericea Collina Group.
• HEIGHT 50cm (20in).
• SPREAD 50cm (20in).

D. collina

☼ ◊ ❋❋❋

D. ARBUSCULA
Habit Semi-prostrate, dwarf, evergreen, shrub.
Flowers Very fragrant, 1.5cm (⅝in) across, borne in dense clusters in late spring and early summer. Deep pink.
Fruits Dry and egg-shaped. Grey-white.
Leaves Linear to oblong, leathery, glossy. Dark green.
• HEIGHT 15cm (6in).
• SPREAD 45cm (18in).

D. arbuscula

☼ ◊ pH ❋❋❋   ♈

D. JEZOENSIS
Habit Slow-growing, rounded, upright, shrub, deciduous in summer.
Flowers Fragrant, 1.5cm (⅝in) across, borne in clusters in early spring. Golden-yellow.
Fruits Oval, shiny. Red.
Leaves Lance-shaped and somewhat shiny. Pale then mid-green.
• HEIGHT 60cm–1m (2–3ft).
• SPREAD 30–45cm.

D. jezoensis

◑ ◊ ❋❋❋

HELIANTHEMUM

The genus *Helianthemum* comprises about 110 species of small, evergreen and semi-evergreen shrubs, most of which inhabit stony alpine meadows or open scrub, particularly in the Mediterranean, but also in N. Africa, and N. and S. America, Asia and Europe. The most popular helianthemums (commonly known as rock roses) are the named cultivars derived from crosses between *H. croceum*, *H. apenninum* and *H. nummularium*. They are valued for their neat, spreading to hummock-forming habit, and attractive, usually grey- or silver-green, finely haired foliage. Their often brilliantly coloured, saucer-shaped flowers are borne in clusters, over long periods in late spring and summer. Helianthemums are ideal for bringing colour into rock gardens and raised beds or, indeed, at the front of flower borders. The smaller species and cultivars, such as *H. lunulatum*, may be used in troughs and suit a dry,

sunny border. They are particularly effective as ground cover over a dry, sunny bank, or for crevices in dry-stone retaining walls. Grow in an open, sunny site, in well-drained, moderately fertile soil that is preferably neutral to alkaline. A light trimming after flowering to keep the plant compact, may produce a second flush of flowers in late summer. Sometimes, helianthemums are rather short-lived and often become sparse and leggy at maturity, so it is best to propagate them regularly, replacing leggy specimens.

Take softwood cuttings in late spring or early summer and root in a cold frame. Pinch out the growing tips of young plants to promote a bushy, well-branched habit. Species can be raised from seed sown as soon as ripe or in the early spring. Overwinter young plants in a cold frame, and set them out in their permanent positions in spring.

H. 'Wisley White'
Habit Low, spreading, evergreen, shrub.
Flowers Saucer-shaped, 2.5cm (1in) across, borne in late spring to mid-summer. Creamy-white, with deep yellow centre.
Leaves Oblong. Grey-green.
• HEIGHT 30cm (12in).
• SPREAD 45cm (18in).

H. 'Wisley White'

☼ ◊ ✽✽✽

H. APENNINUM
Habit Low, loosely mound-forming, evergreen, shrub.
Flowers Saucer-shaped, 2.5cm (1in) across, borne from late spring to mid-summer. White, with deep golden-yellow centre.
Leaves Oval to linear, and downy. Grey-green.
• HEIGHT to 40cm (16in).
• SPREAD 60cm (24in).

H. apenninum
White rock rose

☼ ◊ ✽✽✽

H. 'Rhodanthe Carneum'

Habit Spreading, low, evergreen, shrub.
Flowers Saucer-shaped, 2.5cm (1in) across, borne in late spring and mid-summer. Pale pink, with yellow-flushed centre.
Leaves Narrowly oblong. Grey-green.
• OTHER NAME
H. 'Wisley Pink'.
• HEIGHT 30cm (12in).
• SPREAD 45cm (18in).

H. 'Rhodanthe Carneum'

☼ ◊ ✿✿✿ ♈

H. 'Ben More'

Habit Compact, spreading, twiggy, evergreen, shrub.
Flowers Saucer-shaped, across 2.5cm (1in), borne in loose, terminal clusters from late spring to summer. Deep orange-red.
Leaves Oval to oblong, and glossy. Dark green.
• HEIGHT to 30cm (12in).
• SPREAD 30cm (12in).

H. 'Ben More'

☼ ◊ ✿✿✿

H. 'Raspberry Ripple'

Habit Low, spreading, evergreen, shrub.
Flowers Saucer-shaped, 2.5cm (1in) across, borne in summer. White, with deep raspberry-pink centre spreading out along the petals.
Leaves Linear to oblong. Dark grey-green.
• HEIGHT 20cm (8in).
• SPREAD 30cm (12in).

H. 'Raspberry Ripple'

☼ ◊ ✿✿✿

H. 'Wisley Primrose'

Habit Compact, fast-growing, free-flowering, evergreen, shrub.
Flowers Saucer-shaped, 2.5cm (1in) across, borne over long periods in late spring and summer. Pale primrose-yellow, with golden centre.
Leaves Narrowly oblong. Grey-green.
• HEIGHT 30cm (12in).
• SPREAD 45cm (18in).

H. 'Wisley Primrose'

☼ ◊ ✿✿✿ ♈

H. 'Fire Dragon'

Habit Spreading, evergreen, shrub.
Flowers Saucer-shaped, 2.5cm (1in) across, borne in profusion in late spring and summer. Bright orange-red.
Leaves Elliptic to oblong. Grey-green.
• OTHER NAME
H. 'Mrs Clay'.
• HEIGHT to 30cm (12in).
• SPREAD 30cm (12in).

H. 'Fire Dragon'

☼ ◊ ✿✿✿ ♈

H. LUNULATUM

Habit Compact, upright then spreading, dwarf, evergreen, shrub.
Flowers Saucer-shaped, 15mm (⅝in) across, borne in late spring and early summer. Clear yellow, with prominent orange stamens.
Leaves Lance-shaped to elliptical, and hairy. Grey-green.
• HEIGHT 15cm (6in).
• SPREAD 25cm (10in).

H. lunulatum
Shrubby rock rose

☼ ◊ ✿✿✿

Campanulaceae	

CODONOPSIS VINCIFLORA

Habit Slender, fragile, twining, tuberous, herbaceous, perennial. **Flowers** Saucer-shaped, to 4.5cm (1¾in) across, borne singly on terminal or lateral shoots from mid-summer to autumn. Blue to blue-lilac. **Leaves** Lance-shaped to oval. Mid-green, with blue-green underside.
• NATIVE HABITAT Western China.
• CULTIVATION Needs fertile, light, moist but well-drained soil, in a site with sun or dappled shade. Stake plant or allow to climb small shrubs.
• PROPAGATION By seed in autumn or spring.

☀ ◊
❄ ❄ ❄

HEIGHT
1m (3ft)

SPREAD
60cm (24in)

Iridaceae	

SISYRINCHIUM 'E.K. Balls'

Habit Semi-evergreen, clump-forming, perennial. **Flowers** Star-shaped, 2cm (¾in) across, borne in succession on upright stems in summer. Mauve. **Leaves** Sword-shaped, in basal fans. Mid-green.
• NATIVE HABITAT Garden origin.
• CULTIVATION Suitable for growing in a rock garden, or scree and gravel plantings. Needs a site in full sun with well-drained, moderately fertile soil that is neutral to slightly alkaline.
• PROPAGATION By division in spring.
• OTHER NAME S. 'Balls' Mauve'.

☀ ◊
❄ ❄ ❄

HEIGHT
25cm (10in)

SPREAD
15cm (6in)

Scrophulariaceae	

PARAHEBE CATARRACTAE   ♥

Habit Spreading or erect, evergreen, sub-shrub. **Flowers** Saucer-shaped, 1cm (⅜in) across, borne in sprays in summer. White, heavily veined purple. **Leaves** Oval to lance-shaped and sharp-toothed. Dark green, tinted purple when young.
• NATIVE HABITAT Lowland and mountain meadows, New Zealand.
• CULTIVATION Needs well-drained, moderately fertile soil, in sun. Shelter from cold, dry winds.
• PROPAGATION By seed when ripe or in spring, or by semi-ripe cuttings in summer.

☀ ◊
❄ ❄ ❄

HEIGHT
30cm (12in)

SPREAD
30cm (12in)

Iridaceae	BLUE-EYED GRASS

SISYRINCHIUM GRAMINOIDES

Habit Slender, clump-forming, semi-evergreen, perennial. **Flowers** Star-like, 2cm (⅜in) across, borne throughout summer. Deep blue, with yellow throat. **Leaves** Linear, grass-like. Mid-green.
• NATIVE HABITAT Damp grassland, N. America.
• CULTIVATION Suits a rock or scree garden with neutral to slightly alkaline, moderately fertile soil.
• PROPAGATION By seed in autumn or spring. Self-seeds very freely.
• OTHER NAMES *S. angustifolium, S. bermudiana, S. birameum* of gardens.

HEIGHT
to 30cm
(12in)

SPREAD
15cm (6in)

Dipsacaceae	

SCABIOSA GRAMINIFOLIA

Habit Clump-forming, evergreen, perennial. **Flowers** Solitary, spherical, pincushion-like, to 4cm (1½in) across, borne on slender stems in summer. Lilac to violet. **Leaves** Linear to lance-shaped, grass-like, hairy, in basal tufts. Mid-green.
• NATIVE HABITAT Mountains, southern Europe.
• CULTIVATION Suits a rock garden or border front. Needs dry, well-drained, moderately fertile soil that is neutral to alkaline, preferably in hot sun.
• PROPAGATION By seed in autumn or spring, or by division in spring.

HEIGHT
25cm (10in)

SPREAD
30cm (12in)

Asteraceae/Compositae	PYRENEAN ASTER

ASTER PYRENAEUS

Habit Upright or ascending, clump-forming, perennial. **Flowers** Daisy-like, to 5cm (2in) across, borne from mid- to late summer. Violet or purple, with golden centre. **Leaves** Broadly lance-shaped and slightly toothed. Mid-green.
• NATIVE HABITAT Damp pasture, subalpine meadows, and rocky places, Pyrenees.
• CULTIVATION Suitable for growing in borders. Needs moist but well-drained, fertile soil.
• PROPAGATION By seed in autumn, or by division in spring.

HEIGHT
40–90cm
(16–36in)

SPREAD
30cm (12in)

Campanulaceae	

CODONOPSIS CLEMATIDEA

Habit Tufted, tuberous, herbaceous, perennial.
Flowers Nodding, bell-shaped, 2.5cm (1in) long,
borne in early to mid-summer. Greenish-blue.
Leaves Oval and lightly toothed. Grey-green.
• NATIVE HABITAT Grassy and rocky mountain
slopes, central Asia.
• CULTIVATION Needs light, fertile, moist but
well-drained soil, in sun or dappled shade. Provide
light, twiggy support and shelter from wind.
• PROPAGATION By seed in autumn or spring,
or by division in early spring. Often self-sows.

HEIGHT
70cm (28in)

SPREAD
70cm (28in)

Boraginaceae	SHRUBBY CROMWELL

LITHODORA OLEIFOLIA

Habit Semi-erect, suckering, evergreen, sub-
shrub. **Flowers** Funnel-shaped, 9mm (⅜in) long,
borne in clusters of 3–7 in early summer. Sky-blue,
with pale pink bud. **Leaves** Narrowly oval, with
silky-haired underside. Dull, dark green.
• NATIVE HABITAT Eastern, Spanish Pyrenees.
• CULTIVATION Grow in any well-drained soil in
sun. Trim after flowering to keep plant compact.
• PROPAGATION By rooted suckers in spring,
or by cuttings in mid-summer.
• OTHER NAME *Lithospermum oleifolium*.

HEIGHT
20cm (8in)

SPREAD
30cm (12in)

Campanulaceae	HORNED RAMPION

PHYTEUMA SCHEUCHZERI

Habit Tuft-forming, herbaceous, perennial.
Flowers Tubular, 2.5cm (1in) span, borne in
rounded, spidery heads in summer. Violet-blue.
Leaves Lance-shaped and sparse-toothed,
forming basal clumps. Mid-green.
• NATIVE HABITAT Meadows, European Alps.
• CULTIVATION Suits a rock garden or border front.
Tolerates any well-drained, moderately fertile soil
in sun, but dislikes excessive winter wet.
• PROPAGATION By seed in autumn, or by division
in autumn or early spring. Self-seeds freely.

HEIGHT
to 40cm
(16in)

SPREAD
30cm (12in)

Papaveraceae	PRICKLY BLUE POPPY

MECONOPSIS HORRIDULA

Habit Monocarpic, rosette-forming, perennial.
Flowers Cup-shaped, semi-drooping, long-stalked, to 8cm (3in) across, borne in sprays on spiny stems in early and mid-summer. Pale to deep blue, mauve, or reddish-blue. **Leaves** Oval to narrowly lance-shaped, bristly, with wavy margins. Grey-green, clothed in straw-coloured to purple bristles.
• NATIVE HABITAT High altitudes, Himalaya and Tibet.
• CULTIVATION Ideal for woodland or rock gardens and peat terraces. Grow in leaf-rich, moist but well-drained, neutral to acid, soil with an open texture to prevent winter rot. Needs a cool, humid site in dappled shade, and shelter from cold, dry winds. Prefers areas with cool, damp summers.
• PROPAGATION Sow seed as soon as ripe or in spring, in loamless seed compost but uncovered as the light is needed for germination. Keep seedlings from autumn sowings in a cold greenhouse or frame. Will self-sow in favoured gardens.

☀️ 💧 pH
❄️ ❄️ ❄️

HEIGHT
20–70cm
(8–28in)

SPREAD
45cm (18in)

Campanulaceae	RING BELLFLOWER

SYMPHYANDRA WANNERI

Habit Upright, rosette-forming, monocarpic, evergreen, perennial. *Flowers* Drooping, narrowly bell-shaped, to 3.5cm (1½in) long, borne in clusters in summer. Deep violet-blue. *Leaves* Lance-shaped, toothed, rough-haired. Mid-green.
• NATIVE HABITAT Mountains, southeast Europe.
• CULTIVATION Needs a site in sun or softly dappled shade, with light, well-drained, fertile soil. Usually dies after flowering, but may self-seed.
• PROPAGATION By seed in autumn or early spring.
• OTHER NAME *Campanula wanneri.*

☼ ◊
❀ ❀ ❀

HEIGHT
to 50cm
(20in)

SPREAD
30cm (12in)

Scrophulariaceae	

VERONICA AUSTRIACA subsp. *TEUCRIUM* 'Kapitän'

Habit Mat-forming, evergreen, perennial. *Flowers* Saucer-shaped, 13mm (½in) across, borne in dense spikes during summer. Gentian-blue. *Leaves* Narrowly oval and toothed. Bright green.
• NATIVE HABITAT Garden origin.
• CULTIVATION Suitable for growing in a rock garden or at the front of a border. Grow in well-drained, moderately fertile soil.
• PROPAGATION By division in autumn or spring.
• OTHER NAME *V. teucrium* 'Kapitän'.

☼ ◊
❀ ❀ ❀

HEIGHT
30cm (12in)

SPREAD
50cm (20in)

Boraginaceae	

MOLTKIA SUFFRUTICOSA

Habit Upright, loosely branched, deciduous, sub-shrub. *Flowers* Tubular, 17mm (¾in) long, borne in short, dense clusters in summer. Intense, bright blue. *Leaves* Linear and bristly. Dark green.
• NATIVE HABITAT Mountain grass, northern Italy.
• CULTIVATION Suitable for planting in a rock garden or crevice of rock or a retaining wall. Grow in sharply drained, preferably alkaline soil.
• PROPAGATION By seed in autumn, or by softwood cuttings in mid-summer.
• OTHER NAME *Lithospermum graminifolium.*

☼ ◊
❀ ❀ ❀

HEIGHT
to 40cm
(16in)

SPREAD
30cm (12in)

Boraginaceae	

LITHODORA DIFFUSA 'Heavenly Blue' ♥

Habit Prostrate, hummock-forming, evergreen, shrub. *Flowers* Funnel-shaped, 1cm (½in) across, borne in terminal clusters from late spring to summer. Deep azure-blue. *Leaves* Oval to narrowly paddle-shaped and bristly. Dark green.
• NATIVE HABITAT Garden origin.
• CULTIVATION Needs fertile, acid soil.
• PROPAGATION By semi-ripe cuttings in summer, with gentle heat underneath.
• OTHER NAME *Lithospermum diffusum* 'Heavenly Blue'.

☼ ◊ pH
❀ ❀ ❀

HEIGHT
15cm (6in)

SPREAD
60cm (24in)
or more

Scrophulariaceae	

VERONICA PROSTRATA 'Trehane'

Habit Mat-forming, evergreen, perennial.
Flowers Saucer-shaped, 6–10mm (¼–⅜in) across,
borne in dense, upright spikes in early or mid-
summer. Deep blue. *Leaves* Narrowly oval
and toothed. Yellow-green to gold.
• NATIVE HABITAT Garden origin.
• CULTIVATION Suitable for rock gardens, gravel-
path edges, or at the front of an herbaceous or
mixed border. Grow in full sun in a site with
well-drained, moderately fertile soil.
• PROPAGATION Divide in autumn or early spring.

HEIGHT
15cm (6in)

SPREAD
40cm (16in)
or more

Scrophulariaceae	

VERONICA AUSTRIACA subsp. *TEUCRIUM*

Habit Mat- or cushion-forming, evergreen,
perennial. *Flowers* Saucer-shaped, outward-
facing, 13mm (½in) across, borne in paired sprays
in summer. Deep, bright blue. *Leaves* Narrowly
oval and toothed. Bright green.
• NATIVE HABITAT Grassy and rocky habitats,
in the mountains of temperate northern Europe.
• CULTIVATION Needs well-drained soil.
• PROPAGATION By seed as soon as ripe, or
by division in autumn or spring.
• OTHER NAME *V. teucrium.*

HEIGHT
to 30cm
(12in)

SPREAD
40cm (16in)

Boraginaceae	

MERTENSIA ECHIOIDES

Habit Clumping, perennial. *Flowers* Funnel-
shaped, 7mm (¼in) long, borne in curving clusters
on erect stems, in summer. Deep blue. *Leaves*
Spoon- or lance-shaped, hairy. Dark blue-green.
• NATIVE HABITAT High altitudes, Himalaya.
• CULTIVATION Prefers a site in sun or dappled
shade with gritty, moist but sharply drained soil
enriched with organic matter.
• PROPAGATION By seed in autumn, keeping
seedlings moist and shaded. Divide carefully
as growth begins in early spring.

HEIGHT
20cm (8in)

SPREAD
15cm (6in)

Rosaceae	ALPINE LADY'S MANTLE

ALCHEMILLA ALPINA

Habit Mat-forming or tufted, rhizomatous, perennial. *Flowers* Tiny, star-shaped, 3mm (⅛in) across, borne in loose clusters in summer. Yellow-green. *Leaves* Divided into 5–7 lance-shaped leaflets. Green, with silver, silky-haired underside.
• NATIVE HABITAT Alpine turf and mountain habitats in Europe and Greenland.
• CULTIVATION Thrives in sun or light shade, with moist but well-drained, gritty, fertile soil.
• PROPAGATION By seed in autumn, or by division in early spring or autumn.

☀ ◑
❀ ❀ ❀

HEIGHT
to 12cm
(5in)

SPREAD
to 50cm
(20in)

Geraniaceae	YELLOW ERODIUM

ERODIUM CHRYSANTHUM

Habit Compact, tufted, mound-forming, evergreen, perennial. *Flowers* Saucer-shaped, 2cm (⅘in) across, borne in clusters in summer. Pale sulphur-yellow. *Leaves* Finely dissected, fern-like, paddle- to lance-shaped. Silvery-green.
• NATIVE HABITAT Mountains, Greece.
• CULTIVATION Suits a raised bed or rock garden. Grow in sharply drained, neutral to alkaline soil.
• PROPAGATION By seed when ripe, or by division or basal cuttings in spring. Male and female flowers borne on separate plants; both are needed for seed.

☀ ◌
❀ ❀ ❀

HEIGHT
15cm (6in)

SPREAD
40cm (16in)

Labiatae/Lamiaceae	

ORIGANUM ROTUNDIFOLIUM ♈

Habit Woody-based, rhizomatous, herbaceous or semi-evergreen, perennial. *Flowers* Tubular, 15mm (⅝in) long, borne in nodding whorls in summer. Pale pink, dominated by overlapping, large apple-green bracts. *Leaves* Rounded to heart-shaped and aromatic. Blue-grey.
• NATIVE HABITAT Turkey, Armenia, and Georgia.
• CULTIVATION Ideal pot-grown in an alpine house. Needs sharply drained, alkaline soil, in sun.
• PROPAGATION By seed in autumn or spring, by division in spring, or by cuttings in mid-summer.

☀ ◌
❀ ❀ ❀

HEIGHT
10–30cm
(4–12in)

SPREAD
30cm (12in)

Guttiferae/Clusiaceae	

HYPERICUM OLYMPICUM ♈ f. *UNIFLORUM* 'Citrinum'

Habit Upright, deciduous, sub-shrub. *Flowers* Saucer-shaped, 6cm (2½in) across, borne in summer. Pale lemon-yellow. *Leaves* Broadly oval. Grey-green, with glaucous underside.
• NATIVE HABITAT Garden origin.
• CULTIVATION Ideal for a rock garden, raised bed, or gravel plantings. Needs sun or light shade, with sharply drained, moderately fertile soil.
• PROPAGATION By softwood or semi-ripe cuttings. Self-sown seedlings may come true.

☀ ◌
❀ ❀ ❀

HEIGHT
25cm (10in)

SPREAD
30cm (12in)

Linaceae	

LINUM ARBOREUM

Habit Dwarf, evergreen, shrub. **Flowers** Funnel-shaped, to 3cm (1¼in) across, in compact, terminal clusters, opening from pointed buds; individually short-lived, but borne in succession throughout summer. Rich, deep yellow. **Leaves** Thick and oval, often crowded into rosettes. Dark blue-green.
• NATIVE HABITAT Rocky habitats, southern Aegean to Crete and western Turkey. Plants in the wild are often larger than dimensions given.
• CULTIVATION Excellent for growing on a rock garden, raised bed, or crevices of dry, retaining walls. Also suits planting in large troughs or pans in an alpine house. Grow in a warm site, in full sun, with light, sharply drained, moderately fertile soil. The flowers open fully in warm, sunny weather.
• PROPAGATION By seed in spring or autumn, or by semi-ripe cuttings in summer in a cold frame.

☼ ◊
❄ ❄

HEIGHT
30cm (12in)

SPREAD
30cm (12in)

Scrophulariaceae	

VERBASCUM 'Letitia' ♥

Habit Dense, rounded, stiff-branched, evergreen, sub-shrub. **Flowers** Outward-facing, saucer-shaped, 15mm (⅝in) across, borne in short spikes throughout summer. Bright yellow, with reddish-orange centre. **Leaves** Lance-shaped and irregularly toothed. Grey-green.
• NATIVE HABITAT Garden origin.
• CULTIVATION Suits a rock garden, raised bed, or crevice in a dry, retaining wall. Needs sharply drained, moderately fertile soil in warm sun.
• PROPAGATION By semi-ripe cuttings in summer.

HEIGHT
25cm (10in)

SPREAD
50cm (20in)

Cruciferae/ Brassicaceae	MOUNTAIN ALISON

ALYSSUM MONTANUM

Habit Prostrate, mat-forming, evergreen, perennial. **Flowers** Scented, cross-shaped, 4-petalled, 5mm (⅛in) across, borne in spikes in early summer. Golden-yellow. **Leaves** Paddle-shaped to oval, forming rosettes. Grey.
• NATIVE HABITAT Rocky and stony sites, Europe.
• CULTIVATION Suitable for a rock garden and raised beds. Needs sunny site, with well-drained, preferably gritty, moderately fertile soil.
• PROPAGATION By seed in autumn or spring, or by greenwood cuttings in mid-summer.

HEIGHT
10–15cm
(4–6in)

SPREAD
to 50cm
(20in)

Ranunculaceae	

TROLLIUS ACAULIS

Habit Clumping, herbaceous, perennial.
Flowers Bowl-shaped, terminal, usually solitary, to 5cm (2in) across, borne in summer. Golden-yellow. **Leaves** Rounded, segmented into narrowly lance-shaped lobes. Mid-green.
• NATIVE HABITAT Moist, grassy slopes, Himalaya.
• CULTIVATION Needs leaf- or peat-rich, moist soil that is acid or alkaline, in sun or partial shade.
• PROPAGATION By seed when ripe or in spring (may take 2 years to germinate), or by division as new growth begins or after flowering.

HEIGHT
10–30cm
(4–12in)

SPREAD
15cm (6in)

Onagraceae	SUNDROPS

OENOTHERA PERENNIS

Habit Tufted, clumping, evergreen, perennial.
Flowers Funnel-shaped, 2cm (¾in) across, opening from nodding buds, borne in loose, erect spikes in summer. Yellow. **Leaves** Narrowly spoon-shaped, forming rosettes. Mid-green.
• NATIVE HABITAT Mountains, eastern N. America.
• CULTIVATION Needs well-drained, moderately fertile, gritty or stony soil, in a warm, sunny site.
• PROPAGATION By seed in autumn or early spring, or by careful division in spring.
• OTHER NAME O. pumila.

HEIGHT
20cm (8in)

SPREAD
20cm (8in)

Guttiferae/Clusiaceae	

HYPERICUM CERASTOIDES

Habit Erect, then arching, evergreen, sub-shrub.
Flowers Star-shaped, to 4.5cm (1¾in) across, borne
in clusters of 5 in early summer. Deep yellow.
Leaves Oval or narrow, downy. Grey-green.
• NATIVE HABITAT Woods and rocks, southern
Bulgaria, northeast Greece, and northwest Turkey.
• CULTIVATION Needs moderately fertile, sharply
drained, ideally sandy and slightly acid soil, in sun.
• PROPAGATION By seed or by division, in spring
or autumn.
• OTHER NAME *H. rhodoppeum.*

HEIGHT
15cm (6in)

SPREAD
to 40cm
(16in)

Compositae/Asteraceae	

EURYOPS ACRAEUS

Habit Dense, dome-forming, evergreen, shrub.
Flowers Daisy-like, 2.5cm (1in) across, borne
in summer. Clear, citrus yellow. *Leaves* Leathery,
waxy, linear and flattened, with toothed tips.
Bright silver-grey.
• NATIVE HABITAT Rocky areas, S. Africa.
• CULTIVATION Grow in sharply drained soil, in
warm, sheltered site. Dislikes excessive winter wet.
• PROPAGATION By seed in spring, or by
softwood or semi-ripe cuttings in summer.
• OTHER NAME *E. evansii* of gardens.

HEIGHT
50cm (20in)

SPREAD
50cm (20in)

Polygonaceae	SULPHUR FLOWER

ERIOGONUM UMBELLATUM

Habit Mat-forming, evergreen, perennial. *Flowers*
Tiny, borne in dense clusters to 6cm (2½in) across,
in summer. Cream to sulphur-yellow, with copper
tints at maturity. *Leaves* Spoon-shaped to oval.
Mid-green, with woolly, white undersides.
• NATIVE HABITAT Southwest Canada to
western USA.
• CULTIVATION Grow in poor to moderately
fertile, gritty, sharply drained soil in sun.
• PROPAGATION By seed in autumn, or by rooting
rosette cuttings in spring and early summer.

HEIGHT
30cm (12in)

SPREAD
to 90cm
(36in)

Scrophulariaceae

VERBASCUM DUMULOSUM

Habit Forms large, spreading domes, downy-stemmed, evergreen, sub-shrub.
Flowers Outward-facing, saucer-shaped, 15mm (⅝in) across, borne in short spikes, to 15cm (6in) high, during summer. Bright yellow, with red eye.
Leaves Oval, often scalloped, and densely felted. Grey or grey-green.
• NATIVE HABITAT Dry, stony hillsides, southwest Turkey.
• CULTIVATION Suitable for a rock garden or raised bed, with overhead protection from winter wet.

Best planted on its side in a vertical rock or wall crevice. Needs a warm, sunny site, with gritty or stony, sharply drained, moderately fertile, and preferably alkaline soil. Although cold hardy, it will not tolerate cold in combination with winter wet. May also be grown in an alpine house in a mix of equal parts loam-based potting compost and grit.
• PROPAGATION By seed in late spring in a cold frame, or by semi-ripe cuttings in summer.

☼ ◊
❄ ❄ ❄

HEIGHT
to 25cm
(10in)

SPREAD
to 70cm
(28in)

Ranunculaceae	GRASS-LEAVED BUTTERCUP

RANUNCULUS GRAMINEUS

Habit Slender, upright, clumping, herbaceous, perennial. *Flowers* Cup-shaped, 2cm (¾in) across, borne on upright, branched stems in late spring and early summer. Lemon-yellow. *Leaves* Grass-like and linear to lance-shaped. Blue-green.
• NATIVE HABITAT Mountain pastures, southern Europe.
• CULTIVATION Tolerates any moist but well-drained soil in a sunny or partially shaded site.
• PROPAGATION By division in early spring or autumn, or by seed as soon as ripe.

☼ ◊
❋ ❋ ❋

HEIGHT
to 30cm
(12in)

SPREAD
15cm (6in)

Leguminosae/ Papilionaceae	

GENISTA PILOSA 'Procumbens'

Habit Prostrate, free-flowering, deciduous, shrub, with downy branches. *Flowers* Pea, 1cm (¾in) long, borne in spikes in early summer. Yellow. *Leaves* Lance-shaped. Dark green.
• NATIVE HABITAT Garden origin. Species occurs in heath, open woods, and rocky places.
• CULTIVATION Suitable for a raised bed or rock garden, and will trail over a large rock or bank. Needs a sunny site with light, well-drained, moderately fertile soil. Tolerates poor, dry soils.
• PROPAGATION By semi-ripe cuttings in summer.

☼ ◊
❋ ❋ ❋

HEIGHT
20cm (8in)

SPREAD
50cm (20in)
or more

Leguminosae/ Papilionaceae	

GENISTA LYDIA

Habit Mound-forming, free-flowering, deciduous, shrub, with arching, prickle-tipped branches. *Flowers* Pea, 15mm (⅝in) long, borne in small clusters in early summer. Yellow. *Leaves* Small, narrowly oval. Blue-green.
• NATIVE HABITAT Rocky sites, eastern Balkans.
• CULTIVATION Suitable for a large rock garden or raised bed. Needs a warm, sunny site, with light, well-drained, moderately fertile soil.
• PROPAGATION By seed in autumn or spring, or by semi-ripe cuttings in summer.

☼ ◊
❋ ❋ ❋

HEIGHT
to 60cm
(24in)

SPREAD
90cm (36in)

Crassulaceae	ROSEROOT

RHODIOLA ROSEA

Habit Clumping, herbaceous, with succulent, thick stems, perennial. *Flowers* Tiny, star-shaped, 6mm (¼in) across, borne in dense, terminal heads in summer. Pink bud, opening to yellow-green. *Leaves* Fleshy and oval. Grey-green, with red tips.
• NATIVE HABITAT Rocks, sea cliffs, screes, from sea level to high altitudes, northern hemisphere.
• CULTIVATION Best grown in gritty compost.
• PROPAGATION By seed in spring or autumn, or by division in spring.
• OTHER NAMES *Sedum roseum, S. rhodiola.*

☼ ◊
❋ ❋ ❋

HEIGHT
20–30cm
(8–12in)

SPREAD
30cm (12in)

Papaveraceae	ALPINE POPPY

PAPAVER ALPINUM

Habit Short-lived, tufted, evergreeen, perennial. *Flowers* Cup-shaped, solitary, 4cm (1½in) across, borne in summer. White, orange, or yellow. *Leaves* Hairy, and finely divided into linear segments. Grey-green.
• NATIVE HABITAT Alps and Pyrenees.
• CULTIVATION Grows best in a sunny site, with low-fertility, stony, free-draining soils.
• PROPAGATION By seed in spring. Often self-seeds, but seldom to the point of nuisance. Needs to be propagated regularly.

☼ ◊
❋ ❋ ❋

HEIGHT
15–20cm
(6–8in)

SPREAD
10cm (4in)

Compositae/Asteraceae	GOLDEN HAWKSBEARD

CREPIS AUREA

Habit Tap-rooted, rosette-forming, perennial. *Flowers* Dandelion-like, 3cm (1¼in) across, borne on stems covered in black and white hairs, during summer. Bright orange-yellow. *Leaves* Oval to lance-shaped and deep-toothed. Light green.
• NATIVE HABITAT Rocky places and mountains, in Italy and the Balkans.
• CULTIVATION Good for wall plantings or rocky places. Tolerates any well-drained soil in sun.
• PROPAGATION By seed as soon as ripe. Self-seeds freely, and can become a nuisance.

☼ ◊
❋ ❋ ❋

HEIGHT
10–30cm
(4–12in)

SPREAD
to 30cm
(12in)

Ericaceae	

GAULTHERIA CUNEATA

Habit Dwarf, densely branched, evergreen, shrub.
Flowers Urn-shaped, 6mm (¼in) across, borne
in lateral spikes in late spring. White. **Leaves**
Pointed, oval, toothed, and leathery. Mid-green.
Fruits Globose berries, 6mm (¼in) across. White.
• NATIVE HABITAT Western China.
• CULTIVATION Excellent for growing in a rock
or woodland garden, or a peat bed. Needs moist
but well-drained, leaf-rich, neutral to acid soil.
• PROPAGATION By seed as soon as ripe, or by
semi-ripe cuttings in mid- to late summer.

☼ ◊ pH
❋ ❋ ❋

HEIGHT
30cm (12in)

SPREAD
90cm (36in)

Labiatae/Lamiaceae	

ORIGANUM AMANUM

Habit Spreading, wiry-stemmed, semi-
herbaceous, sub-shrub. **Flowers** Tubular, slightly
curved, 4cm (1½in) long, borne in terminal whorls
in autumn. Bright pink, with green base.
Leaves Aromatic and oval. Bright green.
• NATIVE HABITAT Mountain rocks, Turkey.
• CULTIVATION Under glass, grow in a mix of equal
parts loam, leaf-mould, and grit. Needs sharply
drained, gritty, alkaline soil. Dislikes winter wet.
• PROPAGATION By seed in spring, or by cuttings
of basal shoots in mid-summer.

☼ ◊
❋ ❋

HEIGHT
8cm (3in)

SPREAD
30cm (12in)

Rosaceae	

SORBUS REDUCTA

Habit Suckering, thicket-forming, deciduous,
shrub. **Flowers** Small, saucer-shaped, borne in
clusters 8cm (3in) across, in spring. White.
Leaves Pinnate and glossy. Dark green, rich red
in autumn. **Fruits** Round berries, 1cm (½in)
span. White, flushed crimson.
• NATIVE HABITAT Mountains, western China.
• CULTIVATION Grow in an open site in full sun,
with moderately fertile, well-drained soil.
• PROPAGATION By seed in autumn or spring,
or by softwood cuttings in early summer.

☼ ◊
❋ ❋ ❋

HEIGHT
30–60cm
(12–24in))

SPREAD
1–2m
(3–6ft)
or more

Compositae/Asteraceae	

CELMISIA SEMICORDATA

Habit Clump-forming, somewhat rhizomatous, evergreen, perennial. *Flowers* Daisy-like, 8cm (3in), borne on upright, green-white stems in early and mid-summer. White, with yellow centre. *Leaves* Erect, then recurved, sword- to lance-shaped, leathery, with fine, silky hair. Silver-green, white underneath.

• NATIVE HABITAT Alpine and subalpine pastures, at high altitudes, South Island, New Zealand.
• CULTIVATION Excellent for planting in a raised bed or rock garden, but grows best in cool, moist climates. Needs a sunny or partially shaded site, with slightly acid, moist but well-drained soil that is rich in organic matter.
• PROPAGATION By seed as soon as ripe, or by careful division in spring. Offspring may be hybrids unless isolated, and few viable seeds generally are produced.
• OTHER NAME *C. coriacea* of gardens.

HEIGHT
to 50cm
(20in)

SPREAD
30cm (12in)

Ranunculaceae	

RANUNCULUS CALANDRINIOIDES

Habit Clumping, fleshy-rooted, semi-evergreen, perennial. **Flowers** Cup-shaped, 5cm (2in) across, borne in loose clusters of up to 3 in late winter and early spring. White, flushed pink. **Leaves** Smooth and oval, dying back in summer. Blue-green.
• NATIVE HABITAT Atlas mountains, N. Africa.
• CULTIVATION Needs gritty, sharply drained soil, that is rich in organic matter. Under glass, use equal parts of loam, leaf-mould, and sharp sand.
• PROPAGATION By seed when ripe but still green, or by division in autumn or after flowering.

HEIGHT
20cm (8in)

SPREAD
15cm (6in)

Asteraceae/Compositae	

OZOTHAMNUS SELAGO

Habit Upright, evergreen, hebe-like, sub-shrub. **Flowers** Solitary, cylindrical, borne in summer. Cream. **Leaves** Aromatic, oval to triangular, scale-like. Dark green, with woolly, white underside.
• NATIVE HABITAT South Island, New Zealand.
• CULTIVATION Suitable for growing in a trough, a scree bed, or an alpine house. Needs gritty, sharply drained soil, and protection from winter wet.
• PROPAGATION By seed when ripe, or by semi-ripe cuttings in summer.
• OTHER NAME *Helichrysum selago*.

HEIGHT
to 40cm
(16in)

SPREAD
25cm (10in)

Compositae/Asteraceae	

OZOTHAMNUS CORALLOIDES

Habit Erect, dome-forming, evergreen, sub-shrub. **Flowers** Solitary, cylindrical, borne in summer. Pale yellow. **Leaves** Leathery, diamond-shaped, scale-like. Dark green, woolly-white underneath.
• NATIVE HABITAT New Zealand.
• CULTIVATION Suitable for planting in a trough, a scree bed, or an alpine house. Grow in gritty, sharply drained soil, and protect from winter wet.
• PROPAGATION By seed when ripe, or by semi-ripe cuttings in mid- to late summer.
• OTHER NAME *Helichrysum coralloides*.

HEIGHT
15cm (6in)

SPREAD
15cm (6in)

Salicaceae	

SALIX X BOYDII

Habit Very slow-growing, erect, deciduous, shrub, with gnarled branches. **Flowers** Insignificant female catkins borne occasionally on bare branches in spring. **Leaves** Almost circular, rough-textured, prominently veined, and untoothed. Grey-green.
• NATIVE HABITAT Angus mountains, Scotland.
• CULTIVATION Suitable for planting in a trough or rock garden. Grows best in gritty, moist but sharply drained soil.
• PROPAGATION By hardwood cuttings in winter.
• OTHER NAME *S. 'Boydii'*.

HEIGHT
30cm (12in)

SPREAD
to 1m
(40in)

Cruciferae/ Brassicaceae	TRIFOLIATE BITTERCRESS

CARDAMINE TRIFOLIA

Habit Creeping, rhizomatous, evergreen, patch-forming, perennial. **Flowers** Cross-shaped, to 15mm (⅝in) across, borne in congested sprays in late spring. White, sometimes pink, with yellow anthers. **Leaves** Divided into 3 rounded to diamond-shaped leaflets. Dark green.
• NATIVE HABITAT Central and southern Europe.
• CULTIVATION Ideal for a shady corner of a rock garden in moist, fertile soil. Tolerates deep shade.
• PROPAGATION By seed in autumn or spring, or by division in autumn or after flowering.

☼ ◖
❄ ❄ ❄

HEIGHT
to 15cm
(6in)

SPREAD
30cm or
more (12in)

Cruciferae/ Brassicaceae	

ARABIS CAUCASICA 'Variegata'

Habit Mat-forming, evergreen, perennial. **Flowers** Fragrant, cross-shaped, to 1cm (⅜in) across, borne in loose sprays in spring. White. **Leaves** Oval, toothed, rosetted. Mid-green, edged pale-yellow.
• NATIVE HABITAT Garden origin.
• CULTIVATION Suitable for planting in a rock garden, dry bank, or on the top of a retaining wall. Thrives in any well-drained soil in full sun, and will tolerate hot, dry conditions and poor soils. Trim plant after flowering.
• PROPAGATION By softwood cuttings in summer.

☼ ◌
❄ ❄ ❄

HEIGHT
15cm (6in)

SPREAD
50cm (20in)

Caryophyllaceae	CORSICAN SANDWORT

ARENARIA BALEARICA

Habit Prostrate, mat-forming, moss-like, evergreen, perennial. **Flowers** Solitary, saucer-shaped, 6–10mm (¼–⅜in) across, borne in late spring to summer. White. **Leaves** Tiny and broadly oval. Bright, shining green.
• NATIVE HABITAT Western Mediterranean islands.
• CULTIVATION Will cling tightly to a shady, porous sandstone rockface or damp wall, forming a dense mat of foliage. Needs a moist, shaded site.
• PROPAGATION By seed in autumn, or take rooted cuttings.

☼ ◖
❄ ❄ ❄

HEIGHT
1–2cm
(⅜–¾in)

SPREAD
30cm or
more (12in)

Portulacaceae	

LEWISIA BRACHYCALYX

Habit Dwarf, tufted, herbaceous, perennial.
Flowers Solitary, funnel-shaped, to 5cm (2in)
across, borne in profusion from late spring to
early summer. White, or pale pink. **Leaves** Lance-
shaped, fleshy, in basal rosettes. Dark green.
• NATIVE HABITAT Stony, open meadows and
grassland, southern California and Arizona, USA.
• CULTIVATION Needs sharply drained, neutral to
acid soil. Best in an alpine house to protect from
excessive wet when dormant in summer.
• PROPAGATION By seed in autumn in a cold frame.

☀ ◐
❄❄❄

HEIGHT
8cm (3in)

SPREAD
8cm (3in)

| Fumariaceae/ | DUTCHMAN'S |
Papaveraceae	BREECHES

DICENTRA CUCULLARIA

Habit Tuberous, clump-forming, herbaceous,
perennial. **Flowers** Drooping, heart-shaped, to
2cm (⅜in) long, borne on arching stems in early
spring. White, tipped yellow. **Leaves** Fern-like
and finely divided. Blue-green.
• NATIVE HABITAT Woods, eastern N. America.
• CULTIVATION Suits a woodland or rock garden,
in gritty, fertile soil. Dies back soon after
flowering and needs a dry summer dormancy.
• PROPAGATION By seed as soon as ripe or in
spring. Divide after the leaves have died down.

◐ ◐
❄❄❄

HEIGHT
20cm (8in)

SPREAD
25cm (10in)

Rosaceae	ROCK SPIRAEA

PETROPHYTUM HENDERSONII

Habit Mat-forming, evergreen, sub-shrub.
Flowers Tiny, borne in conical, spike-like
sprays to 8cm (3in) long, in summer. White.
Leaves Spoon-shaped, hairy. Blue-green.
• NATIVE HABITAT Scree and rock crevices,
mountains of western N. America.
• CULTIVATION Excellent for a scree or raised
bed. Needs gritty, sharply drained, preferably
slightly alkaline soil that is not too fertile.
• PROPAGATION By seed in autumn, or by
softwood or semi-ripe cuttings in summer.

☀ ◐
❄❄❄

HEIGHT
10cm (4in)

SPREAD
20cm (8in)

Portulacaceae	

LEWISIA COLUMBIANA

Habit Evergreen, perennial. **Flowers** Open
funnel-shaped, 2.5cm (1in) across, borne in lax
clusters from spring to summer. Deep to pale
pink, with darker veins. **Leaves** Lance-shaped
or linear, in fleshy rosettes. Dark green.
• NATIVE HABITAT Western N. America.
• CULTIVATION Excellent for growing as a pot
plant in an alpine house. Can be grown in troughs
outdoors but protect from winter wet.
• PROPAGATION By seed in autumn, or by offsets
in early summer.

☀ ◐
❄❄❄

HEIGHT
15cm (6in)

SPREAD
15cm (6in)

Caryophyllaceae	

SAGINA SUBULATA 'Aurea'

Habit Mat-forming, stem-rooting, moss-like, evergreen, perennial. **Flowers** Solitary, tiny, 5-petalled, 4mm (⅙in) across, borne in summer. White. **Leaves** Linear, pointed. Yellow-green.
• NATIVE HABITAT Garden origin.
• CULTIVATION Suits a rock garden or paving crevices, where it forms a spreading mat. Needs moist but well-drained, neutral to acid soil. Prefers some mid-day shade but dislikes hot, dry weather.
• PROPAGATION Divide in spring or summer.
• OTHER NAME S. glabra 'Aurea'.

☀ ◊ pH
❀ ❀ ❀

HEIGHT
1cm (⅜in)

SPREAD
20cm (8in)

Liliaceae/Trilliaceae	SNOW TRILLIUM

TRILLIUM NIVALE

Habit Compact, clump-forming, rhizomatous, herbaceous, perennial. **Flowers** Upright, to 4cm (1½in) across, borne in early spring. Pure white, with green sepals. **Leaves** Oval and pointed, in threes. Dark blue-green.
• NATIVE HABITAT Southeast USA.
• CULTIVATION Quite difficult to grow, but suits a rock garden or alpine house. Needs moist, well-drained, fertile, neutral to slightly alkaline soil.
• PROPAGATION By seed as soon as ripe, but may take 5–7 years to flower. Divide after flowering.

☀ ◊
❀ ❀ ❀

HEIGHT
12cm (5in)

SPREAD
10cm (4in)

Papaveraceae	DOUBLE BLOOD ROOT

SANGUINARIA CANADENSIS 'Plena' ♀

Habit Rhizomatous, herbaceous, patch-forming, perennial. **Flowers** Solitary, cup-shaped, double, 7cm (3in) across, borne in spring. Glistening white. **Leaves** Kidney-shaped, lobed. Bluish grey-green.
• NATIVE HABITAT Garden origin.
• CULTIVATION Suits a woodland, rock garden, or peat bed. Needs reliably moist, well-drained fertile soil in partial or dappled shade. Tolerates part-day sun in moist soils, but dislikes being disturbed.
• PROPAGATION Divide after flowering in spring.
• OTHER NAME S. canadensis 'Flore Plena'.

☀ ◊
❀ ❀ ❀

HEIGHT
15cm (6in)

SPREAD
30cm (12in)

Papaveraceae	BLOOD ROOT, RED PUCCOON

SANGUINARIA CANADENSIS

Habit Rhizomatous, herbaceous, patch-forming, perennial. *Flowers* Solitary, cup-shaped, single, to 5cm (2in) across, borne in spring with the leaves. White. *Leaves* Kidney-shaped. Bluish grey-green.
• NATIVE HABITAT Woodlands, eastern N. America.
• CULTIVATION Excellent for a woodland, rock garden, or peat bed. Needs fertile, reliably moist but well-drained soil, in partial or dappled shade. Will tolerate part-day sun in moist soils.
• PROPAGATION Divide after flowering in spring, or sow seed in autumn in a cold frame.

HEIGHT
15cm (6in)

SPREAD
30cm (12in)

Ranunculaceae	ALPINE BUTTERCUP

RANUNCULUS ALPESTRIS

Habit Short-lived, fibrous-rooted, evergreen, perennial. *Flowers* Cupped, to 2cm (⅜in) across, borne from late spring to mid-summer. White. *Leaves* Kidney-shaped, lobed. Dark, glossy green.
• NATIVE HABITAT Mountains, central and southern Europe.
• CULTIVATION Suits an alpine house or scree bed, in gritty, fertile, moist, sharply drained soil.
• PROPAGATION By seed, when still slightly green, in an open frame, but germination is erratic. Otherwise, by division in early spring or autumn.

HEIGHT
10cm (4in)

SPREAD
10cm (4in)

Ranunculaceae	SPRING PASQUE FLOWER

PULSATILLA VERNALIS

Habit Tufted, rosette-forming, evergreen, perennial. *Flowers* Bell-shaped, erect, silky-haired, to 6cm (2½in) across, borne from drooping buds in spring. White, flushed blue-violet. *Leaves* Finely cut, sparsely haired, leathery. Deep green.
• NATIVE HABITAT Alpine turf, from Spain to Scandinavia, and from Bulgaria to Siberia.
• CULTIVATION Grow in moist, sharply drained soil in a scree or alpine house. Protect from winter wet.
• PROPAGATION By seed as soon as ripe.

HEIGHT
10cm (4in)

SPREAD
10cm (4in)

Ericaceae	

CASSIOPE LYCOPODIOIDES

Habit Mat-forming, evergreen, shrub. *Flowers* Bell-shaped, 6mm (¼in) long, borne from the upper leaf axils in late spring. White, with red sepals. *Leaves* Tiny, scale-like, and closely overlapping on the slender stems. Dark green.
• NATIVE HABITAT Northwest N. America, Japan.
• CULTIVATION Suits a sheltered site on a rock garden, in acid soil that is rich in organic matter.
• PROPAGATION By seed in autumn, or by semi-ripe cuttings in summer, preferably in a propagating frame with a misting unit.

HEIGHT
8cm (3in)

SPREAD
25cm (10in)

Ranunculaceae	WHITE LESSER CELANDINE

RANUNCULUS FICARIA f. *ALBUS*

Habit Tufted, tuberous, herbaceous, perennial.
Flowers Solitary, saucer-shaped, 2–3cm (⅗–1⅕in)
across, borne in late winter and early spring.
Cream, fading to white at maturity. *Leaves*
Basal, broadly heart-shaped, dying back soon
after flowering. Dark glossy green.
• NATIVE HABITAT Garden origin. The white-
flowered form occurs naturally in wild populations,
in hedgerows, deciduous woodland, and damp
grassy habitats. It has been selected and
propagated vegetatively in cultivation.

• CULTIVATION Spreads rapidly and, like the
yellow-flowered species, is too invasive for the
rock garden. More suitable for naturalizing in
turf, or for growing in a wild or woodland garden.
Grow in moist soil that is enriched with organic
matter, in partial or deep shade.
• PROPAGATION Divide in spring or autumn.

☼ ◊
❀ ❀ ❀

HEIGHT
15cm (6in)

SPREAD
30cm (12in)
or more

Ericaceae	

CASSIOPE MERTENSIANA

Habit Dense, upright, evergreen, sub-shrub.
Flowers Bell-shaped, to 8mm (⅓in) long, borne
from the upper leaf axils in spring. Creamy-white,
with red or green sepals. **Leaves** Tiny, oval to
lance-shaped, overlapping along stem. Dark green.
• NATIVE HABITAT Arctic and N. America.
• CULTIVATION Suits a sheltered site in a rock
garden, in acid soil that is rich in organic matter.
• PROPAGATION By seed in autumn, or by
semi-ripe cuttings in summer, preferably in
a propagating frame with a misting unit.

HEIGHT
15cm (6in)

SPREAD
25cm (10in)

Diapensiaceae	OCONEE BELLS

SHORTIA GALACIFOLIA

Habit Clump-forming, stoloniferous, evergreen,
perennial. **Flowers** Solitary, half-nodding, funnel-
shaped, to 2.5cm (1in) across, with toothed petals,
borne in late spring. White. **Leaves** ·Leathery,
rounded, and sharply toothed. Dark green.
• NATIVE HABITAT Woodlands, eastern USA.
• CULTIVATION Good for a rock garden, peat bed,
or open woodland glades, in leaf-rich, acid, moist,
well-drained soil. Needs semi or deep shade.
• PROPAGATION By seed as soon as ripe in a cold
frame. Separate rooted runners carefully in spring.

HEIGHT
15cm (6in)

SPREAD
25cm (10in)

Saxifragaceae	FOAMFLOWER

TIARELLA WHERRYI ♥

Habit Compact, clumping, evergreen, perennial.
Flowers Small, star-shaped, borne in spike-like
sprays 15–35cm (5–14in) long, on upright brown
stems, in spring. White or pink-tinted. **Leaves**
Triangular, 3-lobed. Pale green, tinted red.
• NATIVE HABITAT Appalachian Mountains, USA.
• CULTIVATION Suitable for a rock or woodland
garden, in cool, moist soil. Tolerates a shady site.
• PROPAGATION By seed when ripe or in spring,
or by division in spring or early summer.
• OTHER NAME *T. cordifolia* var. *collina*.

HEIGHT
20cm (8in)

SPREAD
30cm (12in)

Caryophyllaceae	HIMALAYAN GYPSOPHILA

GYPSOPHILA CERASTIOIDES

Habit Mat-forming, semi-evergreen, perennial.
Flowers Shallow funnel-shaped, to 15mm (⅝in)
across, borne in loose clusters in late spring. White,
with pink veins or tint. **Leaves** Spoon-shaped or
broadly oval, almost stalkless. Mid-green.
• NATIVE HABITAT Western Himalaya.
• CULTIVATION Good for a raised bed, dry-stone
retaining wall, or rock garden. Needs light, sharply
drained, preferably slightly alkaline soil, in full sun.
• PROPAGATION By seed in winter,
or by division in spring.

HEIGHT
5cm (2in)

SPREAD
15cm (6in)

Ranunculaceae	RUE ANEMONE

ANEMONELLA THALICTROIDES

Habit Clump-forming, tuberous, herbaceous, perennial. **Flowers** Cup-shaped, to 2cm (⅝in) across, borne in sprays of 2–4, from spring to early summer. White or pale pink. **Leaves** Finely divided, delicate, and fern-like. Dark bluish-green.
• NATIVE HABITAT Woodland, eastern N. America.
• CULTIVATION Grow as a pot plant in an alpine house. Outdoors, prefers moist but well-drained, fertile soil. The tubers will rot in over-wet soils.
• PROPAGATION Sow seed as soon as ripe in a cold frame, or divide young plants in early spring.

☀ ◊
✳ ✳ ✳

HEIGHT
10cm (4in)

SPREAD
30cm (12in)

Portulacaceae	

LEWISIA TWEEDYI ♔

Habit Rosette-forming, evergreen, perennial. **Flowers** Open funnel-shaped, to 6cm (2½in) across, borne singly or in clusters of up to 4, from spring to early summer. White to pink, or apricot. **Leaves** Lance-shaped to oval, fleshy. Mid-green.
• NATIVE HABITAT Rock crevices. northwest USA.
• CULTIVATION Grows best as a pot plant in an alpine house. Needs neutral to acid soil that is rich in organic matter, and a dry summer dormancy.
• PROPAGATION By seed in autumn, or by offsets in early summer.

☀ ◊
✳ ✳ ✳

HEIGHT
20cm (8in)

SPREAD
30cm (12in)

Diapensiaceae	

SHORTIA UNIFLORA 'Grandiflora'

Habit Vigorous, mat-forming, evergreen, perennial. **Flowers** Solitary, half-nodding flared bells to 5cm (2in) across, with toothed petals, borne in spring. White or pale pink. **Leaves** Leathery, rounded, toothed, heart-shaped base. Deep green.
• NATIVE HABITAT Woodlands, Japan.
• CULTIVATION Suits a rock garden, peat bed, or open woodland glades, with leaf-rich, moist, well-drained soil. Dislikes dry climates and bright sun.
• PROPAGATION By seed as soon as ripe in a cold frame. Separate rooted runners carefully in spring.

☀ ◊ pH
✳ ✳ ✳

HEIGHT
15cm (6in)

SPREAD
25cm (10in)

Liliaceae/Trilliaceae	

TRILLIUM RIVALE ♔

Habit Compact, erect, rhizomatous, herbaceous, perennial. **Flowers** Semi-upright, to 2.5cm (1in) across, borne in spring. White or pale pink, with purple-spotted base and green sepals. **Leaves** Oval and pointed, borne in threes. Mid blue-green.
• NATIVE HABITAT Mountain woods, western USA.
• CULTIVATION Grows best in pockets in a peat garden. Needs moist but well-drained, neutral to slightly alkaline soil, enriched with organic matter.
• PROPAGATION By ripe seed but it may take 5–7 years to flower. Divide large, established clumps.

☀ ◊
✳ ✳ ✳

HEIGHT
12cm (5in)

SPREAD
15cm (6in)

Caryophyllaceae.	PINK SANDWORT

ARENARIA PURPURASCENS

Habit Mat- or cushion-forming, evergreen, perennial. **Flowers** Star-shaped, to 15mm (⅝in) across, in clusters of 2–4, borne in profusion from late spring to mid-summer. Deep pink. **Leaves** Paired, sharp-pointed, oval to lance-shaped, hairy at the margins. Glossy, dark green.
• NATIVE HABITAT Pyrenees and mountains of northern Spain.
• CULTIVATION Suitable for growing in a rock garden, trough, or scree bed, or for planting in crevices in rock work, walls, and paving. It is especially valued for its flowering period that extends well into summer, when many true alpines are past their flowering peak. Grow in low-fertility, sandy, moist but well-drained soil in sun with some shade from hot summer sun.
• PROPAGATION Sow seed as soon as ripe or in autumn, in containers under an open frame. Divide in spring.

☀ ◊
✿ ✿ ✿

HEIGHT
2–5cm
(¾–2in)

SPREAD
20cm (8in)

Primulaceae	

DIONYSIA CURVIFLORA

Habit Compact, cushion-forming, evergreen,
perennial. *Flowers* Salver-shaped, 6mm (¼in)
across, borne in spring. Pink, with yellow eye.
Leaves Tiny, spoon-shaped to oblong, hairy
above, forming small rosettes. Grey-green.
• NATIVE HABITAT Mountains, southwestern Iran.
• CULTIVATION Suitable for growing in an alpine
house, in very gritty soi. Needs a deep collar of
grit. Keep plant barely moist in winter.
• PROPAGATION By seed as soon as ripe. Root
single rosettes in summer; water from below only.

HEIGHT
5cm (2in)

SPREAD
25cm (10in)

Caryophyllaceae	MOSS CAMPION

SILENE ACAULIS

Habit Cushion- or mat-forming, moss-like,
evergreen, perennial. *Flowers* Solitary, almost
stemless, star-shaped, to 1cm (⅜in) across, borne
in spring. Often not freely borne in cultivation.
Deep pink. *Leaves* Tiny and linear. Bright green.
• NATIVE HABITAT Europe and N. America.
• CULTIVATION Suitable for a scree bed or trough
in gritty, sharply drained soil. Grows well in an
alpine house in a mix of equal parts loam and grit.
• PROPAGATION By seed in autumn, placed in
a cold frame.

HEIGHT
5cm (2in)

SPREAD
20cm (8in)

Cruciferae/ Brassicaceae	

THLASPI CEPAEIFOLIUM subsp.
ROTUNDIFOLIUM

Habit Tuft-forming, short-lived, evergreen,
perennial. *Flowers* Cross-shaped, 4-petalled, 1cm
(⅜in) across, borne in clusters in spring. Deep lilac-
pink. *Leaves* Broadly oval to rounded. Dark green.
• NATIVE HABITAT Rocks, screes, Alps, Apennines.
• CULTIVATION Grow in an alpine house, in a mix
of equal parts loam, leaf-mould, and grit, or in a
scree bed with protection from winter wet.
• PROPAGATION By ripe seed under a cold frame.
• OTHER NAME *T. rotundifolium*.

HEIGHT
10cm (4in)

SPREAD
15cm (6in)

Primulaceae	

DIONYSIA INVOLUCRATA

Habit Dense, cushion-forming, evergreen,
perennial. *Flowers* Salver-shaped, 7–15mm
(¼–⅝in) across, borne in late spring and early
summer. Violet, with a white or red eye.
Leaves Oval, finely toothed. Dark green.
• NATIVE HABITAT Shady cliffs, Pamir Mountains.
• CULTIVATION Grow in an alpine house or in
tufa, with protection from excessive overhead wet.
Needs very gritty soil and a deep collar of grit.
• PROPAGATION By ripe seed in summer. Water
sparingly from below in winter.

HEIGHT
2.8m (9ft)

SPREAD
2.2m (7ft)

Portulacaceae	

LEWISIA 'Pinkie'

Habit Dwarf, rosette-forming, free-flowering, evergreen, perennial. *Flowers* Open funnel-shaped, 2–4cm (⅘–1⅜in) across, borne in compact clusters from spring to summer. Shades of pink. *Leaves* Narrowly spoon- to lance-shaped, fleshy, forming clusters of rosettes. Dark green.
• NATIVE HABITAT Garden origin.
• CULTIVATION Best grown as a pot plant in an alpine house. Outdoors, suits a trough with neutral to acid soil. Needs protection from winter wet.
• PROPAGATION By offset cuttings in early summer.

HEIGHT
15cm (6in)

SPREAD
20cm (8in)

Portulacaceae	

LEWISIA COTYLEDON 'Rose Splendour'

Habit Rosette-forming, free-flowering, evergreen, perennial. *Flowers* Open funnel-shaped, 4cm (1½in) across, borne in compact clusters from spring to summer. Clear rose-pink. *Leaves* Spoon- to lance-shaped, fleshy, forming rosettes. Dark green.
• NATIVE HABITAT Garden origin.
• CULTIVATION Best grown as a pot plant in an alpine house. Outdoors, suits a trough with neutral to acid soil. Needs protection from winter wet.
• PROPAGATION By offsets in early summer, or by seed in autumn. Seedlings may vary.

HEIGHT
20cm (8in)

SPREAD
20cm (8in)

Cruciferae/ Brassicaceae	

AUBRIETA × *CULTORUM* 'Joy'

Habit Vigorous, mat-forming, evergreen, perennial. *Flowers* Short-stemmed, double, to 15mm (½in) across, borne in spring. Mauve. *Leaves* Oval and slightly toothed. Soft mid-green.
• NATIVE HABITAT Garden origin.
• CULTIVATION Good for growing in rock gardens, sunny banks, and walls. Needs neutral to alkaline, well-drained soil in sun. Trim lightly after flowers.
• PROPAGATION By softwood cuttings in early summer, or by semi-ripe cuttings in mid-summer.
• OTHER NAMES *A. deltoidea* 'Joy', *A.* 'Joy'.

HEIGHT
10cm (2in)

SPREAD
20cm (8in)

Plumbaginaceae	

ARMERIA JUNIPERIFOLIA

Habit Cushion-forming, evergreen, sub-shrub. *Flowers* Cupped, 15mm (⅝in) across, borne in rounded heads in late spring. Purple-pink. *Leaves* Hairy, linear, stiff, and rosetted. Grey-green.
• NATIVE HABITAT Alpine pasture and rock crevices, mountains of central Spain.
• CULTIVATION Suits a rock garden or trough in well-drained, moderately fertile soil, in sun.
• PROPAGATION By seed in autumn or spring, or by semi-ripe cuttings in summer.
• OTHER NAME *A. caespitosa.*

HEIGHT
5–8cm
(2–3in)

SPREAD
15cm (6in)

Cruciferae/ Brassicaceae	

ARABIS × *ARENDSII* 'Rosabella'

Habit Compact, mat-forming, evergreen, perennial. *Flowers* Cross-shaped, to 15mm (⅝in) across, borne in short clusters in late spring and early summer. Deep rose-pink. *Leaves* Elliptic, hairy, forming rosettes. Grey-green.
• NATIVE HABITAT Garden origin.
• CULTIVATION Good for a dry bank or in wall crevices. Prefers well-drained soil in sun but will tolerate hot, dry conditions and low-fertility soils.
• PROPAGATION By softwood cuttings in summer.
• OTHER NAME *A. caucasica* 'Rosabella'.

☼ ◊
❀ ❀ ❀

HEIGHT
5–10cm
(2–4in)

SPREAD
20–30cm
(8–12in)

Diapensiaceae	

SHORTIA SOLDANELLOIDES

Habit Mat-forming, stoloniferous, evergreen, perennial. *Flowers* Broad, flared bells to 2.5cm (1in) across, with fringed petals, borne in late spring. Deep pink. *Leaves* Oval to rounded, with a heart-shaped base, toothed, leathery. Glossy green.
• NATIVE HABITAT Woodlands, Japan.
• CULTIVATION Good for growing in a rock garden, peat bed, or open woodland glades, in moist, well-drained, leaf-rich, acid soil. Dislikes dry climates.
• PROPAGATION By seed as soon as ripe in a cold frame. Separate rooted runners carefully in spring.

☼ ◊ pH
❀ ❀ ❀

HEIGHT
10–30cm
(4–12in)

SPREAD
25cm (10in)

Scrophulariaceae	FAIRY FOXGLOVE

ERINUS ALPINUS

Habit Tufted, short-lived, evergreen, perennial. *Flowers* Five-lobed, to 1cm (⅜in) across, borne in short spikes in late spring and summer. Pink, purple, or white. *Leaves* Soft, sticky, lance- to wedge-shaped, lobed, mostly rosetted. Mid-green.
• NATIVE HABITAT Southern and central Europe.
• CULTIVATION Needs light, well-drained soil that is moderately fertile. Tolerates partial shade.
• PROPAGATION Sow seed in autumn in a cold frame, or root rosettes as cuttings in spring. Will generally self-sow in the garden.

☼ ◊
❀ ❀ ❀

HEIGHT
8cm (3in)

SPREAD
10cm (4in)

Portulacaceae	

LEWISIA 'Trevosia'

Habit Rosette-forming, free-flowering, evergreen, perennial. **Flowers** Open funnel-shaped, to 4cm (⅝in) across, borne in long sprays from spring to summer. Salmon-pink. **Leaves** Spoon- to lance-shaped, fleshy, borne in rosettes. Dark green.
• NATIVE HABITAT Garden origin.
• CULTIVATION Best grown as a plant pot in an alpine house. Outdoors, suits a trough with neutral to acid soil. Needs protection from winter wet.
• PROPAGATION By offsets in early summer, or by seed in autumn. Seedlings may vary.

HEIGHT
20cm (8in)

SPREAD
20cm (8in)

Portulacaceae	PURSLANE, SPRING BEAUTY

CLAYTONIA MEGARHIZA var. NIVALIS

Habit Short-lived, tap-rooted, evergreen, perennial. **Flowers** Cup-shaped, 2–3cm (⅘–1⅛in) across, borne in dense clusters in early summer. Deep rose-pink. **Leaves** Fleshy, spoon-shaped, in rosettes. Dark to grey-green.
• NATIVE HABITAT Rocky Mountains, USA.
• CULTIVATION Suits an alpine house. Needs gritty, sharply drained, fertile soil in a sunny site.
• PROPAGATION By seed in autumn in a cold frame. Propagate regularly.
• OTHER NAME *Calandrinia megarhiza* var. *nivalis*.

HEIGHT
5cm (2in)

SPREAD
15cm (6in)

Primulaceae	

ANAGALLIS TENELLA 'Studland'

Habit Mat-forming, evergreen, perennial. **Flowers** Solitary, honey-scented, upright, bell-shaped, 6–10mm (¼–⅜in) across, borne in late spring and early summer. Deep pink. **Leaves** Small, rounded to oval. Bright green.
• NATIVE HABITAT Cool climates in Europe.
• CULTIVATION Thrives in damp sites in a rock garden. Needs moist but well-drained soil. Excellent for growing in shallow pots in an alpine house.
• PROPAGATION Stems self-root freely.

HEIGHT
to 10cm
(4in)

SPREAD
to 40cm
(16in)

Cruciferae/ Brassicaceae	

ARABIS BLEPHAROPHYLLA ♈
'Frühlingszauber'

Habit Mat-forming, evergreen, perennial. *Flowers* Scented, 5mm (¼in) across, borne in short clusters in late spring and early summer. Deep magenta. *Leaves* Oval, toothed, hairy margins. Dark green.
• NATIVE HABITAT Garden origin.
• CULTIVATION Suitable for growing in a rock garden, on a dry bank, or in wall crevices. Will tolerate hot, dry conditions and low-fertility soils.
• PROPAGATION By softwood cuttings in summer
• OTHER NAME *A. blepharophylla* 'Spring Charm'.

☀ ◌
❀ ❀ ❀

HEIGHT
10cm (4in)

SPREAD
20cm (8in)

Ericaceae	ROCK OR MOUNTAIN CRANBERRY

VACCINIUM VITIS-IDAEA subsp. MINUS

Habit Creeping, rhizomatous, mat-forming, evergreen, shrub. *Flowers* Bell-shaped, 6mm (¼in) long, borne in nodding clusters in late spring and early summer. Deep pink. *Leaves* Oval and glossy. Dark green.
• NATIVE HABITAT Alpine habitats, N. America.
• CULTIVATION Suits a rock garden or peat bed, in moist but well-drained, leaf-rich or sandy, acid soil.
• PROPAGATION Sow seed in pots in a cold frame in autumn, or take semi-ripe cuttings during mid- to late summer.

☀ ◌ pH
❀ ❀ ❀

HEIGHT
10–20cm
(4–8in)

SPREAD
60cm (24in)

Compositae/Asteraceae	

ANTENNARIA DIOICA 'Rosea' ♈

Habit Stoloniferous, mat-forming, semi-evergreen, perennial. *Flowers* Small, fluffy, clustered in terminal heads to 2cm (⅜in) long, borne on stems in late spring and early summer. Deep rose-pink. *Leaves* Spoon-shaped. Grey-green, with densely white-felted underside.
• NATIVE HABITAT Garden selection.
• CULTIVATION Suitable for growing in a rock garden or gravel plantings. Tolerant of any moderately fertile, well-drained soil.
• PROPAGATION Separate rooted stems in spring.

☀ ◌
❀ ❀ ❀

HEIGHT
4m (12ft)

SPREAD
2.5m (8ft)

Compositae/Asteraceae	

LEPTINELLA ATRATA subsp. LUTEOLA

Habit Tufted, creeping, evergreen, perennial. *Flowers* Conical, 15mm (⅝in) across, borne in late spring and early summer. Dark red-brown, with creamy-white stigmas at maturity. *Leaves* Finely divided. Grey-green, tinted purple.
• NATIVE HABITAT Alpine habitats, New Zealand.
• CULTIVATION Suitable for growing in a scree bed, with gritty, sharply drained soil.
• PROPAGATION By seed in an open frame when ripe, or by division in spring.
• OTHER NAME *Cotula atrata* var. *luteola*.

☀ ◌
❀ ❀ ❀

HEIGHT
15cm (6in)

SPREAD
20cm (8in)

ANDROSACE

Androsaces, commonly known as rock jasmines, are found in alpine turf, screes, and rock crevices in the mountains of the northern hemisphere. Although androsaces are fully hardy, they need sharp drainage to be able to thrive in areas with wet winters. Those described thrive in scree and raised beds, or in troughs, and they are equally suitable for pot culture in an alpine house.

All androsaces need moist but gritty and sharply drained soil in full sun. In an alpine house, pot them up in a mix of equal parts grit and loam-based compost. In areas with wet winters, protect plant with a sheet of glass or place under a cloche.

Propagate by seed sown as soon as ripe in an open frame, or root single rosettes as cuttings in early or mid-summer.

A. VILLOSA
Habit Cushion-forming, evergreen, perennial.
Flowers Flat, 6–10mm (¼–½in) across, borne in head-like clusters in spring. White, with yellow eye that matures to red.
Leaves Linear to oval, in tightly packed rosettes, silky-haired underside. Grey-green.
• HEIGHT 4cm (1½in).
• SPREAD 20cm (8in).

A. villosa

☼ ◊ ❀❀❀

A. CARNEA
Habit Tufted to loose cushion-forming, evergreen, perennial.
Flowers Cupped, 5–8mm (¼–⅜in) across, borne in compact head-like clusters in spring. Pink, with yellow eye.
Leaves Linear, pointed, hairy-margined, fleshy, in rosettes. Deep green.
• HEIGHT 5cm (2in).
• SPREAD 8–15cm (3–6in).

A. carnea
Pink rock jasmine

☼ ◊ ❀❀❀

A. LANUGINOSA
Habit Mat-forming, with trailing, red-tinted stems.
Flowers Flat, 8–12mm (⅜–½in) across, borne in head-like clusters in summer. Pale pink.
Leaves Elliptic, silky-hairy, rosetted or alternate. Grey-green.
• HEIGHT 10cm (4in), occasionally more.
• SPREAD 30cm or more (12in).

A. lanuginosa

☼ ◊ ❀❀❀ ♎

A. CARNEA subsp. LAGGERI
Habit Densely tufted, evergreen, perennial.
Flowers Up to 8mm (⅜in) across, borne in loose heads in spring. Deep pink.
Leaves Linear, pointed and fleshy. Mid-green.
• OTHER NAME *A. laggeri*.
• HEIGHT 5cm (2in).
• SPREAD 8–15cm (3–6in).

A. carnea subsp. *laggeri*

☼ ◊ ❀❀❀ ♎

A. VILLOSA var. JACQUEMONTII
Habit Mat-forming, stoloniferous, rosetted.
Flowers Flat, 6–10mm (¼–½in) across, borne in heads in spring. Deep pink, with lime eye.
Leaves Oval to linear. Silvery-green, with silky hairs below.
• OTHER NAME *A. jacquemontii*.
• HEIGHT 4cm (1½in).
• SPREAD 20cm (8in).

A. villosa var. *jacquemontii*

☼ ◊ ❀❀❀

A. SARMENTOSA
Habit Stoloniferous, mat-forming, evergreen, perennial
Flowers Flat, 7–9mm (¼–⅜in) across, borne in compact heads in late spring. Deep rose-pink, with yellow-green eye.
Leaves Oval and white-haired. Pale grey-green.
• HEIGHT 5–10cm (2–4in).
• SPREAD 30cm (12in) or more.

A. sarmentosa

☼ ◊ ❀❀❀ ♎

PRIMULA

The genus *Primula* comprises about 400 species, some evergreen, including popular cottage-garden favourites, such as cowslips, primroses, and auriculas. All have basal rosettes of leaves and tubular, bell-shaped, or flat (primrose-like) flowers. Nearly all of the alpine and rock garden species thrive best in climates with cool, moist summers. Most of these come from the mountains of the northern hemisphere (almost half of all primulas are from western China and the Himalaya) growing in alpine turf, stony pastures, shaded cliffs, or rock crevices.

For ease of reference, their cultivation requirements may be grouped as follows.

Group 1 Sun or partial shade, in moist but well-drained soil, rich in organic matter.

Group 2 Partial shade, in deep, moist, neutral to acid soil, rich in organic matter.

Group 3 Partial or deep shade, in peat-rich, gritty, moist but sharply drained soil, with protection from winter wet.

Group 4 In an alpine house or cold frame, in equal parts loam, leaf-mould, and grit. Do not wet the foliage of those with white-mealy leaves when watering. *P. allionii* needs alkaline soil and suits alpine-house culture.

Group 5 Partial shade, or full sun with some mid-day shade, in moist but sharply drained, gritty, slightly alkaline soil.

Some true alpine species, such as *P. marginata* and *P. auricula* and their cultivars, are fully hardy and suit rock gardens. However, their early flowers and mealy leaves can be spoiled by excessive rain, so they are often grown in an alpine house or protected cloches. Propagate by seed as soon as ripe or in late winter and early spring, in a cold frame; by division from autumn to early spring; or by offsets in autumn or early spring. Some, like *P. denticulata* var. *alba*, can be increased by root cuttings in winter.

P. DENTICULATA var. ALBA
Habit Sturdy, rosette-forming, herbaceous, perennial.
Flowers Flat, up to 2cm (⅜in) across, borne in dense, spherical heads on stout, erect stems, in spring. White, with yellow eye.
Leaves Mainly oval to spoon-shaped. Green, with white underside.
• CULTIVATION 1 or 2.
• HEIGHT 45cm (18in).
• SPREAD 45cm (18in).

P. denticulata var. *alba*

☀ ◐ ❋❋❋

P. MARGINATA 'Linda Pope'
Habit Vigorous, evergreen, perennial.
Flowers Flat, to 3cm (1¼in) across, borne in heads of 4–16, in spring. Mauve-blue, with small, white centre.
Leaves Oval, toothed, and smooth. Mid-green, white-farinose.
• CULTIVATION 4 or 5.
• OTHER NAME *P.* 'Linda Pope'.
• HEIGHT 15cm (6in).
• SPREAD 15–23cm (6–9in).

P. marginata 'Linda Pope'

☀ ◊ ❋❋❋ ♀

P. GRACILIPES
Habit Rosette-forming, evergreen, perennial.
Flowers Short-stemmed, funnel-shaped, to 2.5cm (1in) across, borne in late winter to late spring. Purple-pink, with white-edged, orange eye.
Leaves Toothed, oblong to spoon-shaped or oval. Mid-green.
• CULTIVATION 3 or 4.
• HEIGHT 10cm (4in).
• SPREAD 20cm (8in).

P. gracilipes

☼ ◐ ❋❋❋

P. ROSEA
Habit Herbaceous, perennial.
Flowers Flat, to 3cm (1¼in) across, borne in clusters of 4–12, in spring. Deep rose-pink, with yellow eye.
Leaves Smooth, oval to lance-shaped, scalloped or fine-toothed. Mid-green.
• CULTIVATION 2.
• HEIGHT 20cm (8in).
• SPREAD 20cm (8in).

P. rosea

☼ ◐ ❋❋❋   ♛

P. ALLIONII
Habit Evergreen, tufted to cushion-forming, perennial.
Flowers Tubular, flat-faced, to 3cm (1¼in) across, borne in clusters of 1 to 5 in spring. White, or pink to red-purple.
Leaves Lance-shaped, scalloped or fine-toothed, and hairy. Grey-green.
• CULTIVATION 4.
• HEIGHT 10cm (4in).
• SPREAD 20cm (8in).

P. allionii

☼ ◐ ❋❋❋

P. POLYNEURA
Habit Herbaceous, perennial.
Flowers To 2.5cm (1in) across, borne in loose, long-stalked clusters in late spring and early summer. Purple-pink, with yellow eye.
Leaves Hairy, oval to rounded, lobed, forming basal rosettes. Mid-green.
• CULTIVATION 2.
• HEIGHT 45cm (18in).
• SPREAD 45cm (18in).

P. polyneura

☼ ◐ ❋❋❋

P. JULIAE
Habit Stoloniferous, herbaceous, perennial.
Flowers Solitary, long-stalked, saucer-shaped, to 3cm (1¼in) across, in spring. Magenta, with yellow eye.
Leaves Rounded and scalloped. Dark green.
• CULTIVATION 1, 2, or 4.
• HEIGHT 7cm (3in).
• SPREAD 25cm or more (10in).

P. juliae

☼ ◐ ❋❋❋

P. 'Wanda'
Habit Very vigorous, evergreen, perennial.
Flowers Flat, to 3.5cm (1¼in) across, borne in basal clusters over long periods in spring. Deep, claret-red.
Leaves Oval, toothed, and slightly hairy. Purple-green.
• CULTIVATION 1 or 2.
• HEIGHT 10cm (4in).
• SPREAD 30cm (12in).

P. 'Wanda'

☼ ◐ ❋❋❋   ♛

P. *MARGINATA*
'Pritchard's Variety'
Habit Virtually
evergreen, perennial.
Flowers Shallow, flat,
3cm (1¼in) across,
borne in long-stalked
clusters in spring. Deep
lavender-blue.
Leaves Toothed and
oval. Mid-green, with
white farinose margins.
• CULTIVATION 4 or 5.
• HEIGHT 15cm (6in).
• SPREAD 30cm (12in).

P. marginata
'Pritchard's Variety'

☀ ◊ ❀❀❀

P. *CAPITATA*
Habit Virtually
herbaceous, perennial.
Flowers Funnel-shaped,
1cm (⅜in) across, fragrant,
borne in rounded clusters
on white-mealy stems, in
summer. Purple.
Leaves Oblong to
lance-shaped and mealy.
Pale to mid-green.
• CULTIVATION 2.
• HEIGHT 40cm (16in).
• SPREAD 40cm (16in).

P. capitata

◑ ◊ ❀❀❀

P. *VULGARIS*
'Double Sulphur'
Habit Vigorous,
evergreen, perennial.
Flowers Funnel-shaped,
double, to 2.5–4cm
(1–1⅝in) across, borne
in spring. Pale yellow.
Leaves Lance-shaped
to oval, scalloped to
toothed, deeply veined
and quilted. Bright green.
• CULTIVATION 2.
• HEIGHT 20cm (8in).
• SPREAD 25cm (10in).

P. vulgaris
'Double Sulphur'

◑ ◊ ❀❀❀

P. AURICULA
Habit Evergreen, often white-mealy, perennial.
Flowers Fragrant, flat, to 2.5cm (1in) across, borne in long-stalked clusters of 2–30, during spring. Deep yellow.
Leaves Fleshy, smooth, oval to spoon-shaped or rounded. Pale to grey-green, often mealy.
• CULTIVATION 4 or 5.
• HEIGHT 20cm (8in).
• SPREAD 25cm (10in).

P. auricula
Auricula

☼ ◊ ❀❀❀   ♛

P. ELATIOR
Habit Clump-forming, perennial.
Flowers Funnel-shaped, fragrant, to 2.5cm (1in) across, borne in one-sided clusters on upright stalks, in spring. Yellow.
Leaves Oval to oblong, scalloped, hairy, in basal rosettes. Bright-green.
• CULTIVATION 1 or 2.
• HEIGHT 20–30cm (8–12in).
• SPREAD 15–25cm (6–10in).

P. elatior
Oxlip

☼ ◊ ❀❀❀   ♛

P. VERIS
Habit Clump-forming, perennial.
Flowers Funnel-shaped, fragrant, 1.5–2.5cm (⅝–1in) long, borne in one-sided clusters of 2–16 on upright stems, in spring. Deep yellow.
Leaves Oblong to oval, crinkled, hairy, and often scalloped or toothed. Mid-green.
• CULTIVATION 1 or 3.
• HEIGHT 15–25cm (6–10in).
• SPREAD 15–25cm (6–10in).

P. veris
Cowslip

☼ ◊ ❀❀❀   ♛

Convallariaceae/ Liliaceae	

POLYGONATUM HOOKERI

Habit Slow-growing, creeping, rhizomatous, herbaceous, perennial. *Flowers* Solitary, upright, bell-shaped, to 15mm (⅝in) across, borne in late spring and early summer. Pale to deep pink. *Leaves* Narrowly elliptic. Mid- to dark green.
• NATIVE HABITAT Woodland, Eastern Himalaya.
• CULTIVATION Suitable for growing in a peat bed or trough. Needs moist but well-drained soil that is rich in organic matter.
• PROPAGATION Sow seed in autumn in a cold frame, or divide in spring or after flowering.

☀ ◐
❄ ❄ ❄

HEIGHT
5–10cm
(2–4in)

SPREAD
30cm (12in)

Cruciferae/ Brassicaceae	

AUBRIETA × *CULTORUM* 'Argenteovariegata'

Habit Mat-forming, evergreen, perennial. *Flowers* Single, to 15mm (⅝in) across, borne in spring. Pinkish-mauve. *Leaves* Oval and slightly toothed. Soft mid-green, with silver-white margins.
• NATIVE HABITAT Garden origin.
• CULTIVATION Needs neutral to alkaline, well-drained soil in sun. Trim lightly after flowering.
• PROPAGATION By softwood cuttings in early summer, or by semi-ripe cuttings in mid-summer.
• OTHER NAME *A. deltoidea* 'Argenteovariegata'.

☀ ◐
❄ ❄ ❄

HEIGHT
5cm (2in)

SPREAD
50cm (20in)

Scrophulariaceae	

MAZUS REPTANS

Habit Creeping, mat-forming, evergreen, perennial. *Flowers* Solitary, 2-lipped, 10–15mm (⅜–⅝in) across, borne in late spring and summer. Purple-blue, with white-, red- and yellow-spotted lips. *Leaves* Lance-shaped to oval and coarsely toothed. Shiny, mid-green.
• NATIVE HABITAT Damp habitats, Himalaya.
• CULTIVATION Grows best in a sheltered site in sun, with moist but well-drained soil .
• PROPAGATION By seed in spring or autumn in a cold frame, or by division in spring.

☀ ◐
❄ ❄

HEIGHT
5cm (2in)

SPREAD
30cm (12in)

Primulaceae	HAIRY SNOWBELL

SOLDANELLA VILLOSA

Habit Vigorous, clump-forming, evergreen, perennial. *Flowers* Nodding, bell-shaped, 15mm (⅝in) long, with fringed petals, borne on long, hairy stalks in mid-spring. Violet. *Leaves* Kidney-shaped. Mid-green, with paler underside.
• NATIVE HABITAT Alpine rocks, western Pyrenees.
• CULTIVATION Ideal for a peat bed. Needs fertile, moist but sharply drained soil in sun but with shade from hottest sun. Top-dress with grit.
• PROPAGATION By seed as soon as ripe in a cold frame. Divide after flowering.

☀ ◐
❄ ❄ ❄

HEIGHT
to 20cm
(8in)

SPREAD
20cm (8in)

| Cruciferae/ | |
| Brassicaceae | |

AUBRIETA × *CULTORUM* **'J.S. Baker'**

Habit Vigorous, mat-forming, evergreen, perennial. *Flowers* Single, to 15mm (½in) across, borne in clusters in spring. Purple, with white eye. *Leaves* Oval and slightly toothed. Soft mid-green.
• NATIVE HABITAT Garden origin.
• CULTIVATION Suitable for rock gardens, sunny banks, and walls. Grow in well-drained, neutral to alkaline soil in sun. Trim plant after flowering.
• PROPAGATION By softwood cuttings in early summer, or by semi-ripe cuttings in summer.
• OTHER NAME *A. deltoidea* 'J. S. Baker'.

HEIGHT
5cm (2in)

SPREAD
50cm (20in)

| Cruciferae/ | |
| Brassicaceae | |

AUBRIETA × *CULTORUM* **'Hartswood Purple'**

Habit Vigorous, mat-forming, evergreen, perennial. *Flowers* Single, 15mm (½in) across, borne in clusters in spring. Violet-purple. *Leaves* Oval to oblong, slightly toothed. Soft mid-green.
• NATIVE HABITAT Garden origin.
• CULTIVATION Grow in well-drained, neutral to alkaline soil in sun. Trim lightly after flowering.
• PROPAGATION By softwood cuttings in early summer, or by semi-ripe cuttings in mid-summer.
• OTHER NAME *A.* 'Carnival'.

HEIGHT
10cm (4in)

SPREAD
50cm (20in)

| Polygalaceae | |

POLYGALA CHAMAEBUXUS var. *GRANDIFLORA*

Habit Low-spreading, evergreen, shrub. *Flowers* Pea-like, 15mm (⅝in) long, borne in late spring and early summer. Yellow, with purple-pink wings. *Leaves* Lance-shaped and leathery. Dark green.
• NATIVE HABITAT Alps, Carpathian mountains.
• CULTIVATION Needs moist, leaf-rich soil.
• PROPAGATION By softwood or semi-ripe cuttings in summer, or by seed when ripe in an open frame.
• OTHER NAMES *P. chamaebuxus* var. *purpurea*, *P. chamaebuxus* var. *rhodoptera*.

HEIGHT
5–15cm
(2–6in)

SPREAD
30cm (12in)

| Ranunculaceae | HEPATICA |

HEPATICA NOBILIS

Habit Slow-growing, clumping, semi-evergreen, perennial. *Flowers* Saucer-shaped, 2.5cm (1in) across, borne in early spring. Purple, white, or pink. *Leaves* Leathery, rounded or kidney-shaped, divided into 3 lobes. Mid-green, often mottled.
• NATIVE HABITAT Woodland, Europe.
• CULTIVATION Needs fertile, moist, well-drained soil. Mulch with leaf-mould in autumn or spring.
• PROPAGATION By seed as soon as ripe in an open frame, or by careful division in spring.
• OTHER NAMES *Anemone hepatica*, *Hepatica triloba*.

HEIGHT
10cm (4in)

SPREAD
15cm (6in)

Polygalacae	

POLYGALA CALCAREA 'Lillet'

Habit Robust, creeping, prostrate, free-flowering, evergreen, sub-shrub. *Flowers* Pea-like, with broad, wing-like petals and a keel with a fringed tip, to 3cm (1¼in) long, borne in terminal clusters over long periods from late spring to early summer. Intense, deep blue with white lips. *Leaves* Oval and leathery. Mid-green.
• NATIVE HABITAT Garden origin.
• CULTIVATION Suitable for growing in a trough or raised bed, and ideal as a pot plant in an alpine house. This cultiva is generally more robust and easier to grow than the species, and produces intensely coloured flowers. Grow in sharply drained, moderately fertile soil that is enriched with organic matter, in a sunny site. Protect from excessive winter wet.
• PROPAGATION By softwood cuttings in early summer, or by semi-ripe cuttings in mid- to late summer.

HEIGHT
5cm (2in)

SPREAD
20cm (8in)

Cruciferae/ Brassicaceae	

AUBRIETA 'Cobalt Violet'

Habit Vigorous, mat-forming, evergreen, perennial. **Flowers** Single, short-stemmed, to 15mm (⅝in) across, borne in spring. **Leaves** Small, oval to oblong, entire or toothed, hairy. Mid-green.
• NATIVE HABITAT Garden origin.
• CULTIVATION Grow in neutral to alkaline, well-drained soil in sun, and trim lightly after flowering.
• PROPAGATION Take softwood cuttings in early summer, or semi-ripe ones in summer.
• OTHER NAMES *A.* x *cultorum* 'Cobalt Violet', *A. deltoidea* 'Cobalt Violet'.

HEIGHT
10cm (4in)

SPREAD
to 20cm
(8in)
or more

Berberidaceae	

JEFFERSONIA DUBIA

Habit Tufted, herbaceous, perennial. **Flowers** Solitary, cup-shaped, 3cm (1¼in) across, borne in late spring or early summer. Lavender-blue, or white. **Leaves** Rounded or kidney-shaped and notched at apex. Blue-green, often tinted purple.
• NATIVE HABITAT Damp woods, northeast Asia.
• CULTIVATION Good for a peat bed or shaded rock garden, in moist soil enriched with organic matter.
• PROPAGATION By seed in an open frame as soon as ripe. Divide well-established plants in spring.
• OTHER NAME *Plagiorhegma dubia.*

HEIGHT
20cm (8in)

SPREAD
30cm (12in)

Ranunculaceae	JAPANESE HEPATICA

HEPATICA NOBILIS var. JAPONICA

Habit Tufted, slow-growing, semi-evergreen, perennial. **Flowers** Star-shaped, 2.5cm (1in) across, borne in early spring. Blue. **Leaves** Rounded or kidney-shaped, with pointed lobes. Dark green.
• NATIVE HABITAT Woodland, Japan.
• CULTIVATION More compact than the species. Needs moist but well-drained, neutral to alkaline soil that is rich in organic matter. Apply an annual mulch of leaf-mould in autumn.
• PROPAGATION By seed as soon as ripe in pots in a cold frame, or by careful division in spring.

HEIGHT
8cm (3in)

SPREAD
15cm (6in)

Boraginaceae	OYSTER PLANT

MERTENSIA MARITIMA

Habit Prostrate, spreading, semi-evergreen, perennial. **Flowers** Bell-shaped, 8mm (⅜in) across, borne in branched, terminal heads in early summer. Bright blue. **Leaves** Fleshy, spoon-shaped, glaucous, tasting of oysters. Blue-green.
• NATIVE HABITAT Northern Europe, Greenland.
• CULTIVATION Best in a deep bed of coarse sand or grit, with sharply drained, low-fertility soil. Very prone to slug damage.
• PROPAGATION By seed in autumn, or by careful division in spring.

HEIGHT
10cm (4in)

SPREAD
30cm (12in)

Ranunculaceae

HEPATICA TRANSSILVANICA

Habit Slow-growing, semi-evergreen, clump-forming, perennial. *Flowers* Cup-shaped, many-petalled, 4cm (1½in) across, with 3 leaf-like bracts immediately below, borne in early spring before the leaves have developed fully. Usually bright blue, sometimes white or pale pink. *Leaves* Rounded or kidney-shaped, hairy, and divided into 3 oval, scalloped lobes. Pale to mid-green.
• NATIVE HABITAT Woodland, Romania.
• CULTIVATION Excellent for planting in shady areas in a rock or woodland garden, and thrives in sites with heavy soil. Needs moist but well-drained soil that is neutral to alkaline and enriched with organic matter. Apply an annual mulch of leaf-mould in autumn or late spring, and protect from birds in spring. Tends to be slow establishing large clumps.
• PROPAGATION By seed as soon as ripe in a cold frame, or by careful division in spring. The stout rootstock resents disturbance and divisions may be slow to re-establish.
• OTHER NAME *H. angulosa.*

HEIGHT
15cm (6in)

SPREAD
20cm (8in)

Scrophulariaceae	COLUMBIA SYNTHYRIS

SYNTHYRIS STELLATA

Habit Rhizomatous, clump-forming, semi-evergreen, perennial. *Flowers* Bell-shaped, 6mm (¼in) long, borne in dense, oblong clusters in spring and early summer. Violet-blue. *Leaves* Rounded, heart-shaped, and jagged-toothed. Dark green.
• NATIVE HABITAT Woodlands, northwest USA.
• CULTIVATION Needs moist but well-drained soil rich in organic matter, in partial or deep shade.
• PROPAGATION By seed in autumn in an open frame, or by division in spring.

☼ ◊
❄ ❄ ❄

HEIGHT
15cm (6in)

SPREAD
25cm (10in)

Boraginaceae	

ANCHUSA CESPITOSA ♟

Habit Mound-forming, bristly, perennial. *Flowers* Forget-me-not-like, 12mm (½in) across, borne in clusters in spring. Intense blue, with white eye. *Leaves* Linear, in rosettes. Dark green.
• NATIVE HABITAT Mountain rocks, Crete.
• CULTIVATION Best grown as a pot plant in an alpine house. Needs moist but sharply drained, moderately fertile soil in sun. Dislikes excess wet.
• PROPAGATION By seed in spring, by root cuttings in winter, or by careful division.
• OTHER NAME *A. caespitosa*.

☼ ◊
❄ ❄ ❄

HEIGHT
5–10cm
(2–4in)

SPREAD
10–20cm
(4–8in)

Salicaceae	NET-LEAVED WILLOW

SALIX RETICULATA ♟

Habit Dwarf, prostrate, stem-rooting, deciduous, shrub. *Flowers* Male or female, upright, slender, catkins, 2.5cm (1in) long, borne in early spring. Yellow, with pink tips. *Leaves* Rounded to oval, glossy. Dark green, with white-haired underside.
• NATIVE HABITAT Rocky mountain habitats, northern Europe, northern Asia, and N. America.
• CULTIVATION Suits a trough with fertile, gritty, sharply drained soil. Dislikes drought conditions.
• PROPAGATION By softwood cuttings in summer, or by hardwood cuttings in winter.

☼ ◊
❄ ❄ ❄

HEIGHT
8cm (3in)

SPREAD
30cm (12in)

Compositae/Asteraceae	

LEPTINELLA ATRATA

Habit Tufted, creeping, mat-forming, evergreen, perennial. **Flowers** Rounded, fluffy, 15mm (⅝in) across, borne in late spring. Deep purple, with yellow anthers at maturity. **Leaves** Fern-like and finely divided. Grey-green, tinted purple.
• NATIVE HABITAT Alpine habitats, New Zealand.
• CULTIVATION Suitable for growing in a scree bed, with gritty, sharply drained soil
• PROPAGATION By seed in an open frame when ripe, or by division in spring.
• OTHER NAME *Cotula atrata*.

☀ ◊
❀ ❀ ❀

HEIGHT
15cm (6in)

SPREAD
20cm (8in)

Euphorbiaceae	

EUPHORBIA MYRSINITES ♀

Habit Semi-prostrate, evergreen, with milky juice, perennial. **Flowers** Borne in terminal clusters, to 8cm (3in) across, in spring. Bright greenish-yellow, with numerous bracts. **Leaves** Oval, pointed, and fleshy, arranged in spirals. Blue-green.
• NATIVE HABITAT Dry, rocky places, from southern and eastern Europe, to Turkey and central Asia.
• CULTIVATION Suits a sheltered raised bed or rock garden in sun. Needs light, well-drained soil.
• PROPAGATION By seed as soon as ripe or in spring in a cold frame. Often self-sows.

☀ ◊
❀ ❀ ❀

HEIGHT
10cm (4in)

SPREAD
50cm (20in)

Umbelliferae/Apiaceae	

HACQUETIA EPIPACTIS ♀

Habit Clump-forming, rhizomatous, herbaceous, perennial. **Flowers** Tiny, to 4cm (1½in) across, borne in dense clusters in late winter and early spring. Yellow, with apple-green bracts below. **Leaves** Lobed, rounded, toothed, glossy. Emerald.
• NATIVE HABITAT Central and eastern Europe.
• CULTIVATION Grow in a rock garden, woodland, or peat bed, in moist, neutral to acid, leaf-rich soil.
• PROPAGATION Sow ripe seed in a cold frame, divide in spring, or take root cuttings in winter.
• OTHER NAME *Dondia epipactis*.

☀ ◊
❀ ❀ ❀

HEIGHT
5cm (2in), taller after flowering

SPREAD
15–30cm (6–12in)

Cruciferae/ Brassicaceae	

DRABA RIGIDA

Habit Cushion-forming, evergreen, perennial. **Flowers** Cross-shaped, 4–5mm (⅛–¼in) across, borne in clusters in late spring. Yellow. **Leaves** Small, linear to oval, hairy-margined, forming dense rosettes. Dark green.
• NATIVE HABITAT Mountain screes, Turkey.
• CULTIVATION Grows best in an alpine house, with a mix of equal parts loam, leaf-mould and grit, top-dressed with grit. Water sparingly in winter.
• PROPAGATION By seed in a cold frame in autumn or early spring. Root rosette cuttings in late spring.

☀ ◊
❀ ❀ ❀

HEIGHT
5cm (2in)

SPREAD
20cm (8in)

Cruciferae/Brassicaceae	YELLOW WHITLOW GRASS

DRABA AIZOIDES

Habit Tufted- or cushion-forming, evergreen, perennial. **Flowers** Cross-shaped, 8–12mm (⅓–½in) across, borne in dense clusters in late spring. Bright yellow. **Leaves** Linear to lance-shaped, bristle-margined, forming dense rosettes. Dark green.
• NATIVE HABITAT Mountain screes and other rocky habitats, central and southern Europe.
• CULTIVATION Suitable for planting in a rock garden, scree bed, raised bed, or trough, and for growing in tufa. Needs gritty, sharply drained soil in full sun. Protect plants from excess winter wet.

Alternatively, grow in an alpine house, in a mix of equal parts loam, leaf-mould, and grit, top-dressed with grit. Water plant from below.
• PROPAGATION Sow seed in a cold frame in autumn, or root individual rosettes as cuttings in late spring. Often self-sows in gardens under favourable conditions.

☼ ◊
❄ ❄ ❄

HEIGHT
10cm (4in)

SPREAD
25cm (10in)

Primulaceae	

DIONYSIA ARETIOIDES 🏆

Habit Cushion-forming, evergreen, perennial.
Flowers Scented, solitary, stemless, to 1cm (⅜in)
across, with notched petals, borne in early spring.
Bright yellow. **Leaves** Aromatic, oblong to spoon-
shaped, softly hairy, recurved margins. Grey-green.
• NATIVE HABITAT Mountain cliffs, northern Iran.
• CULTIVATION Grow in tufa or in a trough with
sharply drained soil, and top-dress with grit to keep
the plant collar dry. Keep just moist in winter.
• PROPAGATION By seed as soon as ripe in a cold
frame. Root rosette cuttings in summer.

☼ ◊
❄ ❄ ❄

HEIGHT
7cm (3in)

SPREAD
to 30cm
(12in)

Cruciferae/ Brassicaceae	

DRABA LONGISILIQUA 🏆

Habit Soft cushion-forming, evergreen, perennial.
Flowers Cross-shaped, to 1cm (⅜in) across, borne
in dense clusters in spring. Yellow. **Leaves** Oval,
grey-hairy, in firm, tight rosettes. Silvery-green.
• NATIVE HABITAT Screes in the Caucasus.
• CULTIVATION Grow in a scree bed with
protection from winter wet, or in an alpine house,
in a mix of equal parts loam, leaf-mould and grit,
top-dressed with grit. Avoid wetting the foliage.
• PROPAGATION Sow seed in containers in a cold
frame in autumn. Root rosettes in late spring.

☼ ◊
❄ ❄ ❄

HEIGHT
9cm (3½in)

SPREAD
to 25cm
(10in)

Cruciferae/ Brassicaceae	

DRABA MOLLISSIMA

Habit Soft cushion-forming, evergreen, perennial.
Flowers Cross-shaped, to 8mm (⅜in) across,
borne in tight clusters in late spring. Bright yellow.
Leaves Oblong, hairy, in rosettes. Grey-green.
• NATIVE HABITAT Screes in the Caucasus.
• CULTIVATION Grows best as a pot plant in
an alpine house, in a mix of equal parts loam,
leaf-mould, and grit, top-dressed with grit.
Avoid wetting the foliage.
• PROPAGATION Sow seed in containers in
a cold frame in autumn.

☼ ◊
❄ ❄ ❄

HEIGHT
8cm (3in)

SPREAD
to 20cm
(8in)

Primulaceae	

DIONYSIA TAPETODES

Habit Dense, cushion-forming, evergreen,
perennial. **Flowers** Solitary, stemless, long-tubed,
to 1cm (⅜in) across, borne in spring and early
summer. Yellow. **Leaves** Small, oval, oblong,
or spoon-shaped, forming rosettes. Mid-green.
• NATIVE HABITAT Northeast Iran and Afghanistan.
• CULTIVATION Excellent as a pot plant in an
alpine house, and can also be grown in tufa. Keep
the plant collar dry, and protect from winter wet.
• PROPAGATION By seed when ripe in a cold
frame. Root rosettes as cuttings in summer.

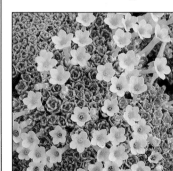

☼ ◊
❄ ❄ ❄

HEIGHT
5cm (2in)

SPREAD
to 20cm
(8in)

Primulaceae

VITALIANA PRIMULIFLORA

Habit Tufted, mat- or cushion-forming, evergreen perennial, with creeping stems. **Flowers** Solitary, almost stemless, tubular with 5 spreading lobes, giving a star-shaped outline, to 2cm (⅘in) across, borne in spring. Bright yellow. **Leaves** Narrow, oblong to lance-shaped, pointed, usually hairy. Pale green, with silver margins.

• NATIVE HABITAT Screes, rocks, and alpine and subalpine meadows in the mountains from southwest and central Europe to southeastern Alps and Apennines.

• CULTIVATION Suitable for growing in a trough, scree bed, or rock garden in moist but sharply drained, gritty, moderately fertile soil. Protect from winter wet. Alternatively, grow in an alpine house in a mix of 1 part loam and leaf-mould, with 3 parts grit.

• PROPAGATION By seed as soon as ripe in containers in a cold frame. Separate offsets in spring and early summer.

• OTHER NAMES *Androsace vitaliana,* *Douglasia vitaliana.*

HEIGHT
to 2.5cm
(1in)

SPREAD
To 25cm
(10in)

Cruciferae/ Brassicaceae	

MORISIA MONANTHOS

Habit Tap-rooted, rosette-forming, evergreen, perennial. **Flowers** Cross-shaped, short-stemmed, to 15mm (⅝in) across, borne in late spring and early summer. Golden-yellow. **Leaves** Lance-shaped, divided into slightly fleshy segments. Dark green.
• NATIVE HABITAT Sandy areas, Corsica, Sardinia.
• CULTIVATION Needs gritty, very sharply drained soil and protection from excessive winter wet.
• PROPAGATION By seed in containers in a cold frame, in spring. Take root cuttings in winter.
• OTHER NAME *M. hypogaea.*

☼ ◊
✿ ✿ ✿

HEIGHT
5.5m (18ft)

SPREAD
3m (10ft)

Ranunculaceae	

TROLLIUS PUMILUS

Habit Tufted, perennial. **Flowers** Solitary, cup-shaped, opening flat, 2–3.5cm (⅘–1⅜in) across, borne in late spring and early summer. Bright yellow. **Leaves** Divided into 5 toothed, oblong to lance-shaped lobes. Mid-green.
• NATIVE HABITAT Damp mountain meadows, Himalaya, eastern Tibet, and western China.
• CULTIVATION Grow in deep, moist, fertile soil, in sun or partial shade.
• PROPAGATION Divide as growth begins in spring. Sow seed when ripe in containers in a cold frame.

☼ ◊
✿ ✿ ✿

HEIGHT
to 30cm
(12in)

SPREAD
to 20cm
(8in)

Ranunculaceae	

RANUNCULUS FICARIA FLORE-PLENO

Habit Tuberous, herbaceous, perennial.
Flowers Solitary, pompon-like, to 3cm (1⅛in) across, borne in early spring. Bright yellow.
Leaves Basal, broadly heart-shaped, glossy, dying back soon after flowering. Dark green.
• NATIVE HABITAT Europe, northwest Africa, and southwest Asia.
• CULTIVATION Spreads rapidly, but is not as invasive as the species. Suits wild gardens or may be naturalized in turf, in sun or deep shade.
• PROPAGATION Divide in spring or autumn.

☼ ◊
✿ ✿ ✿

HEIGHT
5cm (2in)

SPREAD
30cm (12in)
or more

Ranunculaceae	

RANUNCULUS FICARIA
var. *AURANTIACUS*

Habit Tuberous, herbaceous, perennial.
Flowers Solitary, saucer-shaped, to 3cm (1⅛in) wide, borne in early spring. Copper-orange.
Leaves Basal, broadly heart-shaped, glossy, dying back soon after flowering. Dark green.
• NATIVE HABITAT Europe and northwest Africa.
• CULTIVATION Suitable for naturalizing in turf. Needs a site in sun or deep shade. Spreads rapidly.
• PROPAGATION Divide in spring or autumn.
• OTHER NAME *R. ficaria* 'Cupreus'.

☼ ◊
✿ ✿ ✿

HEIGHT
5cm (2in)

SPREAD
30cm (12in)
or more

SAXIFRAGA

The genus *Saxifraga* includes a wide range of species of alpine plant, many of which suit rock gardens, troughs and alpine-house culture. They are grouped according to their cultivation requirements.

Group 1 Moist but well-drained soil, in partial or deep shade.

Group 2 Moist, sharply drained, fertile, neutral to alkaline soil, in light shade.

Group 3 Moist but sharply drained, moderately fertile, neutral to alkaline soil, protected from the hottest summer sun.

Group 4 Sharply drained, alkaline soil, in full sun. In an alpine house, use shallow pans and a mix of 2 parts loam, and 1 part limestone chippings.

Sow seed when fresh, or root rosette cuttings in late spring or early summer.

S. GRANULATA
Habit Clump-forming, summer-herbaceous, perennial, with stem and root bulbils.
Flowers Saucer-shaped, 15mm (⅝in) across, borne in clusters of 10–20, in late spring. White.
Leaves Kidney-shaped, toothed, in fairly large rosettes. Mid-green.
• CULTIVATION 2.
• HEIGHT 25cm (10in).
• SPREAD 30cm (12in).

S. granulata
Fair maids of France, Meadow saxifrage

☀ ◊ ❉ ❉ ❉

S. HIRSUTA
Habit Mound-forming, evergreen, perennial.
Flowers Star-shaped, to 8mm (⅜in) across, borne in loose clusters in spring or early summer. White.
Leaves Kidney-shaped to rounded, toothed. Mid-green, often with purple underside.
• CULTIVATION 1.
• HEIGHT to 20cm (8in).
• SPREAD 20cm (8in).

S. hirsuta
Kidney saxifrage

☀ ◊ ❉ ❉ ❉

S. CUNEIFOLIA
Habit Carpet-forming, evergreen, perennial.
Flowers Star-shaped, 7mm (¼in) across, borne in loose clusters in spring and early summer. White.
Leaves Wedge-shaped, sometimes oval or rounded, toothed and leathery. Fresh green.
• CULTIVATION 1.
• HEIGHT 20cm (8in).
• SPREAD 30cm (12in).

S. cuneifolia
Shield-leaved saxifrage

☀ ◊ ❉ ❉ ❉

S. LONGIFOLIA
Habit Monocarpic, evergreen, perennial.
Flowers Saucer-shaped, 1cm (⅜in) across, borne in large, arching, pyramidal spray to 70cm (28in) long, in summer. White.
Leaves Linear, lime-encrusted, in a single, large, tough rosette. Silver-grey.
• CULTIVATION 4.
• HEIGHT 60cm (24in).
• SPREAD 20cm (8in).

S. longifolia
Pyrenean saxifrage

☀ ◊ ❉ ❉ ❉

S. 'Tumbling Waters'
Habit Tufted, evergreen, perennial.
Flowers Open saucer-shaped, 1cm (⅜in) across, borne in spring. White.
Leaves Linear, in large rosettes. Silver-green.
• CULTIVATION 4.
• OTHER NAME
S. longifolia 'Tumbling Waters'.
• HEIGHT 45cm(18in).
• SPREAD 20cm (8in).

S. 'Tumbling Waters'

S. SCARDICA
Habit Cushion-forming, evergreen, perennial.
Flowers Cupped, upturned, 15mm (⅝in) across, borne in clusters on red-tinted stems, in spring. White.
Leaves Oblong and fleshy, forming rosettes. Blue-green.
• CULTIVATION 3.
• HEIGHT 8cm (3in).
• SPREAD 15cm (6in).

S. scardica

S. BURSERIANA
Habit Cushion-forming, evergreen, perennial.
Flowers Solitary, cup-shaped, 1cm (⅜in) across, borne on red stems in early spring. White.
Leaves Pointed, firm, and narrowly lance-shaped, in small, compact rosettes. Grey-green.
• CULTIVATION 3.
• HEIGHT 5cm (2in).
• SPREAD 15cm (6in).

S. burseriana

S. × GEUM
Habit Mat-forming, evergreen, perennial.
Flowers Star-shaped, 8mm (⅛in) across, borne in loose sprays during summer. White.
Leaves Spoon-shaped, long-stalked, and sparsely haired, with scalloped margins, in large rosettes. Mid-green.
• CULTIVATION 1.
• HEIGHT 20cm (8in).
• SPREAD 20cm (8in).

S. × geum

S. × IRVINGII 'Jenkinsiae'
Habit Dense, cushion-forming, evergreen, perennial.
Flowers To 2cm (⅝in) across, borne in spring. Pale pink, dark-centred.
Leaves Wedge-shaped, rosetted. Grey-green.
• CULTIVATION 3.
• OTHER NAME
S. × jenkinsiae.
• HEIGHT 5cm (2in).
• SPREAD 20cm (8in).

S. × irvingii 'Jenkinsiae'

S. COTYLEDON
Habit Tufted, evergreen, perennial.
Flowers Cupped, to 1cm (⅜in) across, borne in loose sprays to 70cm (28in) long, in spring. White, often marked red.
Leaves Lance-shaped, with lime-encrusted teeth, in large rosettes. Pale green.
• CULTIVATION 4.
• HEIGHT 30cm (12in).
• SPREAD 20cm (8in).

S. cotyledon

S. 'Kathleen Pinsent'
Habit Rosette-forming, evergreen, perennial.
Flowers Open cup-shaped, to 2cm (⅝in) across, borne in arching sprays during late spring and early summer. Pink.
Leaves Narrow spoon-shaped, with recurved tips. Silver-grey.
• CULTIVATION 4.
• HEIGHT 20cm (8in).
• SPREAD 20cm (8in).

S. 'Kathleen Pinsent'

S. 'Southside Seedling'
Habit Tufted, evergreen, perennial.
Flowers Open cup-shaped, 1cm (⅜in) across, borne in large sprays in spring and early summer. White, spotted red.
Leaves Oblong to spoon-shaped, forming large rosettes. Pale green.
• CULTIVATION 4.
• HEIGHT 30cm (12in).
• SPREAD 20cm (8in).

S. 'Southside Seedling'

S. FREDERICI-AUGUSTI subsp. GRISEBACHII 'Wisley Variety'

Habit Cushion-forming, evergreen, perennial. **Flowers** To 6mm (¼in) across, borne on leafy, hairy stems in late spring. Red-purple, green tips. **Leaves** Spoon-shaped, in flat rosettes. Silver.
• CULTIVATION 4.
• HEIGHT 10cm (4in).
• SPREAD 10cm (4in).

S. frederici-augusti subsp. grisebachii 'Wisley Variety'

☼ ◊ ❀❀❀ ♈

S. OPPOSITIFOLIA

Habit Flat, mat-forming, evergreen, perennial. **Flowers** Solitary, almost stemless, cup-shaped, to 2cm (¾in) across, borne in spring or sometimes late winter. Red-purple to pink, or white. **Leaves** Tiny, stiff, oval or oblong. Dark green.
• CULTIVATION 2.
• HEIGHT 2.5cm (1in).
• SPREAD 20cm (8in).

S. oppositifolia
Purple saxifrage

☼ ◖ ❀❀❀

S. × ANGLICA 'Cranbourne'

Habit Cushion-forming, evergreen, perennial. **Flowers** Solitary, cup-shaped, almost stemless, to 2cm (¼in) across, borne in early summer. Lilac-purple. **Leaves** Linear, forming dense rosettes. Grey-green.
• CULTIVATION 3.
• HEIGHT 2.5cm (1in).
• SPREAD 20cm (8in).

S. × anglica 'Cranbourne'

☼ ◊ ❀❀❀ ♈

S. STRIBRNYI

Habit Cushion-forming, evergreen, perennial. **Flowers** Cupped, 1cm (⅜in) across, borne in spikes on crook-like stems, in late spring and early summer. Deep violet-purple. **Leaves** Pointed, lance-shaped, lime-encrusted, in rosettes. Blue-green.
• CULTIVATION 4.
• HEIGHT 10cm (4in).
• SPREAD 20cm (8in).

S. stribrnyi

☼ ◊ ❀❀❀

S. SEMPERVIVUM

Habit Cushion-forming, evergreen, perennial. **Flowers** Open cup-shaped, 6mm (¼in) across, borne in spikes on silver-haired stems, in spring. Deep red-purple. **Leaves** Linear and lime-encrusted. Silver-green.
• CULTIVATION 4.
• OTHER NAME
S. porophylla var. *thessalica*.
• HEIGHT 10cm (4in).
• SPREAD 20cm (8in).

S. sempervivum

☼ ◊ ❀❀❀

S. × BOYDII
'Hindhead Seedling'
Habit Tight cushion-forming, evergreen, perennial.
Flowers Solitary, cupped, erect, to 3cm (1¼in) across, borne in spring. Pale yellow.
Leaves Linear to lance-shaped, and pointed. Blue-green.
• CULTIVATION 3.
• OTHER NAME
S. 'Hindhead Seedling'.
• HEIGHT 5cm (2in).
• SPREAD 5cm (2in).

S. × *boydii*
'Hindhead Seedling'

☀ ◊ ❋❋❋

S. × APICULATA
Habit Cushion-forming, evergreen, perennial.
Flowers Cup-shaped, 8mm (⅜in) across, borne in clusters in early spring. Yellow.
Leaves Linear to lance-shaped, forming tight rosettes. Dark green.
• CULTIVATION 3.
• HEIGHT 10cm (4in).
• SPREAD 30cm (12in).

S. × *apiculata*

☀ ◊ ❋❋❋   ♆

S. SANCTA
Habit Spreading, hummock-forming, evergreen, perennial.
Flowers Open cup-shaped, 8mm (⅜in) across, borne in compact clusters in spring. Deep yellow.
Leaves Narrowly lance-shaped, forming tight rosettes. Dark green.
• CULTIVATION 3.
• OTHER NAME
S. *juniperifolia* subsp. *sancta*.
• HEIGHT 5cm (2in).
• SPREAD 20cm (8in).

S. *sancta*

☀ ◊ ❋❋❋

S. 'Carmen'
Habit Cushion-forming, evergreen, perennial.
Flowers Upright, cupped, 8mm (⅜in) across, borne in spring. Bright yellow.
Leaves Linear, pointed, in rosettes. Dark green.
• CULTIVATION 3.
• OTHER NAME
S. × *elizabethae*.
• HEIGHT 2.5cm (1in).
• SPREAD 10–15cm (4–6in).

S. 'Carmen'

☀ ◊ ❋❋❋

S. EXARATA
subsp. MOSCHATA
'Cloth of Gold'
Habit Tufted, evergreen, perennial.
Flowers Star-like, 8mm (⅜in) across, sparsely borne in flat-topped clusters in late spring and early summer. White.
Leaves Entire or lobed, in soft rosettes. Yellow.
• CULTIVATION 1.
• HEIGHT 10cm (4in).
• SPREAD 30cm (12in).

S. *exarata*
subsp. *moschata*
'Cloth of Gold'

☀ ◊ ❋❋❋

Caryophyllaceae	

SILENE ALPESTRIS

Habit Branching, loosely tufted, evergreen, perennial. *Flowers* Saucer-shaped, 1cm (⅜in) across, with fringed petals, borne in open sprays in early summer. White, sometimes pink-flushed. *Leaves* Linear to lance-shaped. Mid-green.
• NATIVE HABITAT Eastern Alps, Europe.
• CULTIVATION Grow in gritty, sharply drained, neutral to slightly alkaline soil.
• PROPAGATION By seed in autumn, in containers in a cold frame. Take basal cuttings in spring.
• OTHER NAME *Heliosperma alpestris.*

HEIGHT
15cm (6in)

SPREAD
20cm (8in)

Gesneriacae	

HABERLEA RHODOPENSIS 'Virginalis'

Habit Rosette-forming, evergreen, perennial. *Flowers* Trumpet-shaped, two-lipped, to 2.5cm (1in) across, borne in lax clusters in spring and early summer. Pure white. *Leaves* Coarsely scalloped, oval, and softly hairy. Dark green.
• NATIVE HABITAT Shady, rocky places and mountains of Bulgaria and northeastern Greece.
• CULTIVATION Needs moist but well-drained, gritty, fertile soil that is neutral to acid.
• PROPAGATION By leaf cuttings or division, both in spring. Sow seed at 13°C (55°F) in spring.

HEIGHT
to 15cm (6in)

SPREAD
to 25cm (10in)

Rosaceae	

POTENTILLA ALBA

Habit Spreading, clumping, evergreen, perennial. *Flowers* Saucer-shaped, 2.5cm (1in) across, borne in loose clusters in late spring and early summer. White, with golden anthers. *Leaves* Palmate, with oblong to oval leaflets. Light green, hairy below.
• NATIVE HABITAT Central and southern Europe.
• CULTIVATION Suitable for growing in scree beds, rock gardens, and border fronts. Needs poor to moderately fertile, well-drained soil.
• PROPAGATION Divide in autumn or spring. Sow seed when ripe, in containers in a cold frame.

HEIGHT
8cm (3in)

SPREAD
to 30cm (12in)

Portulacaceae	BITTERROOT

LEWISIA REDIVIVA (White form)

Habit Tufted, rosette-forming, herbaceous, perennial. *Flowers* Broadly funnel-shaped, 5cm (2in) across, with narrow petals, borne in early spring to summer. White. *Leaves* Linear to club-shaped, dying back after flowering. Dark green.
• NATIVE HABITAT Open, stony mountain grassland in Canada and western USA.
• CULTIVATION Needs sharp drainage. Dislikes excess wet during winter and summer dormancy.
• PROPAGATION By seed in containers in a cold frame, in autumn.

HEIGHT
5cm (2in)

SPREAD
10cm (4in)

Campanulaceae	

CYANANTHUS LOBATUS 'Albus'

Habit Tufted, spreading, tap-rooted, herbaceous, perennial. **Flowers** Single, funnel-shaped, with 5 lobes 2–4cm (¾–1⅜in) across, borne in late summer. White. **Leaves** Oval, deeply lobed. Dull green.
• NATIVE HABITAT Cool moist habitats in China and Himalaya.
• CULTIVATION Grow in moderately fertile, moist but well-drained soil that is neutral to slightly acid.
• PROPAGATION By softwood cuttings in late spring or early summer. Sow seed as soon as ripe, or in early spring, in containers in a cold frame.

HEIGHT
5cm (2in)

SPREAD
to 30cm
(12in)

Caryophyllaceae	

ARENARIA MONTANA ♀

Habit Vigorous, spreading, prostrate, evergreen, perennial. **Flowers** Saucer-shaped, to 2cm (⅝in) across, borne in early summer. White. **Leaves** Paired, narrowly lance-shaped. Greyish-green.
• NATIVE HABITAT Mountains, southwest Europe.
• CULTIVATION Good for growing on a rock garden, or in rock or paving crevices. Easily grown in poor, sandy, moist but sharply drained soil.
• PROPAGATION Divide after flowering, take basal cuttings in early summer, or sow seed in autumn, in containers in a cold frame.

HEIGHT
to 5cm
(2in)

SPREAD
to 30cm
(12in)

Geraniaceae	

GERANIUM FARRERI ♀

Habit Tap-rooted, rosette-forming, herbaceous, perennial. **Flowers** Saucer-shaped, to 3.5cm (1½in) across, with wavy margins, borne in early summer. Pale pink, with black anthers. **Leaves** Kidney-shaped, divided. Mid-green, with red margins.
• NATIVE HABITAT Mountains, western China.
• CULTIVATION Outdoors, grow in a scree bed and protect from winter wet. In an alpine house, use a mix of equal parts loam, leaf-mould, and grit.
• PROPAGATION By seed when ripe in containers in a cold frame, or take basal cuttings in spring.

HEIGHT
to 12cm
(5in)

SPREAD
to 15cm
(6in)

Onagraceae	

EPILOBIUM CHLORIFOLIUM var.
KAIKOURENSE

Habit Woody-based, clump-forming, evergreen, perennial. **Flowers** Funnel-shaped, with spreading lobes 15mm (⅝in) across, borne in summer. White or pale pink. **Leaves** Oval, toothed. Bronze-green.
• NATIVE HABITAT Stony slopes, New Zealand.
• CULTIVATION Grow in fertile, moist but well-drained soil, with shade from the hottest sun.
• PROPAGATION By seed when ripe or in spring, in containers in a cold frame. By division in autumn or spring.

HEIGHT
to 30cm
(12in)

SPREAD
To 15cm
(6in)

Cruciferae/ Brassicaceae	

IBERIS SAXATILIS

Habit Evergreen, sub-shrub. *Flowers* Cross-shaped, borne in flattened clusters 3–4cm (1½–1¾in) across, in late spring and summer. White, sometimes tinted purple. *Leaves* Linear, fleshy, almost cylindrical. Dark green.
• NATIVE HABITAT Southern Europe.
• CULTIVATION Needs well-drained, moderately fertile soil that is neutral to alkaline.
• PROPAGATION Take softwood cuttings in early summer or semi-ripe cuttings in mid-summer. Sow seed when ripe in containers in a cold frame.

☼ ◊
❀ ❀ ❀

HEIGHT
to 15cm
(6in)

SPREAD
to 30cm
(12in)

Geraniaceae	

GERANIUM SESSILIFLORUM subsp. *NOVAE-ZELANDIAE* 'Nigricans'

Habit Rosette-forming, evergreen, perennial. *Flowers* Upright, funnel-shaped, 7mm (¼in) across, borne in loose clusters in summer. Grey-white. *Leaves* Divided. Olive-bronze.
• NATIVE HABITAT Garden origin.
• CULTIVATION Good for scree or rock gardens, in moist but well-drained, poor to moderately fertile soil. Self-sows freely; seedlings come true.
• PROPAGATION Sow seed when ripe in containers in a cold frame.

☼ ◊
❀ ❀ ❀

HEIGHT
to 8cm
(3in)

SPREAD
15cm (6in)

Cornaceae	CREEPING DOGWOOD, DWARF CORNEL

CORNUS CANADENSIS 🏆

Habit Creeping, rhizomatous, evergreen, perennial. *Flowers* Tiny, borne in dense clusters, with 4–6 bracts to 2cm (¾in) long, in late spring and early summer. Green, with white bracts. *Fruits* Rounded berry. Bright red. *Leaves* Oval to lance-shaped, in terminal whorls. Bright green.
• NATIVE HABITAT Woods, USA and Greenland.
• CULTIVATION Prefers a site in partial shade, with moist, leaf-rich acid soil.
• PROPAGATION By division in spring or autumn.
• OTHER NAME *Chamaepericlymenum canadense.*

☼ ◊ pH
❀ ❀ ❀

HEIGHT
to 15cm
(6in)

SPREAD
indefinite

Compositae/Asteraceae	NEW ZEALAND DAISY

CELMISIA RAMULOSA

Habit Branching, evergreen, sub-shrub. **Flowers** Daisy, 2.5cm (1in) across, borne on sticky white stems in late spring and early summer. White, with yellow disc. **Leaves** Linear to oblong, overlapping, stiff. Dark green, with white-woolly underside.
• NATIVE HABITAT Moorland and scree, high altitudes, mountains of New Zealand.
• CULTIVATION Grow in moist but well-drained, acid soil that is rich in organic matter, in sun or light shade. Grows best in cool, moist climates.
• PROPAGATION Root rosettes as cuttings in spring.

☼ ◊ pH
❋ ❋ ❋

HEIGHT
to 25cm
(10in)

SPREAD
to 25cm
(10in)

Scrophulariaceae	

OURISIA CAESPITOSA

Habit Mat-forming, evergreen, perennial.
Flowers Tubular, 2-lipped, 15mm (⅝in) across, borne in whorls on leafless stems, in summer. White, with yellow throat. **Leaves** Broadly oval to spoon-shaped, entire or notched. Grey-green.
• NATIVE HABITAT Alpine areas, New Zealand.
• CULTIVATION Grow in reliably moist but well-drained soil, preferably in cool, damp climates. Good for a rock garden, peat bed, or wall crevice.
• PROPAGATION By seed as soon as ripe or in spring, in a cold frame. Divide in spring.

☼ ◊
❋ ❋ ❋

HEIGHT
5cm (2in)

SPREAD
to 20cm
(8in)

Solanaceae	WHITE CUP

NIEREMBERGIA REPENS

Habit Mat-forming, stem-rooting, perennial.
Flowers Upright, open bell, 2.5–5cm (1–2in) across, borne in summer. White, with yellow eye. **Leaves** Rounded, spoon-shaped. Light green.
• NATIVE HABITAT Andes.
• CULTIVATION Suitable for planting in paving crevices. Grow in dry, sandy soils in a warm, sunny site. Tends to be invasive, so site away from small, more precious alpines.
• PROPAGATION By seed or division in spring.
• OTHER NAME *N. rivularis.*

☼ ◊
❋ ❋

HEIGHT
5cm (2in)

SPREAD
60cm (24in)
or more

Compositae/Asteraceae	

ANACYCLUS PYRETHRUM var. DEPRESSUS

Habit Mat-forming, evergreen, perennial. **Flowers** Daisy, to 5cm (2in) across, borne in summer. White with red reverse and yellow disc. **Leaves** Finely divided, forming rosettes. Grey-green.
• NATIVE HABITAT Stony slopes, Atlas Mountains.
• CULTIVATION Needs gritty, sharply drained, moderately fertile soil. Protect from winter wet.
• PROPAGATION Take softwood cuttings in spring. Sow seed in autumn in containers in a cold frame.
• OTHER NAME *A. depressus.*

☼ ◊
❋ ❋

HEIGHT
2.5–5cm
(1–2in) or
more

SPREAD
10cm (4in)

Rosaceae	MOUNTAIN AVENS

DRYAS OCTOPETALA

Habit Mat-forming, evergreen, sub-shrub.
Flowers Upright, cup-shaped, to 4cm (1⅝in)
across, borne in late spring and early summer.
White. **Leaves** Oblong, scalloped and glossy.
Dark green. **Fruits** Fluffy, silky-haired seedheads.
• NATIVE HABITAT Moorland, northern Europe.
• CULTIVATION Suitable for growing on a rock
garden. Prefers gritty, well-drained, fertile soil.
• PROPAGATION By seed when ripe in a cold
frame, by softwood cuttings in early summer,
or by separation of rooted stems in spring.

☀ ○
❀ ❀ ❀

HEIGHT
10cm (4in)

SPREAD
90cm (36in)
or more

Compositae/Asteraceae	STEMLESS CARLINE THISTLE

CARLINA ACAULIS

Habit Rosette-forming, prickly, herbaceous,
perennial. **Flowers** Measuring 10cm (4in) across,
borne at the centre of the rosettes in mid- and late
summer. Silvery-white, with brown disc. **Leaves**
Deeply cut, oval, with spiny margins. Green.
• NATIVE HABITAT Southern and eastern Europe.
• CULTIVATION Grow in poor, sharply drained soil.
• PROPAGATION Sow seed in autumn in containers
in a cold frame.

☀ ○
❀ ❀ ❀

HEIGHT
to 10cm
(4in)

SPREAD
to 25cm
(10in)

Ranunculaceae	

THALICTRUM KIUSIANUM

Habit Mat-forming, rhizomatous, herbaceous,
perennial. **Flowers** Many-petalled, to 1cm (⅜in)
across, borne in few-flowered, fluffy clusters in
early summer. Pale pink-mauve. **Leaves** Finely
divided, fern-like, with oval lobes. Blue-green.
• NATIVE HABITAT Damp shady habitats, Japan.
• CULTIVATION Ideal for a rock garden, peat bed,
or trough. Grow in moist, sandy, leaf-rich soil.
• PROPAGATION Sow seed when ripe or in early
spring, in containers in a cold frame. Divide
carefully, in spring, as new growth begins.

◐ ◊
❀ ❀ ❀

HEIGHT
to 10cm
(4in)

SPREAD
to 30cm or
more (12in)

Caprifoliaceae	TWIN FLOWER

LINNAEA BOREALIS

Habit Mat-forming, stem-rooting, evergreen,
sub-shrub. **Flowers** Paired, nodding bell-shaped,
to 1cm (⅜in) long, borne in summer. Palest pink.
Leaves Paired, oval to rounded, scalloped, glossy.
Dark green, with pale green or buff underside.
• NATIVE HABITAT Woods, tundra, and heath
in Eurasia and N. America.
• CULTIVATION Needs moist, fertile, acid soil.
• PROPAGATION Separate rooted stems between
autumn and spring, root softwood cuttings in early
summer. Sow seed in autumn in a cold frame.

◐ ◊ pH
❀ ❀ ❀

HEIGHT
to 8cm
(3in)

SPREAD
90cm (36in)
or more

CORYDALIS

The genus *Corydalis* comprises about 300 species of annuals, biennials, and perennials, often from scree, woods, and mountain meadows. For ease of reference, cultivation needs are grouped as follows:
Group 1 Full sun or partial shade, in fertile, well-drained soil.
Group 2 Full sun, in moderately fertile, sharply drained soil.

Group 3 Partial shade and moist but well-drained, leaf-rich, fertile soil.
Group 4 In an alpine house, in a mix of equal parts loam, leaf-mould and grit.

Propagate by dividing spring-flowering species in late summer before growth resumes, or summer-flowering species in spring. Sow seed as soon as ripe in a cold frame. Germination may be erratic.

C. OCHROLEUCA
Habit Clump-forming, fibrous-rooted, evergreen, perennial.
Flowers Two-lipped, 15mm (⅝in) long, borne in oblong clusters in late spring and summer. Creamy-white, with yellow tip.
Leaves Finely divided and oval. Pale green.
• CULTIVATION 1.
• HEIGHT 30cm (12in).
• SPREAD 30cm (12in).

C. ochroleuca

☼ ◊ ✿ ✿ ✿

C. MALKENSIS
Habit Compact, tuberous, herbaceous, perennial.
Flowers Two-lipped, 2.5cm (1in) long, borne in spikes in spring. Cream.
Leaves Finely divided and oval. Pale green.
• CULTIVATION 2 or 3.
• OTHER NAME
C. caucasica var. *alba* of gardens.
• HEIGHT 8–15cm (3–6in).
• SPREAD to 10cm (4in).

C. malkensis

☼ ◊ ✿ ✿ ✿

C. POPOVII
Habit Tuberous, herbaceous, perennial.
Flowers Two-lipped, to 4.5cm (1¾in) long, borne in loose spikes in late spring. White or pale violet, with maroon lips.
Leaves Finely divided and oval. Blue-green.
• CULTIVATION 4.
• HEIGHT 15cm (6in).
• SPREAD 12cm (5in).

C. popovii

◐ ◊ ✿ ✿ ✿

C. DIPHYLLA
Habit Tuberous, herbaceous, perennial.
Flowers Two-lipped, to 3cm (1⅛in) long, borne in loose spikes in spring. Pale violet, with white spurs and red-violet lips.
Leaves Narrowly lance-shaped and finely divided. Glaucous, mid-green.
• CULTIVATION 2.
• HEIGHT 15cm (6in).
• SPREAD 10cm (4in).

C. diphylla

☼ ◊ ✿ ✿ ✿

C. SOLIDA
'George Baker'
Habit Clump-forming, tuberous, herbaceous, perennial.
Flowers Two-lipped, 2cm (¾in) long, borne in erect spikes in spring. Deep salmon-rose.
Leaves Finely dissected. Greyish-green.
• CULTIVATION 1 or 2.
• OTHER NAME *C. solida* 'G. P. Baker'.
• HEIGHT 15cm (6in).
• SPREAD 20cm (8in).

C. solida
'George Baker'

C. CASHMERIANA
Habit Tufted, tuberous, perennial.
Flowers Two-lipped, 1cm (½in) long, with curved spurs, borne in sprays in summer. Bright blue.
Leaves Finely divided, with oval to elliptic lobes. Bright green.
• CULTIVATION 3.
• HEIGHT 10–25cm (4–10in).
• SPREAD 8–15cm (3–6in).

C. cashmeriana

C. FLEXUOSA
'China Blue'
Habit Scaly-rooted, summer-dormant, rhizomatous, perennial.
Flowers Two-lipped, 2.5cm (1in) long, borne in oblong clusters in late spring and summer. Bright blue.
Leaves Finely divided, and oval. Bluish-green.
• CULTIVATION 3.
• HEIGHT 30cm (12in).
• SPREAD 40cm (16in) or more.

C. flexuosa
'China Blue'

C. CHEILANTHIFOLIA
Habit Rosette-forming, fibrous-rooted, evergreen, perennial.
Flowers Two-lipped, 15mm (⅝in) long, borne in dense spikes in spring and summer. Deep yellow.
Leaves Fern-like and finely divided. Pale to mid-green.
• CULTIVATION 1.
• HEIGHT 30cm (12in).
• SPREAD 25cm (10in).

C. cheilanthifolia

C. WILSONII
Habit Tap-rooted, rosetted, evergreen, perennial.
Flowers Two-lipped, 2cm (⅝in) long, borne in lax spikes in spring and summer. Canary-yellow, with green tips.
Leaves Fleshy, divided, and smooth. Blue-green.
• CULTIVATION 4.
• HEIGHT 10–20cm (4–8in).
• SPREAD 20–30cm (8–12in).

C. wilsonii

C. LUTEA
Habit Rhizomatous, mound- or tuft-forming, evergreen, perennial.
Flowers Two-lipped, to 2cm (⅝in) long, borne in spikes from spring to autumn. Golden-yellow.
Leaves Fern-like and arching. Pale green.
• CULTIVATION 1, 2, or 3.
• OTHER NAME *Pseudofumaria lutea.*
• HEIGHT 40cm (16in).
• SPREAD 30cm (12in).

C. lutea

PHLOX

The genus *Phlox* comprises 67 species of evergreen, semi-evergreen, and herbaceous perennials, with a few annuals and sub-shrubs. They bear heads or clusters of usually salver- but occasionally funnel-shaped flowers, with 5 spreading petal lobes. Many phloxes, mostly those found in dry, rocky mountain habitats or woodlands in North America, are suitable in scale for a rock garden and are easily grown. Many are also suitable for planting in or trailing over walls, and used as border edging. Phloxes are valued for their foliage, and the profusion of small, usually brilliantly coloured flowers, borne during spring and summer. The flowers, which are often so abundant that they almost obscure the foliage, are also attractive to butterflies. For ease of reference, their cultivation requirements may be grouped as follows:

Group 1 Fertile, moist but well-drained soil that is enriched with organic matter, in partial shade.

Group 2 Well-drained, fertile soil in sun, or in light, dappled shade in areas with low rainfall.

Group 3 Poor to moderately fertile, gritty, sharply drained soil, in full sun. Best suited to rock gardens, raised beds, and troughs. Grow as a pot plant in an alpine house, in a mix of equal parts loam, leaf-mould, and sharp sand.

Take softwood cuttings of leafy, non-flowering shoots in spring. Separate self-rooted stem sections of trailing species and cultivars in spring or early autumn. Sow seed in pots in a cold frame, as soon as ripe or in early spring. In areas with cold, wet winters, overwinter young plants in a cold frame, and set them out in their permanent positions in spring.

P. STOLONIFERA 'Ariane'
Habit Spreading, stoloniferous, semi-evergreen, perennial.
Flowers Salver-shaped, 3cm (1⅛in) across, borne in early summer. White, with yellow eye.
Leaves Oval. Dark green.
• CULTIVATION 1.
• HEIGHT 10–15cm (4–6in).
• SPREAD 30cm (12in).

P. stolonifera 'Ariane'

☀ ◐ ❄❄❄

P. ADSURGENS 'Wagon Wheel'
Habit Stem-rooting, mat-forming, evergreen, perennial.
Flowers To 25mm (1in) across, borne in late spring and early summer. Salmon-pink.
Leaves Rounded to narrowly oval. Mid-green.
• CULTIVATION 1.
• HEIGHT 30cm (12in).
• SPREAD 30cm (12in) or more.

P. adsurgens 'Wagon Wheel'

☀ ◐ ❄❄❄

P. 'Kelly's Eye'
Habit Vigorous, mound-forming, evergreen, perennial.
Flowers Salver-shaped, 15mm (⅝in) across, borne during late spring and early summer. Pale pink, with red-purple eye.
Leaves Narrowly lance-shaped. Dark green.
• CULTIVATION 2.
• HEIGHT 10cm (4in).
• SPREAD 30cm (12in).

P. 'Kelly's Eye'

☀ ◐ ❄❄❄   ♡

P. NIVALIS 'Camla'
Habit Trailing or mat-forming, evergreen, sub-shrub.
Flowers Salver-shaped, 15mm (⅝in) across, borne in lax clusters in summer. Warm pink.
Leaves Lance-shaped and hairy. Mid-green.
• CULTIVATION 2.
• HEIGHT 20cm (8in).
• SPREAD 30cm (12in).

P. nivalis 'Camla'

☀ ◐ ❄❄❄

P. SUBULATA 'Marjorie'
Habit Mound-forming, evergreen, perennial.
Flowers Star-shaped, , 30mm (1¼in) wide, borne in clusters in late spring and early summer. Deep pink, with yellow eye edged dark pink.
Leaves Linear to elliptic, hairy. Bright green.
• CULTIVATION 2.
• HEIGHT 10cm (4in).
• SPREAD 20cm (8in).

P. subulata 'Marjorie'

☼ ◊ ❋❋❋

P. DOUGLASII 'Crackerjack'
Habit Compact, mound-forming, evergreen, perennial.
Flowers Salver-shaped, 15mm (⅝in) across, borne in late spring and early summer. Magenta.
Leaves Stiff and narrowly lance-shaped. Dark green.
• CULTIVATION 2.
• HEIGHT 12cm (5in).
• SPREAD 20cm (8in).

P. douglasii 'Crackerjack'

☼ ◊ ❋❋❋ ♛

P. NANA 'Arroya'
Habit Spreading, semi-evergreen or deciduous, perennial.
Flowers Solitary, salver-shaped, 25mm (1in) across, borne throughout summer. Bright magenta, with white eye.
Leaves Narrowly lance-shaped. Grey-green.
• CULTIVATION 3.
• HEIGHT 20cm (8in).
• SPREAD 30cm (12in).

P. nana 'Arroya'

☼ ◊ ❋❋❋

P. DOUGLASII 'Red Admiral'
Habit Mound-forming, evergreen, perennial.
Flowers Salver-shaped, 15mm (⅝in) across, borne in clusters during late spring and early summer. Deep crimson.
Leaves Narrowly lance-shaped. Dark green.
• CULTIVATION 2.
• HEIGHT 20cm (8in).
• SPREAD 30cm (12in).

P. douglasii 'Red Admiral'

☼ ◊ ❋❋❋ ♛

P. NANA 'Mary Maslin'
Habit Spreading, semi-evergreen or deciduous, perennial.
Flowers Solitary, salver-shaped, 25mm (1in) across, borne in lax clusters in summer. Scarlet, with yellow eye.
Leaves Linear to narrow lance-shaped and downy. Grey-green.
• CULTIVATION 3.
• HEIGHT 20cm (8in).
• SPREAD 30cm (12in).

P. nana 'Mary Maslin'

☼ ◊ ❋❋❋

P. DOUGLASII 'Boothman's Variety'
Habit Mound-forming, evergreen, perennial.
Flowers Salver-shaped, 15mm (⅝in) across, borne in late spring and early summer. Violet-pink, with dark eye.
Leaves Narrowly lance-shaped. Dark green.
• CULTIVATION 2.
• HEIGHT 20cm (8in).
• SPREAD 30cm (12in).

P. douglasii 'Boothman's Variety'

☼ ◊ ❋❋❋ ♛

P. DIVARICATA 'Dirigo Ice'
Habit Stem-rooting, spreading, semi-evergreen, perennial.
Flowers Salver-shaped, to 30mm (1¼in) across, borne in lax clusters in early summer. Clear pale blue.
Leaves Oval and hairy. Mid-green.
• CULTIVATION 1.
• HEIGHT 35cm (14in).
• SPREAD 50cm (20in).

P. divaricata 'Dirigo Ice'

☼ ◊ ❋❋❋

P. BIFIDA
Habit Mound-forming, evergreen, perennial.
Flowers Scented, star-shaped, 20mm (⅘in) across, deeply cleft, borne in lax clusters in spring. Deep lavender-blue to white.
Leaves Linear, spiny and hairy. Mid-green.
• CULTIVATION 2 or 3.
• HEIGHT 20cm (8in).
• SPREAD 15cm (6in).

P. bifida
Sand phlox

☀ ◊ ❀❀❀

P. 'Chatahoochee'
Habit Tufted, short-lived, semi-evergreen, perennial.
Flowers Salver-shaped, to 25mm (1in) across, borne in summer and early autumn. Lavender-blue, with maroon eye.
Leaves Lance-shaped. Mid-green, flushed purple when young.
• CULTIVATION 1 or 2.
• HEIGHT 15cm (6in).
• SPREAD 30cm (12in).

P. 'Chatahoochee'

☀ ◗ ❀❀   ♈

P. 'Emerald Cushion'
Habit Mound-forming, evergreen, perennial.
Flowers Salver-shaped, to 25mm (1in) wide, with notched petals, borne in lax clusters in late spring and early summer. Pale violet.
Leaves Linear to elliptic. Light green.
• CULTIVATION 2.
• HEIGHT 8cm (3in).
• SPREAD 20cm (8in).

P. 'Emerald Cushion'

☀ ◊ ❀❀❀

P. DIVARICATA subsp. LAPHAMII
Habit Stem-rooting, spreading, semi-evergreen, perennial.
Flowers Salver-shaped, to 30mm (1⅛in) across, borne in heads in early summer. Pale to deep lilac-blue.
Leaves Oval and hairy. Mid-green.
• CULTIVATION 1.
• HEIGHT 35cm (14in).
• SPREAD 50cm (20in).

P. divaricata subsp. **laphamii**

☀ ◗ ❀❀❀

P. SUBULATA 'G.F. Wilson'
Habit Vigorous, cushion-forming, evergreen, perennial.
Flowers Star-shaped, 30mm (1⅛in) wide, borne in lax clusters in late spring and early summer. Deep lavender-blue.
Leaves Linear to elliptic and hairy. Bright green.
• CULTIVATION 2.
• HEIGHT 10cm (4in).
• SPREAD 20cm (8in).

P. subulata 'G.F. Wilson'

☀ ◊ ❀❀❀

Caryophyllaceae	

GYPSOPHILA REPENS
'Dorothy Teacher'

Habit Mat-forming, semi-evergreen, perennial.
Flowers Saucer-shaped, 15mm (⅝in) across, borne
in sprays in summer. Pale to dark pink. *Leaves*
Paired, linear or sickle-shaped. Blue-green.
• NATIVE HABITAT Garden origin.
• CULTIVATION Best grown on a rock garden,
raised bed, or sunny bank, in light, gritty,
sharply drained, and slightly alkaline soil.
• PROPAGATION By division in spring, or take
basal cuttings.

HEIGHT
5cm (2in)

SPREAD
to 40cm
(16in)

Campanulaceae	

HYPSELA RENIFORMIS

Habit Vigorous, stem-rooting, creeping, perennial.
Flowers Solitary, tubular, with pointed lobes,
8mm (⅜in) across, borne in late spring and summer.
White to pale pink, with crimson veins. *Leaves*
Rounded to kidney-shaped. Bright green.
• NATIVE HABITAT Moist sites, S. America.
• CULTIVATION Tolerates sun or shade, in gritty,
fertile soil. Best planted away from small alpines.
• PROPAGATION Divide or sow seed at 6–12°C
(43–54°F), both in spring.
• OTHER NAME *H. longiflora.*

HEIGHT

2cm (⅝in)

SPREAD
indefinite

Caryophyllaceae	TUNIC FLOWER

PETRORHAGIA SAXIFRAGA

Habit Tufted to mat-forming, semi-evergreen,
perennial. *Flowers* Saucer-shaped, 1cm (⅜in)
across, borne in delicate clusters during summer.
White or pink, with dark pink veins. *Leaves*
Paired, linear, pointed, grass-like. Deep green.
• NATIVE HABITAT Sandy and rocky sites in
southern and central Europe.
• CULTIVATION Prefers gritty, low-fertility soil.
• PROPAGATION Sow seed in autumn, in
containers in a cold frame; will self-seed freely.
• OTHER NAME *Tunica saxifraga.*

HEIGHT
10cm (4in)

SPREAD
20cm (8in)

Geraniaceae	

GERANIUM SANGUINEUM var. STRIATUM

Habit Spreading, rhizomatous, part-evergreen, hummock-forming, perennial. **Flowers** Saucer-shaped, to 4cm (1⅜in) across, borne in summer. Pale pink, with deep veins. **Leaves** Deeply cut, sparsely toothed. Dark green.
• NATIVE HABITAT Cumbria, United Kingdom.
• CULTIVATION Ideal for borders and rock gardens, in any well-drained, moderately fertile soil.
• PROPAGATION By division in spring.
• OTHER NAME *G. sanguineum* var. *lancastriense*.

☼ ◊
❅ ❅ ❅

HEIGHT
10cm (4in)

SPREAD
30cm or
more (12in)

Scrophulariaceae	

OURISIA MICROPHYLLA

Habit Cushion-forming, semi-evergreen, perennial. **Flowers** Solitary, salver-shaped, 1cm (⅜in) across, borne in profusion in late spring and early summer. Pale pink, with white eye. **Leaves** Heath-like, close to the stems. Pale green.
• NATIVE HABITAT Alpine areas, Chile, Argentina.
• CULTIVATION Grows best in an alpine house. Prefers cool, damp climates, and needs reliably moist but well-drained soil.
• PROPAGATION By seed as soon as ripe or in spring, in a cold frame. Divide in spring.

❅ ❅ ❅

HEIGHT
5cm (2in)

SPREAD
15cm (6in)

Rubiaceae	

ASPERULA SUBEROSA

Habit Soft, clump-forming, spreading, evergreen, perennial. **Flowers** Tubular, with spreading lobes, 6mm (¼in) long, borne in clusters in early summer. Pink. **Leaves** Small, lance-shaped, hairy, whorled. Grey-green.
• NATIVE HABITAT Mountains, Greece, Bulgaria.
• CULTIVATION Needs sharply drained, moderately fertile soil. Dislikes excessive winter wet.
• PROPAGATION Divide in spring or autumn, or sow seed in containers in a cold frame, in autumn.
• OTHER NAME *A. athoa* of gardens.

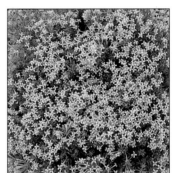

☼ ◊
❅ ❅ ❅

HEIGHT
to 8cm
(3in)

SPREAD
to 20cm
(8in)

Geraniaceae	

ERODIUM CORSICUM

Habit Mat- or cushion-forming perennial. **Flowers** Saucer-shaped, 2cm (⅝in) across, borne in clusters of 1–3, from late spring to summer. Rose-pink, with darker veins. **Leaves** Oval, silver-downy, and crumpled. Grey-green.
• NATIVE HABITAT Sea cliffs, Corsica, Sardinia.
• CULTIVATION Suitable for growing in a trough or raised bed. Needs gritty, sharply drained, neutral to slightly alkaline soil. Protect from winter wet.
• PROPAGATION Divide in spring, or sow seed in containers in a cold frame as soon as ripe.

☼ ◊
❅ ❅

HEIGHT
8cm (3in)

SPREAD
20cm (8in)

Caryophyllaceae	

SAPONARIA × OLIVANA

Habit Firm, cushion-forming, evergreen, perennial. **Flowers** Solitary, flat, 5-petalled, 15mm (⅝in) across, borne on short stems all over the cushions in summer. Pale pink. **Leaves** Narrowly lance-shaped. Mid-green.
• NATIVE HABITAT Garden origin.
• CULTIVATION Suitable for a rock garden, trough, or raised and scree beds. Prefers gritty, sharply drained soil that is neutral to alkaline.
• PROPAGATION Root stem tip cuttings in early summer.

☼ ◌
❀ ❀ ❀

HEIGHT
5cm (2in)

SPREAD
15cm (6in)

Cruciferae/ Brassicaceae	

AETHIONEMA 'Warley Rose'

Habit Compact, tufted, semi- or evergreen, sub-shrub. **Flowers** Cross-shaped, 7mm (¼in) across, borne in elongating clusters in late spring and early summer. Rich pink. **Leaves** Linear. Blue-green.
• NATIVE HABITAT Garden origin.
• CULTIVATION Suitable for growing in a rock garden, raised bed, or wall crevice. Needs a site with fertile, well-drained, alkaline soil.
• PROPAGATION Take softwood cuttings in late spring or early summer. Tends to be short-lived, so propagate regularly to maintain stock.

☼ ◌
❀ ❀ ❀

HEIGHT
15–20cm
(6–8in)

SPREAD
15–20cm
(6–8in)

Polygonaceae	

PERSICARIA AFFINIS 'Donald Lowndes'

Habit Mat-forming, evergreen, perennial. **Flowers** Small, cup-shaped, borne in spikes to 8cm (3in) long, in mid- to late summer. Pale pink, deep rose at maturity. **Leaves** Lance-shaped. Bright green.
• NATIVE HABITAT Garden origin.
• CULTIVATION Ideal at the base of rockwork. Will thrive in reliably moist soil, in sun or partial shade.
• PROPAGATION By division in spring or autumn.
• OTHER NAME *Polygonum affine* 'Donald Lowndes'.

☼ ◗
❀ ❀ ❀

HEIGHT
to 20cm
(8in)

SPREAD
30cm (12in)

Geraniaceae	

GERANIUM DALMATICUM

Habit Creeping, rhizomatous, tough-stemmed, semi-evergreen, perennial. **Flowers** Almost flat, to 3.5cm (1⅜in) across, borne in clusters in summer. Pale to bright pink. **Leaves** Deeply divided. Glossy, light green.
• NATIVE HABITAT Montenegro and Albania.
• CULTIVATION Suitable for a rock garden, scree bed or at the front of a flower border. Needs sharply drained soil that is rich in organic matter.
• PROPAGATION Divide in spring, or sow seed as soon as ripe, in containers in a cold frame.

☼ ◌
❀ ❀ ❀

HEIGHT
to 15cm
(6in)

SPREAD
to 50cm or
more (20in)

Caryophyllaceae	ALPINE CAMPION, ALPINE CATCHFLY

LYCHNIS ALPINA

Habit Tufted, herbaceous, perennial. *Flowers* Saucer-shaped, 2cm (⅜in) across, with notched petals, borne in dense, terminal clusters in summer. Bright purplish-pink. *Leaves* Oblong to lance-shaped, forming rosettes. Dark green.
• NATIVE HABITAT Montane and subarctic habitats, northern hemisphere.
• CULTIVATION Suitable for a rock garden or raised bed in well-drained, moderately fertile soil.
• PROPAGATION Divide in early spring, or sow seed when ripe in containers in a cold frame.

☼ ◊
❀ ❀ ❀

HEIGHT
15cm (6in)

SPREAD
15cm (6in)

Labiatae/Lamiaceae	CORSICAN MINT

MENTHA REQUIENII

Habit Creeping, mat-forming, stem-rooting, evergreen, perennial. *Flowers* Tiny, two-lipped, 2mm (½in) long, borne in whorls in summer. Lilac. *Leaves* Strongly peppermint-scented, oval to rounded. Bright green.
• NATIVE HABITAT Sandy areas, Corsica, Sardinia.
• CULTIVATION Ideal for planting in paving crevices. Prefers low-fertility, gritty or sandy soil that is moist but well-drained.
• PROPAGATION Divide in spring or autumn.
• OTHER NAME *M. corsica.*

☼ ◗
❀ ❀ ❀

HEIGHT
to 1cm (⅜in)

SPREAD
indefinite

Asteraceae/Compositae	WALL DAISY

ERIGERON KARVINSKIANUS ♈

Habit Vigorous, rhizomatous, tufted, mounded, evergreen, perennial. *Flowers* Daisy, 2cm (⅜in) across, borne in summer. White with yellow disc, maturing to pink and purple. *Leaves* Oval to lance-shaped, hairy. Grey-green.
• NATIVE HABITAT Mexico and Panama.
• CULTIVATION Ideal for wall crevices and pockets in a rock garden. Needs fertile, well-drained soil.
• PROPAGATION Divide or take basal cuttings in spring. Sow seed in spring in pots in a cold frame.
• OTHER NAME *E. mucronatus.*

☼ ◊
❀ ❀

HEIGHT
15–30cm (6–12in)

SPREAD
90cm or more (36in)

Plumbaginaceae	

ACANTHOLIMON GLUMACEUM

Habit Cushion-forming, evergreen, perennial.
Flowers Funnel-shaped, borne in short, dense
clusters in summer. Deep pink. **Leaves** Spiny,
stiff, narrowly lance-shaped, rosetted. Dark green.
• NATIVE HABITAT Caucasus, Turkey, Armenia.
• CULTIVATION Suitable for growing on a rock
garden or scree bed. Needs a warm site with very
well-drained, moderately fertile soil in full sun.
• PROPAGATION Sow seed as soon as ripe in
containers in a cold frame. Layer stem tips
into sandy compost in spring.

HEIGHT
to 8cm
(3in)

SPREAD
20–30cm
(8–12in)

Cruciferae/	STONE CRESS
Brassicaceae	

AETHIONEMA ARMENUM

Habit Compact, evergreen or semi-evergreen,
sub-shrub. **Flowers** Cross-shaped, 5mm (¼in)
across, borne in dense clusters in late spring.
Pale pink. **Leaves** Linear to oblong. Blue-green.
• NATIVE HABITAT Open sites, mountains of
Turkey and the Caucasus.
• CULTIVATION Suitable for a rock garden or wall
crevice. Grow in fertile, well-drained, alkaline soil.
• PROPAGATION By softwood cuttings in late spring
or early summer, or by seed in spring. Propagate
regularly. Will self-sow in favoured gardens.

HEIGHT
15–20cm
(6–8in)

SPREAD
15–20cm
(6–8in)

Caryophyllaceae	

SAPONARIA CAESPITOSA

Habit Tufted, mat-forming, evergreen, perennial.
Flowers Salver-shaped, 1cm (⅜in) across, borne
in few-flowered heads in summer. Pink to purple.
Leaves Narrowly lance-shaped. Mid-green.
• NATIVE HABITAT Pyrenees.
• CULTIVATION Suitable for a rock garden, trough,
or raised and scree beds. Needs gritty, sharply
drained soil that is neutral to alkaline.
• PROPAGATION Root stem tip cuttings in early
summer. Sow seed in containers in a cold frame,
in autumn or spring.

HEIGHT
15cm (6in)

SPREAD
15cm (6in)

Geraniaceae

ERODIUM x *VARIABILE* 'Ken Aslet'

Habit Spreading, mat-or cushion-forming, perennial, with prostrate stems. *Flowers* Solitary, single, 1cm (⅜in) across, 5-petalled, borne throughout summer. Deep pink, with darker veins and paler centre. *Leaves* Oval, scalloped or lobed, heart-shaped at the base. Mid-green.
• NATIVE HABITAT Garden origin. A selection of the hybrid between *E. corsicum* and *E. reichardii*.
• CULTIVATION Suitable for growing in a rock garden, raised bed, or trough, and ideal for planting in the crevices of well-drained paving. Needs a site in full sun with gritty, sharply drained, neutral to alkaline soil that is enriched with organic matter. Protect from excessive winter wet, with an overhead cloche or glass. Where grown in an alpine house, use a mix of equal parts loam, leaf-mould, and grit.
• PROPAGATION By division in spring.

HEIGHT
10cm (4in)

SPREAD
30cm (12in)

Caryophyllaceae	TUMBLING TED, ROCK SOAPWORT

SAPONARIA OCYMOIDES

Habit Spreading, mat-forming, perennial.
Flowers Flat, 1cm (⅜in) across, borne in loose
clusters in summer. Pink. *Leaves* Oval to lance-
shaped, hairy. Bright green.
• NATIVE HABITAT Mountains, Spain to Yugoslavia.
• CULTIVATION Suitable for a larger rock garden or
sunny bank. Needs gritty, sharply drained, neutral
to alkaline soil. Trim plant lightly after flowering.
• PROPAGATION Root stem tip cuttings in early
summer. Sow seed in containers in a cold frame,
in autumn or early spring.

HEIGHT
8cm (3in)

SPREAD
45cm (18in)
or more

Geraniaceae	

GERANIUM CINEREUM 'Ballerina'

Habit Compact, tufted, semi-evergreen,
perennial. *Flowers* Upright, saucer-shaped, to
2.5cm (1in) across, borne from late spring to early
autumn. Purplish-pink, with darker eye and veins.
Leaves Rounded, deeply lobed. Grey-green.
• NATIVE HABITAT Garden origin.
• CULTIVATION Ideal for rock gardens, raised beds,
or on top of dry retaining walls. Needs sharply
drained soil, that is rich in organic matter.
• PROPAGATION By division or take basal cuttings,
both in spring.

HEIGHT
15cm (6in)

SPREAD
to 30cm
(12in)

Rosaceae	PINK CINQUEFOIL

POTENTILLA NITIDA

Habit Tufted, semi-evergreen, perennial.
Flowers Solitary or paired, saucer-shaped, 2.5cm
(1in) across, borne in summer. Pale to deep pink,
rarely white. *Leaves* Three-lobed, with lance-
shaped segments. Silver-haired.
• NATIVE HABITAT Alps and Apennines.
• CULTIVATION Suitable for a trough or scree bed.
Grows best in low-fertility, sharply drained, gritty
soil, but is not always free-flowering.
• PROPAGATION By division in autumn or spring, or
sow seed when ripe, in containers in a cold frame.

HEIGHT
to 10cm
(4in)

SPREAD
15cm (6in)

Labiatae/Lamiaceae	

TEUCRIUM POLIUM

Habit Semi-deciduous, mound-forming, woolly-
stemmed, sub-shrub. *Flowers* Two-lipped, to 1cm
(⅜in) long, borne in flat-topped clusters in summer.
Pink-purple, or pale yellow. *Leaves* Oblong to
lance-shaped, wrinkled and woolly. Grey-green.
• NATIVE HABITAT Mediterranean, western Asia.
• CULTIVATION Prefers a site with poor, gritty soil.
• PROPAGATION By seed as soon as ripe, in
containers in a cold frame. Root softwood or
semi-ripe cuttings in early or mid-summer with
bottom heat.

HEIGHT
30cm (12in)

SPREAD
30cm (12in)

Portulacaceae	BITTERROOT

LEWISIA REDIVIVA [Pink form]

Habit Herbaceous, rosette-forming, perennial.
Flowers Broadly funnel-shaped, 5cm (2in) across, with narrow, overlapping petals, borne in early spring and summer. Pink. *Leaves* Linear to club-shaped, succulent, dying back after flowering. Dark green.
• NATIVE HABITAT Western Canada, western USA.
• CULTIVATION Grow in pots in an alpine house or in a cold frame, and keep dry after flowering.
• PROPAGATION Sow seed as soon as ripe in containers in a cold frame, in autumn.

HEIGHT
5cm (2in)

SPREAD
10cm (4in)

Caryophyllaceae	

SILENE SCHAFTA ♥

Habit Clump-forming, semi-evergreen, perennial. *Flowers* Flat, long-tubed, 2cm (⅘in) across, with notched petals, borne in open clusters in late summer and autumn. Deep magenta.
Leaves Lance-shaped. Bright green.
• NATIVE HABITAT Subalpine rocks. western Asia.
• CULTIVATION Suitable for growing on a raised bed or at the front of a border. Needs well-drained soil that is neutral to slightly alkaline soil.
• PROPAGATION By seed in containers in a cold frame, in autumn. Take basal cuttings in spring.

HEIGHT
25cm (10in)

SPREAD
30cm (12in)

Geraniaceae	

GERANIUM CINEREUM var. ♥
SUBCAULESCENS

Habit Vigorous, tufted, semi-evergreen, perennial. *Flowers* Saucer-shaped, 2.5cm (1in) across, borne in late spring. Brilliant magenta, with black eye. *Leaves* Deeply lobed. Dark grey-green.
• NATIVE HABITAT Balkans, northeast Turkey.
• CULTIVATION Suitable for growing in a rock garden or raised bed, in sharply drained soil.
• PROPAGATION Divide or take basal cuttings, in spring. Sow seed in a cold frame in spring.
• OTHER NAME *G. subcaulescens.*

HEIGHT
15cm (6in)

SPREAD
30cm (12in)

THYMUS

The genus *Thymus*, commonly known as thyme, comprises about 350 species of aromatic evergreen perennials, sub-shrubs, and shrubs. Many of them suit a rock garden or raised bed, while the prostrate species and cultivars also suit paving crevices, releasing scent when crushed.

Need well-drained, neutral to alkaline, gritty soil in full sun. Trim lightly after flowering to keep the plant neat. Several species, such as *T. cilicicus*, dislike winter wet and are best grown in an alpine house, in equal parts of loam, leaf-mould, and grit.

Take semi-ripe cuttings in mid- to late summer. Separate self-rooted stems and grow on in pots until well-established. Sow seed of species in early spring or autumn, in a cold frame.

T. VULGARIS
'Silver Posie'
Habit Bushy, mound-forming, evergreen, sub-shrub.
Flowers Two-lipped, borne in rounded clusters in late spring and early summer. Pale mauve.
Leaves Aromatic and oval. Grey-green, with white margins.
• HEIGHT 15–30cm (6–12in).
• SPREAD 30cm (12in).

T. vulgaris
'Silver Posie'

☼ ◊ ❀❀❀

T. 'Doone Valley'
Habit Mat-forming, spreading, evergreen, sub-shrub.
Flowers Two-lipped, borne in rounded clusters during summer. Lavender-pink, opening from red buds.
Leaves Lance-shaped and irregular. Deep olive-green, with yellow spots.
• HEIGHT 12cm (5in).
• SPREAD 35cm (14in).

T. 'Doone Valley'

☼ ◊ ❀❀❀

T. PULEGIOIDES
Habit Spreading, strongly aromatic, evergreen, sub-shrub.
Flowers Two-lipped, borne in short, interrupted spikes in late spring and early summer. Pink to purple.
Leaves Oblong to lance-shaped. Mid-green.
• HEIGHT 5–25cm (2–10in).
• SPREAD 30cm (12in).

T. pulegioides
Large thyme

☼ ◊ ❀❀❀

T. LONGIFLORUS
Habit Densely branched, evergreen, sub-shrub.
Flowers Two-lipped, 8mm (⅜in) long, borne in egg-shaped clusters during summer. Pink, with distinctive greenish-purple bracts.
Leaves Narrow, elliptical to linear, hairy. Greyish-green.
• HEIGHT 30cm (12in).
• SPREAD 25cm (10in).

T. longiflorus
Long-flowered thyme

☼ ◊ ❀❀

T. CAESPITITIUS
Habit Mat-forming, highly aromatic, evergreen, sub-shrub.
Flowers Two-lipped, borne in rounded clusters in summer. Pale lilac to lilac-pink.
Leaves Minute, narrowly spoon-shaped, hairy. Mid-green.
• OTHER NAMES
T. azoricus, *T. micans*
• HEIGHT 2.5cm (1in).
• SPREAD 20cm (8in).

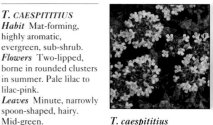
T. caespititius

☼ ◊ ❀❀❀

T. LEUCOTRICHUS
Habit Dwarf, mound-forming, creeping, evergreen, sub-shrub.
Flowers Two-lipped, borne in large, rounded clusters, in early summer. Pale purplish-pink.
Leaves Narrowly lance-shaped, hairy. Grey-green.
• HEIGHT 15cm (6in).
• SPREAD 20cm (8in).

T. leucotrichus

☼ ◊ ❀❀❀

T. CILICICUS
Habit Compact, upright, evergreen, sub-shrub.
Flowers Two-lipped, borne in dense, rounded clusters in early summer. Lilac to mauve.
Leaves Linear, with finely hairy underside and margins. Dark green.
• HEIGHT 15cm (6in).
• SPREAD 20cm (8in).

T. cilicicus

☼ ◊ ❀ ❀

T. SERPYLLUM 'Annie Hall'
Habit Mat-forming, spreading, evergreen, sub-shrub.
Flowers Two-lipped, borne in rounded clusters in summer. Purple-pink.
Leaves Elliptical to oval. Pale green.
• HEIGHT 8–10cm (3–4in).
• SPREAD 25cm (10in).

T. serpyllum 'Annie Hall'

☼ ◊ ❀ ❀ ❀

T. RICHARDII subsp. NITIDUS 'Peter Davis'
Habit Dwarf, bushy, free-flowering, evergreen, sub-shrub.
Flowers Two-lipped, borne in rounded clusters in late spring. Pink.
Leaves Oval and aromatic. Grey-green.
• HEIGHT 15cm (6in).
• SPREAD 15cm (6in).

T. richardii subsp. *nitidus* 'Peter Davis'

☼ ◊ ❀ ❀ ❀

T. HERBA-BARONA
Habit Dwarf, mat-forming, evergreen, perennial.
Flowers Two-lipped, borne in loose, interrupted, oblong or rounded clusters during summer. Pale pink.
Leaves Oval to lance-shaped, caraway-scented. Dark green.
• HEIGHT 10cm (4in).
• SPREAD 20cm (8in).

T. herba-barona
Caraway thyme

☼ ◊ ❀ ❀ ❀

T. DOERFLERI 'Bressingham'
Habit Prostrate, mat-forming, evergreen sub-shrub.
Flowers Two-lipped, borne in lax clusters in summer. Clear pink.
Leaves Linear and very fragrant. Grey-green.
• HEIGHT 10cm(4in).
• SPREAD 35cm (14in).

T. doerfleri 'Bressingham'

☼ ◊ ❀ ❀ ❀

T. x CITRIODORUS
Habit Rounded, bushy evergreen, shrub.
Flowers Two-lipped, with leaf-like bracts, borne in interrupted, oblong clusters during summer. Pale lavender-pink.
Leaves Oval to lance-shaped, lemon-scented. Mid-green.
• HEIGHT 30cm (12in).
• SPREAD 25cm (10in).

T. x citriodorus
Lemon-scented thyme

☼ ◊ ❀ ❀ ❀

T. SERPYLLUM COCCINEUS
Habit Mat- or mound-forming, evergreen, sub-shrub.
Flowers Two-lipped, borne in rounded clusters in summer. Crimson-pink.
Leaves Elliptical to oval. Mid-green.
• HEIGHT 25cm (10in).
• SPREAD 45cm (18in).

T. serpyllum coccineus

☼ ◊ ❀ ❀ ❀   ♔

OXALIS

The genus *Oxalis*, commonly known as shamrock or sorrel, comprises about 500 species of tuberous, bulbous, fibrous-rooted, or rhizomatous annuals and perennials, some of which are pernicious weeds. Oxalis are widely distributed in the wild, being found in a range of habitats from open sites to woodland. Many of the most ornamental species come from South America and South Africa.

The plants described here are suitable for rock gardens, raised beds, troughs, or pots in an alpine house. The native *Oxalis acetosella* and its cultivars are best grown in a woodland garden, shady border, or naturalized beneath shrubs, as they are generally too invasive for the rock garden. Many of the hardy species, as well as various cultivars are suitable for growing in a rock garden, raised bed, trough. In colder areas, the less-hardy species should be grown in a warm greenhouse.

The cultivated species of *Oxalis* are valued for their silky, widely funnel- or cup-shaped flowers that open from furled umbrella-like buds. In many species, both the flowers and foliage fold or close up at night and during wet or dull weather. The flowers frequently only open fully in sunlight or bright light.

Oxalis should be grown in full sun, with well-drained, moderately fertile soil. In an alpine house, use a mix of equal parts loam, leaf-mould, and grit. Keep pot-grown plants just moist when dormant. (Note that *O. lobata* is dormant in summer). *O. acetosella* needs leaf-rich, fertile, moist but well-drained soil that is rich in organic matter, in deep or partial shade.

Propagate by division in spring. Small sections of the rhizomatous species will root readily with bottom heat. Sow seed of species in late winter or early spring, in pots in a cold frame.

O. ENNEAPHYLLA
Habit Tufted, clump-forming, perennial, with short, scaly rhizomes.
Flowers Solitary, scented, funnel-shaped, to 2.5cm (1in) across, borne in spring and early summer. White to red-pink, with deeper veins.
Leaves Pleated, with heart-shaped lobes, fleshy. Blue-grey.
• HEIGHT 8cm (3in).
• SPREAD 15cm (6in).

O. enneaphylla

O. ACETOSELLA
Habit Mat-forming, creeping, rhizomatous, perennial.
Flowers Solitary, cup-shaped, to 2cm (⅔in) across, borne during spring. White or deep pink, with pale purple veins.
Leaves Clover-like, with heart-shaped lobes. Pale green.
• HEIGHT 5cm (2in).
• SPREAD indefinite.

O. acetosella
Wood sorrel

O. OBTUSA
Habit Mat-forming, rhizomatous, herbaceous, perennial, spreading by runners and bulbils.
Flowers Solitary, funnel-shaped, to 2cm (⅔in) wide, borne in spring. Rose-pink, or brick-red, with yellow throat.
Leaves Rounded, with heart-shaped lobes. Grey-green.
• HEIGHT 5cm (2in).
• SPREAD 20cm (8in).

O. obtusa

O. ADENOPHYLLA
Habit Clump-forming, bulbous, herbaceous, perennial.
Flowers Solitary, funnel-shaped, to 2.5cm (1in) across, borne in late spring. Purplish-pink, with dark veins and purple throat.
Leaves Rounded, with heart-shaped lobes. Grey-green.
• HEIGHT 10cm (4in).
• SPREAD 15cm (6in).

O. adenophylla

O. ENNEAPHYLLA 'Rosea'

Habit Tufted, clumping, herbaceous, perennial, with scaly rhizomes.
Flowers Solitary, funnel-shaped, to 2.5cm (1in) across, borne in spring and early summer. Pale purple-pink, with deeper pink veins.
Leaves Umbrella-like, fleshy, with narrowly-oblong and pleated lobes. Blue-grey.
• HEIGHT 8cm (3in).
• SPREAD 15cm (6in).

O. enneaphylla 'Rosea'

O. DEPRESSA

Habit Clump-forming, bulbous, herbaceous, perennial.
Flowers Solitary, funnel-shaped, to 2cm (¾in) across, borne during summer. Deep rose-pink.
Leaves Divided, with oval to triangular lobes. Grey-green.
• OTHER NAME *O. inops.*
• HEIGHT 5cm (2in).
• SPREAD 20cm (8in).

O. depressa

O. TETRAPHYLLA

Habit Clump-forming, bulbous, perennial.
Flowers Funnel-shaped, 2–3cm (¾–1⅛in) across, borne in clustered heads during summer. Deep pink, with yellow-green throat.
Leaves Divided, with heart-shaped lobes. Mid-green with a brown-purple basal band.
• HEIGHT 15cm (6in).
• SPREAD 15cm (6in).

O. tetraphylla
Good luck plant,
Lucky clover

O. TETRAPHYLLA 'Iron Cross'

Habit Clump-forming, bulbous, perennial.
Flowers Funnel-shaped, 2–3cm (¾–1⅛in) across, borne in clustered heads in summer. Pink, with yellow-green throat.
Leaves Divided, with heart-shaped lobes. Green, with "V"-shaped, deep-purple basal mark.
• HEIGHT 15cm (6in).
• SPREAD 15cm (6in).

O. tetraphylla
'Iron Cross'

O. LOBATA

Habit Clump-forming, bulbous, herbaceous, perennial.
Flowers Funnel-shaped, to 2cm (¾in) across, borne during autumn. Bright yellow.
Leaves Divided, with heart-shaped lobes. Bright green.
• OTHER NAME *O. perdicaria.*
• HEIGHT 10cm (4in).
• SPREAD 10cm (4in).

O. lobata

DIANTHUS

The genus *Dianthus* comprises more than 300 species of evergreen sub-shrubs, perennials, and annuals, including a group of compact, fully hardy, perennial alpine species together with the hybrids and cultivars derived from them. The alpine pinks occur naturally in a range of mountain habitats, from dry, rocky, grassy habitats at low altitude, to scree, moraine, and rock crevices at high altitude. Most are found on limestone rocks and prefer slightly alkaline soils, but will tolerate neutral to slightly acid conditions. The smaller pinks are ideal for rock gardens and scree beds, and especially for the tops of dry-stone, retaining walls, raised beds, and troughs, where those with a strong fragrance can be appreciated at close quarters. The more vigorous varieties can also be used for edging along borders and paths, or in scree plantings. Most alpine pinks have a neat, cushion- or mat-forming habit, with paired, linear to narrowly lance-shaped leaves, which are often grey- or silvery-green and sometimes stiff and prickly. Alpine pinks are particularly valued for their flowers, which are borne in summer and range from 1–4cm (⅖–1⅜in) across. The flowers are either solitary or borne in few-flowered clusters, and may be single, semi-double, or double.

Grow in a gritty, well-drained, moderately fertile, neutral to alkaline soil, in full sun. *D. pavonius* and *D. microlepis* prefer acid soils that are rich in organic matter. Dead-head to keep the plant vigorous and neat, unless seed is needed for propagation.

Sow seed of alpine species from autumn to early spring, in pots in a cold frame. Cultivars will not always come true. Take cuttings of non-flowering shoots, or Irishman's cuttings (see p.172) of self-layering, mat-forming types in summer.

D. 'Pike's Pink'
Habit Compact, cushion-forming, evergreen, perennial.
Flowers Solitary, double, about 2.5cm (1in) across, clove-scented, borne in summer. Pale pink, with darker base.
Leaves Narrowly lance-shaped, sharply pointed. Grey-green.
• HEIGHT 15cm (6in).
• SPREAD 15cm (6in).

D. 'Pike's Pink'

D. ERINACEUS
Habit Dense cushion-forming, evergreen, hedgehog-like, perennial.
Flowers Solitary or paired, often sparse, 15mm (½in) across, with toothed and bearded petals, borne on short stems in summer. Pink.
Leaves Stiff and linear to narrowly lance-shaped, sharply pointed. Mid-green.
• HEIGHT 5cm (2in).
• SPREAD 50cm (20in) or more.

D. erinaceus
Hedgehog pink

D. MICROLEPIS

Habit Compact, cushion-forming, evergreen, perennial.
Flowers Solitary, 15mm (⅝in) across, with slightly toothed petals, borne during early summer. Pink or purple.
Leaves Linear, soft. Silver-grey to green.
• HEIGHT 5cm (2in).
• SPREAD 15cm (6in).

D. microlepis

:☼: ◊ pH ✻✻✻

D. 'Little Jock'

Habit Cushion-forming, evergreen, perennial.
Flowers Solitary, semi-double, strongly scented, about 2.5cm (1in) across, with fringed petals, borne in summer. Pale pink, with maroon eye.
Leaves Pointed and narrowly lance-shaped Grey-green.
• HEIGHT 10cm (4in).
• SPREAD 10cm (4in).

D. 'Little Jock'

:☼: ◊ ✻✻✻

D. MYRTINERVIS

Habit Dense, evergreen, mat-forming, perennial.
Flowers Solitary, 1cm (⅜in) across, borne just above the leaves in summer. Deep pink, with paler eye.
Leaves Tiny and elliptical to oblong. Bright green.
• TIPS Best grown in a scree bed or trough.
• HEIGHT 5cm (2in).
• SPREAD 20cm (8in).

D. myrtinervis

:☼: ◊ ✻✻✻

D. 'La Bourboule'

Habit Compact, tuft-forming or matted, evergreen, perennial.
Flowers Strongly scented, 1.5–2cm (⅝–¾in) across, borne in clusters in summer. Clear pink.
Leaves Narrowly lance-shaped and pointed, but soft. Greyish-green.
• OTHER NAME
D. 'La Bourbille'.
• HEIGHT 5cm (2in).
• SPREAD 8cm (3in).

D. 'La Bourboule'

:☼: ◊ ✻✻✻   ♈

D. CARTHUSIANORUM

Habit Tufted, evergreen, perennial,
Flowers Solitary, to 2cm (⅞in) across, with toothed, bearded petals, borne in clusters during summer. Dark red-pink, or white.
Leaves Linear, soft. Pale green.
• HEIGHT to 40cm (16in).
• SPREAD 20–30cm (8–12in).

D. carthusianorum
Carthusian pink

:☼: ◊ ✻✻✻

D. GRATIANO-POLITANUS

Habit Mat-forming, evergreen, perennial.
Flowers Solitary, strong-scented, to 3cm (1¼in) across, with bearded, toothed petals, borne in summer. Deep pink.
Leaves Linear, soft. Grey-green.
• OTHER NAME
D. caesius.
• HEIGHT 15cm (6in).
• SPREAD 40cm (16in).

D. gratianopolitanus
Cheddar pink

:☼: ◊ ✻✻✻   ♈

D. ALPINUS
Habit Cushion- or mat-forming, evergreen, perennial.
Flowers Solitary, to 4cm (1½in) wide, with bearded, toothed petals, borne in summer. Deep pink to crimson, with paler spots.
Leaves Narrow-oblong, blunt, soft, and glossy. Dark green.
• TIPS Needs gritty soil that is rich in organic matter.
• HEIGHT 8cm (3in).
• SPREAD 25cm (10in).

D. alpinus
Alpine pink

☼ ◊ ❀❀❀ 　　 ♔

D. PAVONIUS
Habit Mat-forming, evergreen, perennial.
Flowers Solitary, to 3cm (1¼in) across, with toothed, bearded petals, borne in summer. Pale to deep pink, with buff reverse.
Leaves Pointed and linear. Grey-green.
• OTHER NAME *D. neglectus*.
• HEIGHT 8cm (3in).
• SPREAD to 20cm (8in).

D. pavonius

☼ ◊ pH ❀❀❀ 　 ♔

D. DELTOIDES 'Leuchtfunk'
Habit Mat-forming, evergreen, perennial.
Flowers Solitary, 2cm (⅝in) across, with toothed, bearded petals, borne in summer. Cerise.
Leaves Narrowly lance-shaped, soft. Dark green.
• OTHER NAME *D.* 'Flashing Light'.
• HEIGHT 20cm (8in).
• SPREAD 30cm (12in) or more.

D. deltoides 'Leuchtfunk'

☼ ◊ ❀❀❀

D. 'Annabelle'
Habit Compact, clump-forming, free-flowering, evergreen, perennial.
Flowers Solitary, double, strongly scented, about 2cm (⅝in) across, borne in summer. Cerise-pink.
Leaves Linear, pointed, soft. Grey-green.
• HEIGHT 10cm (4in).
• SPREAD 10cm (4in).

D. 'Annabelle'

☼ ◊ ❀❀❀

D. ALPINUS 'Joan's Blood'
Habit Cushion- or mat-forming, evergreen, perennial.
Flowers Solitary, 4cm (1¾in) wide, with bearded, toothed petals, borne during summer. Deep magenta.
Leaves Linear to lance-shaped. Dark green.
• HEIGHT 8cm (3in).
• SPREAD 10cm (4in).

D. alpinus 'Joan's Blood'

☼ ◊ ❀❀❀ 　 ♔

Plumbaginaceae	

ARMERIA MARITIMA 'Vindictive'

Habit Cushion-forming, evergreen, perennial.
Flowers Small, cup-shaped, borne on stiff stems
in dense, rounded heads to 2cm (¾in) across,
in late spring and summer. Deep rose-pink.
Leaves Linear. Dark green.
• NATIVE HABITAT Garden origin.
• CULTIVATION Good for growing in a rock garden
or as path edging. Needs well-drained, poor
or moderately fertile soil in an open site.
• PROPAGATION Divide in early spring, or root
basal cuttings in summer.

HEIGHT
20cm (8in)

SPREAD
30cm (12in)

Dipsacaceae	

PTEROCEPHALUS PERENNIS

Habit Mat-forming, evergreen, perennial. **Flowers**
Tubular, borne in dense, flattened, scabious-like
heads to 4cm (1½in) across, in summer. Pale pink-
purple. **Leaves** Oval, scalloped, hairy. Grey-green.
• NATIVE HABITAT Dry, rocky slopes, Greece.
• CULTIVATION Suitable for growing in a rock
garden or raised bed. Tolerates well-drained soil
in full sun, but dislikes very acid soils.
• PROPAGATION By seed in pots in a cold frame
in autumn, or by stem-tip cuttings in summer.
• OTHER NAME *P. parnassia.*

HEIGHT
8cm (3in)

SPREAD
20cm (8in)

Globulariaceae	GLOBE DAISY

GLOBULARIA MERIDIONALIS

Habit Mat-forming, evergreen, sub-shrub.
Flowers Tiny, 2-lipped, borne in dense heads to
2cm (¾in) across, in summer. Lavender. **Leaves**
Lance-shaped, leathery, glossy. Dark green.
• NATIVE HABITAT Southeast Alps, central
and southern Apennines, and Greece.
• CULTIVATION Grows best in troughs or on raised
beds, with sharply drained, neutral to alkaline soil.
• PROPAGATION By seed in autumn in containers
under a cold frame, or root rosettes in spring.
• OTHER NAMES *G. bellidifolia, G. pygmaea.*

HEIGHT
to 10cm
(4in)

SPREAD
to 30cm
(12in)

Campanulaceae	

PHYSOPLEXIS COMOSA

Habit Tufted, herbaceous, perennial. **Flowers**
Bottle-shaped, borne in rounded, terminal clusters,
to 2cm (¾in) across, in summer. Pale violet with
dark violet tips. **Leaves** Oval to heart-shaped
and deeply toothed. Dark green.
• NATIVE HABITAT Rocks, southeastern Alps.
• CULTIVATION Grows best in pots in an alpine
house, or in troughs or on tufa outdoors. Very
susceptible to slug damage.
• PROPAGATION By seed in a cold frame in autumn.
• OTHER NAME *Phyteuma comosum.*

HEIGHT
8cm (3in)

SPREAD
10cm (4in)

Labiatae/Lamiaceae	LARGE SELF-HEAL

PRUNELLA GRANDIFLORA

Habit Vigorous, semi-evergreen, perennial.
Flowers Two-lipped, to 3cm (1¼in) long, borne
in dense whorls on upright stems, during summer.
Purple. **Leaves** Paired, oval to lance-shaped
and toothed. Dark green.
• NATIVE HABITAT Woods and meadows, Europe.
• CULTIVATION Tolerates any soil in sun or part-
shade. Good as groundcover but invasive so
avoid siting near smaller plants. Self-seeds freely.
• PROPAGATION Divide in spring or autumn,
or sow seed at 6–12°C (43–54°F) in spring.

HEIGHT
15cm (6in)

SPREAD
90cm (3ft)
or more

Campanulaceae	GRASSY BELLS

EDRAIANTHUS SERPYLLIFOLIUS

Habit Tufted, mat-forming, evergreen, perennial.
Flowers Solitary, erect, bell-shaped, to 2cm (⅝in)
long, borne in early summer. Deep violet.
Leaves Linear to spoon-shaped. Dark green.
• NATIVE HABITAT Mountains of Croatia, Bosnia,
Herzegovina, and Albania.
• CULTIVATION Grow in light, sharply drained
alkaline soil, and protect from excess winter wet.
• PROPAGATION Sow seed in an open frame in
autumn, or take stem-tip cuttings in early summer.
• OTHER NAME *Wahlenbergia serpyllifolia.*

HEIGHT
5cm (2in)

SPREAD
15cm (6in)

Compositae/Asteraceae	ALPINE ASTER

ASTER ALPINUS

Habit Clump-forming, spreading, semi-evergreen,
perennial. **Flowers** Solitary, daisy-like, to 5cm
(2in) across, borne on upright stems in early to
mid-summer. Violet, with a yellow disc. **Leaves**
Spoon- to narrowly lance-shaped. Mid-green.
• NATIVE HABITAT Meadows, stony places, Alps.
• CULTIVATION Suitable for planting in a large
rock garden or at the front of a flower border.
Prefers a site with well-drained soil.
• PROPAGATION Sow seed in pots in a cold
frame or divide, both in early spring or autumn.

HEIGHT
to 25cm
(10in)

SPREAD
45cm (18in)

Leguminosae/ Papilionaceae	

PAROCHETUS COMMUNIS

Habit Tuberous-rooted, carpeting, perennial.
Flowers Pea, solitary or paired, 2.5cm across,
borne in succession from late summer to autumn.
Bright blue. **Leaves** Clover-like, with heart-
shaped leaflets. Mid-green, with bronze markings.
• NATIVE HABITAT Himalaya and southwest China.
• CULTIVATION Needs moist but well-drained soil,
and protection from excessive winter wet.
• PROPAGATION By division or separation of
rooted runners in spring. Needs to be propagated
regularly as it tends to be short-lived.

HEIGHT
10cm (4in)

SPREAD
30cm or
more (12in)

Campanulaceae	

CYANANTHUS MICROPHYLLUS ♟

Habit Mat-forming, stout-rooted, herbaceous, perennial. **Flowers** Solitary, broad funnel-shaped, 2.5cm (1in) across, borne in late summer. Violet-blue. **Leaves** Oval to oblong. Dark green.
• NATIVE HABITAT Nepal to southeast Tibet.
• CULTIVATION Grows best in a peat bed or rock garden with moderately fertile, moist but well-drained soil that is neutral to slightly acid.
• PROPAGATION By softwood cuttings in late spring or early summer. Sow seed as soon as ripe or in early spring, in containers in a cold frame.

☼ ◊
❋ ❋ ❋

HEIGHT
2.5cm (1in)

SPREAD
to 25cm
(10in)

Campanulaceae	

EDRAIANTHUS PUMILIO ♟

Habit Cushion-forming, evergreen, perennial.
Flowers Solitary, erect, bell-shaped, 1cm (⅜in) long, borne in early summer. Pale to deep violet.
Leaves Linear and finely-haired. Silver-green.
• NATIVE HABITAT Mountains of southern Croatia.
• CULTIVATION Grow in light, sharply drained alkaline soil. Protect the overwintering buds from excessive wet.
• PROPAGATION Sow seed in pots in a cold frame in autumn, or take stem-tip cuttings in early summer.
• OTHER NAME *Wahlenbergia pumilio.*

☼ ◊
❋ ❋ ❋

HEIGHT
2.5cm (1in)

SPREAD
to 15cm
(6in)

Gesneriaceae	

RAMONDA MYCONI ♟

Habit Rosette-forming, evergreen, perennial.
Flowers Flat, 5-petalled, 2.5cm (1in) across, borne in late spring and early summer. Violet-blue or pink, with yellow anthers. **Leaves** Leathery, oval, crinkled. Dark green, with rusty hairs underneath.
• NATIVE HABITAT Pyrenees, northeast Spain.
• CULTIVATION Plant between peat blocks, or sideways in crevices to protect from excessive wet.
• PROPAGATION By leaf cuttings in early autumn, or by ripe seed in a shaded, cold frame.
• OTHER NAME *R. pyrenaica.*

☼ ◐ ◊
❋ ❋ ❋

HEIGHT
10cm (4in)

SPREAD
20cm (8in)

Iridaceae	

SISYRINCHIUM IDAHOENSE

Habit Semi-evergreen, tufted, perennial.
Flowers Star-shaped, to 2.5cm (1in) across, borne on erect stems during summer. Deep violet-blue, with yellow throat. **Leaves** Sword-shaped. Mid-green.
• NATIVE HABITAT Mountains, across the USA.
• CULTIVATION Prefers a site with gritty, poor or moderately fertile soil that is neutral to alkaline.
• PROPAGATION Sow seed in containers in a cold frame in autumn or early spring. Self-seeds freely.
• OTHER NAMES *S. bellum* of gardens, *S. macounii.*

☼ ◊
❋ ❋ ❋

HEIGHT
12cm (5in)

SPREAD
15cm (6in)

Globulariaceae	GLOBE DAISY

GLOBULARIA CORDIFOLIA ♥

Habit Mat-forming, evergreen, perennial.
Flowers Tiny, two-lipped, borne in stemless,
rounded heads, to 2cm (¾in) across, in summer.
Lavender-blue. *Leaves* Spoon-shaped, glossy,
notched at the tip. Dark green.
• NATIVE HABITAT Rocky, mountain habitats,
central and southern Europe, and western Turkey.
• CULTIVATION Grow in sharply drained, neutral
to alkaline soil, in a rock garden or retaining wall.
• PROPAGATION By seed in autumn in containers
in a cold frame, or root rosettes in spring.

HEIGHT
to 5cm
(2in)

SPREAD
to 20cm
(8in)

Compositae/Asteraceae	

TOWNSENDIA GRANDIFLORA

Habit Short-lived, evergreen, perennial or
biennial. *Flowers* Daisy-head, 3cm (1¼in) across,
borne in summer. Violet-blue, with a greenish-
yellow disc. *Leaves* Elliptical and leathery.
Dark green, bronze-tinted.
• NATIVE HABITAT Central USA.
• CULTIVATION Suitable for growing in pots in
an alpine house. Needs gritty, sharply drained
soil and protection from excessive winter wet.
• PROPAGATION Sow seed as soon as ripe or in
early spring, in containers under a cold frame.

HEIGHT
to 15cm
(6in)

SPREAD
10cm (4in)

Boraginaceae	

OMPHALODES LUCILIAE

Habit Semi-evergreen, perennial. *Flowers*
Forget-me-not-like, to 8mm (⅜in) across,
borne in terminal sprays in summer. Clear pale
blue, opening from pink buds. *Leaves* Oval
or oblong. Pale grey-blue.
• NATIVE HABITAT Greece, Turkey, western Iran.
• CULTIVATION Grows best in tufa or very gritty,
sharply drained, alkaline soil in troughs and
raised beds. Very susceptible to slug damage.
• PROPAGATION Divide in early spring, or sow
seed in spring, in containers in a cold frame.

HEIGHT
10cm (4in)

SPREAD
to 15cm
(6in)

Campanulaceae	

PRATIA PEDUNCULATA

Habit Prostrate, stem-rooting, invasive, evergreen, perennial. **Flowers** Star-shaped, 6mm (¼in) across, borne in summer. Pale blue. **Leaves** Oval to rounded. Bright green.
• NATIVE HABITAT Damp, shady places, Australia.
• CULTIVATION Good for paving crevices and as low ground-cover in a rock garden. Prefers fertile, loamy, moist but well-drained soil.
• PROPAGATION Divide during the growing season or take self-rooted cuttings in spring and summer.
• OTHER NAME *Lobelia pedunculata.*

☀ ◐
❅ ❅ ❅

HEIGHT
15mm
(1/2in)

SPREAD
indefinite

Campanulaceae	

TRACHELIUM ASPERULOIDES

Habit Cushion-forming, evergreen, perennial. **Flowers** Star-shaped, 6mm (¼in) across, borne in late summer. Lavender-blue or white. **Leaves** Small, rounded, overlapping. Glossy mid-green.
• NATIVE HABITAT Southern Greece.
• CULTIVATION Grows best in a pot in an alpine house. Outdoors, grow in a trough with sharply drained, alkaline soil. Protect from winter wet.
• PROPAGATION Sow seed as soon as ripe in containers in a cold frame.
• OTHER NAME *Diosphaera asperuloides.*

☀ ◐
❅ ❅ ❅

HEIGHT
to 5cm
(2in)

SPREAD
to 15cm
(6in)

Rubiaceae	CREEPING BLUETS

HEDYOTIS MICHAUXII

Habit Mat-forming, stem-rooting, evergreen, perennial. **Flowers** Salver-shaped, 4–10 lobed, to 1cm (⅜in) across, borne in late spring and early summer. Pale blue, with white eye. **Leaves** Rounded to oval. Glossy-green.
• NATIVE HABITAT Damp woods and rocks, USA.
• CULTIVATION Grow in moist but well-drained, preferably acid soil that is rich in organic matter.
• PROPAGATION Divide in spring or autumn, or sow seed in spring in containers under a cold frame.
• OTHER NAME *H. serpyllifolia.*

☀ ◐ pH
❅ ❅ ❅

HEIGHT
7cm (3in)

SPREAD
to 30cm or
more
(12in)

Polygalaceae	

POLYGALA CALCAREA 'Bulley's Form'

Habit Creeping, prostrate, evergreen, sub-shrub.
Flowers Pea-like, 6mm (¼in) long, borne in
terminal clusters, to 3cm (1¼in) long, in late spring
to early summer. Intense, deep blue, with white
fringed lip. **Leaves** Oval and leathery. Mid-green.
• NATIVE HABITAT Garden origin.
• CULTIVATION Good for a rock garden or trough,
in sharply drained, moderately fertile soil.
• PROPAGATION By softwood cuttings in early
summer, or by semi-ripe ones in mid- to
late summer.

HEIGHT
5cm (2in)

SPREAD
to 20cm
(8in)

Polygalaceae	CHALK MILKWORT

POLYGALA CALCAREA

Habit Creeping, prostrate, evergreen, sub-shrub.
Flowers Pea-like, 6mm (¼in) long, borne in
terminal clusters, to 3cm (1¼in) long, in late spring
and early summer. Deep blue, with a white,
fringed lip. **Leaves** Oval and leathery. Mid-green.
• NATIVE HABITAT Grassland, western Europe.
• CULTIVATION Good for a rock garden or trough,
in sharply drained, moderately fertile soil.
• PROPAGATION By softwood cuttings in early
summer, or by semi-ripe ones in mid- to late
summer. By seed in autumn in a cold frame.

HEIGHT
5cm (2in)

SPREAD
to 20cm
(8in)

Gunneraceae	

GUNNERA MAGELLANICA

Habit Carpeting, perennial. **Flowers** Tiny,
borne in oblong clusters, 1.5–12cm (⅝–5in)
long, in summer. Green. **Fruits** Very small,
egg-shaped to rounded. Red. **Leaves** Kidney-
shaped, cupped, and scalloped. Shiny, dark green.
• NATIVE HABITAT Damp habitats, S. America
and Falkland Islands.
• CULTIVATION Grow in moist, fertile soil in part-
shade. Prefers a site in areas with cool summers.
• PROPAGATION Divide in spring, or sow seed
as soon as ripe. Keep cool but frost-free in winter.

HEIGHT
15cm (6in)

SPREAD
30cm (12in)
or more

Saxifragaceae	

MITELLA BREWERI

Habit Clump-forming, rhizomatous, evergreen,
perennial. **Flowers** Tiny, bell-shaped, with fringed
petals, borne in spikes 2–4cm (⅝–1⅝in) long in late
spring and early summer. Yellow-green. **Leaves**
Broadly oval, hairy, lobed. Mid-green.
• NATIVE HABITAT Western to central N. America.
• CULTIVATION Suitable for growing in a peat bed,
woodland garden, or shady corner of a rock garden.
Needs moist but well-drained, leaf-rich, acid soil.
• PROPAGATION Divide in spring, or sow seed
in autumn, in containers in a cold frame.

HEIGHT
15cm (6in)

SPREAD
20cm (8in)

Scrophulariaceae	CREEPING SNAPDRAGON

ASARINA PROCUMBENS

Habit Trailing, evergreen, perennial. *Flowers*
Snapdragon-like, 2-lipped, to 3.5cm (1½in) long,
borne in summer. Pale yellow, with darker throat
and purple veins. *Leaves* Paired, shallowly lobed,
kidney-shaped, sticky-haired. Grey-green.
• NATIVE HABITAT Shady rocks, Pyrenees.
• CULTIVATION Suitable over rocks and walls, or
beneath conifers. Needs well-drained, sandy soil.
• PROPAGATION By seed at 16°C (61°F) in early
spring, or by tip-cuttings in summer.
• OTHER NAME *Antirrhinum asarina.*

HEIGHT
5cm (2in)

SPREAD
to 60cm
(24in)

Papaveraceae	

PAPAVER FAURIEI

Habit Short-lived, tufted, semi-evergreen, annual
or perennial. *Flowers* Solitary, bowl-shaped,
2–3cm (⅜–⅛in) across, borne in summer.
Pale yellow to greenish-yellow. *Leaves* Lance-
shaped and deeply lobed, bristly. Grey-green.
• NATIVE HABITAT N. Kurile Islands and Japan.
• CULTIVATION Grow in a site with moderately
fertile, sharply drained soil, and protect from
excessive winter wet.
• PROPAGATION By seed in spring in a cold frame.
• OTHER NAME *P. miyabeanum* of gardens.

HEIGHT
to 10cm
(4in)

SPREAD
to 10cm
(4in)

Polygalaceae	SHRUBBY MILKWORT

POLYGALA·CHAMAEBUXUS

Habit Dwarf, spreading, evergreen, shrub.
Flowers Pea-like, 15mm (⅝in) long, borne in
late spring and early summer. Yellow, maturing
to brown-crimson, with white or yellow wings.
Leaves Lance-shaped and leathery. Dark green.
• NATIVE HABITAT Western central Europe.
• CULTIVATION Good for growing in a rock garden,
in sharply drained, moderately fertile soil.
• PROPAGATION By softwood cuttings in early
summer, by semi-ripe ones in mid- to late summer,
or by seed in autumn or early spring.

~~IGHT~~
5–15cm
(2–6in)

SPREAD
to 30cm
(12in)

Labiatae/Lamiaceae	

SCUTELLARIA ORIENTALIS

Habit Rhizomatous, woody-based, evergreen, mat-forming, perennial. **Flowers** Two-lipped, 1.5–3cm (⅝–1⅛in) long, borne in 4-angled clusters on hairy stems, in summer. Bright yellow, often with red lips. **Leaves** Oblong to broadly oval, toothed. Dark grey-green.
• NATIVE HABITAT Mountains, southeast Europe.
• CULTIVATION Suits a rock garden or border in light, gritty, well-drained, neutral to alkaline soil.
• PROPAGATION Sow seed in autumn in containers in a cold frame, or divide in spring.

☼ ◊
❋ ❋ ❋

HEIGHT
25cm (10in)

SPREAD
30cm (12in)

Compositae/Asteraceae	

ERIGERON AUREUS 'Canary Bird'

Habit Mound-forming, evergreen, perennial. **Flowers** Solitary, daisy, 2cm (⅜in) across, borne in summer. Bright canary-yellow. **Leaves** Broadly oval to spoon-shaped, leathery, hairy. Grey-green.
• NATIVE HABITAT Garden origin.
• CULTIVATION Ideal as a pot plant in an alpine house. Outdoors, suits scree or raised beds and troughs. Needs moist but sharply drained soil and protection from excessive winter wet.
• PROPAGATION By division or basal cuttings, both in spring.

☼ ◊
❋ ❋ ❋

HEIGHT
10cm (4in)

SPREAD
15cm (6in)

Onagraceae	OZARK SUNDROPS

OENOTHERA MACROCARPA ♻

Habit Vigorous, evergreen, perennial, with trailing, red-tinted stems. **Flowers** Solitary, cup-shaped, to 12.5cm (5in) across, borne in succession from late spring to early autumn. Bright yellow. **Leaves** Lance-shaped, toothed. Pale to mid-green.
• NATIVE HABITAT Rocky areas, USA.
• CULTIVATION Suitable for a sunny bank or scree bed. Prefers poor, gritty, sandy, or stony soils.
• PROPAGATION By seed in spring, in pots in a cold frame, or by stem tip cuttings in summer.
• OTHER NAME *O. missouriensis.*

☼ ◊
❋ ❋ ❋

HEIGHT
15cm (6in)

SPREAD
to 50cm
(20in)

Rosaceae	

POTENTILLA ERIOCARPA

Habit Carpet-forming, rhizomatous, semi-evergreen, perennial. **Flowers** Saucer-shaped, to 4cm (1⅝in) across, borne singly or in small clusters in early summer. Deep yellow. **Leaves** Divided, toothed, wedge-shaped. Bright green.
• NATIVE HABITAT Himalaya, western China.
• CULTIVATION Suitable for growing in a rock garden, at the foot of rock work or at the front of a border. Needs gritty, well-drained soil.
• PROPAGATION By division or seed in containers in a cold frame, both in autumn or spring.

☼ ◊
❋ ❋ ❋

HEIGHT
8cm (3in)

SPREAD
30cm (12in)

Linaceae

LINUM FLAVUM 'Compactum'

Habit Compact, upright, woody-based, evergreen, perennial. *Flowers* Upward-facing, funnel-shaped, to 2.5cm (1in) across, borne in dense branched, terminal clusters, opening in full sunshine, during summer. Flowers are individually short-lived, but are produced in succession over long periods. Bright yellow. *Leaves* Spoon- to lance-shaped. Dark green.
• NATIVE HABITAT Garden origin. The species is found in scrub and on dry grassy slopes, in the hills and mountains of central and southern Europe.

• CULTIVATION Grow in light, moderately fertile, well-drained soil that is rich in organic matter, in a warm, sunny, sheltered site. Protect from excessive winter wet.
• PROPAGATION Sow seed in autumn or spring, in containers under a cold frame. Take stem-tip cuttings in early summer. Propagate regularly as they are often short-lived.

HEIGHT
15cm (6in)

SPREAD
20cm (6in)

ANEMONE

The genus *Anemone* comprises about 120 species of perennials, most of which suit growing in flower borders. For ease of reference, their cultivation requirements may be grouped as follows:

Group 1 Moist but well-drained soil, enriched with organic matter, in partial shade. Tolerate drier conditions when dormant in summer.

Group 2 Well-drained soil that is enriched with organic matter, in sun or partial shade.

Group 3 Light, sandy soil in full sun.

Sow seed of species when fresh in containers in a cold frame. Divide rhizomatous species in spring or after the leaves have faded. Separate tubers when dormant in summer.

A. NEMOROSA
'Bracteata Pleniflora'
Habit Rhizomatous, patch-forming, herbaceous, perennial.
Flowers Star-shaped, semi-double, borne in late spring. White, often with a green ruff.
Leaves Deeply divided. Mid-green.
• CULTIVATION 1 or 2.
• HEIGHT 12cm (5in).
• SPREAD 30cm (12in).

A. nemorosa
'Bracteata Pleniflora'

☼ ◊ ❋❋❋

A. BLANDA
'White Splendour'
Habit Tuberous, herbaceous, perennial.
Flowers Solitary, star-shaped, 5cm (2in) across, borne during spring. White, with a pink tint on the outside.
Leaves Deeply divided. Dark green.
• CULTIVATION 1 or 2.
• HEIGHT 15cm (6in).
• SPREAD 15cm (6in).

A. blanda
'White Splendour'

☼ ◊ ❋❋❋   ♈

A. MULTIFIDA
Habit Vigorous, clump-forming, semi-evergreen, perennial.
Flowers Cupped, 2.5cm (1in) wide, borne in sprays of 2–3 in summer. Creamy-yellow.
Leaves Rounded, lobed, Shiny, deep green.
• CULTIVATION 2.
• OTHER NAMES
A. globosa, A. magellanica.
• HEIGHT 30cm (12in).
• SPREAD 15cm (6in).

A. multifida

☼ ◊ ❋❋❋

A. × *LIPSIENSIS*
Habit Rhizomatous, herbaceous, perennial.
Flowers Solitary, flat, to 2cm (⅝in) across, borne in spring. Creamy-yellow.
Leaves Rounded and deeply lobed. Mid-green.
• CULTIVATION 1 or 2.
• OTHER NAMES *A.* × *intermedia, A.* × *seemannii.*
• HEIGHT 5–15cm (2–6in).
• SPREAD to 45cm (18in).

A. × *lipsiensis*

☼ ◊ ❋❋❋

A. BLANDA **'Radar'**
Habit Tuberous, herbaceous, perennial.
Flowers Solitary, flattened star-shaped, 4cm (1½in) across, borne in spring. Rich magenta, with white centre.
Leaves Deeply divided. Dark green.
• CULTIVATION 1 or 2.
• HEIGHT 15cm (6in).
• SPREAD 15cm (6in).

A. blanda **'Radar'**

☼ ◊ ❋❋❋   ♈

A. HORTENSIS
Habit Tuberous, herbaceous, perennial.
Flowers Solitary, single, 2–4cm (¾–1½in) across, borne in spring. Deep mauve-pink, with paler underside.
Leaves Deeply divided. Mid-green.
• CULTIVATION 2 or 3.
• HEIGHT to 30cm (12in).
• SPREAD 12–15cm (5–6in).

A. hortensis

☼ ◊ ❋❋❋

A. PAVONINA
Habit Tuberous, herbaceous, perennial.
Flowers Solitary, saucer-shaped, 2–10cm (1⅛–4in) across, borne in early to mid-spring. Pink, red, or purple, often white-eyed.
Leaves Deeply divided. Mid- to dark green.
• CULTIVATION 2 OR 3.
• HEIGHT 25cm (10in).
• SPREAD 15cm (6in).

A. pavonina
Peacock anemone

☼ ◊ ✿✿✿

A. NEMOROSA 'Robinsoniana'
Habit Rhizomatous, herbaceous, perennial.
Flowers Single, star-shaped, to 4cm (1½in) across, borne in spring. Soft mid-blue, with blue-grey reverse.
Leaves Deeply divided. Mid-green.
• CULTIVATION 1 or 2.
• HEIGHT 12–18cm (5–7in).
• SPREAD 30cm (12in).

A. nemorosa 'Robinsoniana'

☼ ◑ ◖ ✿✿✿   ♈

A. OBTUSILOBA
Habit Compact, tufted, fibrous-rooted, semi-evergreen, perennial.
Flowers Solitary, 2cm (¾in) across, borne during late spring and early summer. White, blue or, occasionally, yellow.
Leaves Rounded and lobed. Mid-green.
• CULTIVATION 2.
• HEIGHT 15cm (6in).
• SPREAD 20cm (8in).

A. obtusiloba

☼ ◊ ✿✿✿

A. APENNINA
Habit Rhizomatous, patch-forming, herbaceous, perennial.
Flowers Solitary, to 4cm (1½in) across, borne during spring. Bright blue, or pink-flushed white.
Leaves Rounded, lobed, and toothed. Mid-green.
• CULTIVATION 1 or 2.
• HEIGHT 20cm (8in).
• SPREAD 20cm (8in).

A. apennina

☼ ◖ ✿✿✿   ♈

A. BLANDA [Blue form]
Habit Tuberous, herbaceous, perennial.
Flowers Solitary, saucer-shaped, 2.5–4cm (1–1⅝in) across, borne in spring. Mid- to deep blue.
Leaves Deeply divided. Dark green.
• CULTIVATION 1 or 2.
• HEIGHT 15cm (6in).
• SPREAD 15cm (6in).

A. blanda [Blue form]

☼ ◑ ◊ ✿✿✿

A. BLANDA 'Ingramii'
Habit Tuberous, herbaceous, perennial.
Flowers Solitary, star-shaped, 2.5–4cm (1–1⅝in) wide, borne during spring. Deep blue.
Leaves Deeply divided. Dark green.
• CULTIVATION 1 or 2.
• OTHER NAME
A. blanda 'Atrocaerulea'.
• HEIGHT 15cm (6in).
• SPREAD 15cm (6in).

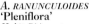

A. blanda 'Ingramii'

☼ ◊ ✿✿✿

A. RANUNCULOIDES 'Pleniflora'
Habit Rhizomatous, herbaceous, perennial.
Flowers Solitary, double, 2–3cm (¾–1⅛in) across, borne in spring. Yellow.
Leaves Deeply lobed and toothed. Mid-green.
• CULTIVATION 1 or 2.
• OTHER NAME
A. r. 'Flore Pleno'.
• HEIGHT 5–10cm (2–4in).
• SPREAD 45cm (18in).

A. ranunculoides 'Pleniflora'

☼ ◖ ✿✿✿

A. RANUNCULOIDES
Habit Patch-forming, rhizomatous, herbaceous, perennial.
Flowers Solitary, 2–3cm (¾–1⅛in) across, borne in spring. Deep yellow.
Leaves Deeply lobed and toothed. Mid-green.
• CULTIVATION 1 or 2.
• HEIGHT 5–10cm (2–4in).
• SPREAD 45cm (18in).

A. ranunculoides

☼ ◖ ✿✿✿   ♈

CAMPANULA

The genus *Campanula* comprises about 300 species of annuals, biennials, and perennials, some of which are evergreen. Campanulas are valued for their tubular, bell-, funnel-, or star-shaped flowers, which are often borne over long periods. The genus includes many small species and cultivars that are perfect for rock gardens, raised beds, and scree plantings, Most of those described here are robust and easily grown. The smallest, for example *Campanula zoysii* or *C. raineri*, are excellent for troughs, but are very susceptible to slug damage. *C. cochleariifolia* is particularly effective if allowed to colonize areas of gravel paving crevices or the tops of dry-stone, retaining walls by self-sowing. *C. poscharskyana* and *C. portenschlagiana* will thrive on a sunny bank or in a wall crevice. Both species are vigorous, so site them away from smaller less-robust alpines. They also suit growing in containers such as window boxes, patio planters, or hanging baskets and are robust enough to be planted at the front of a well-drained, mixed or herbaceous border.

Grow in moist but well-drained soil in full sun or light, dappled or partial shade. *C. zoysii* and *C. raineri* need sharper drainage than the other species described, and must have protection from excessive winter wet, either with a propped pane of glass outdoors, or in an alpine house. Grow in very gritty, sharply drained soil, in a scree bed, in tufa, or in a trough. In an alpine house, use a loam-based potting compost, with up to one-third by volume of added grit.

Divide rhizomatous species and cultivars in autumn or early spring. Take cuttings of new growth or root individual rosettes cuttings, both in early summer. Sow seed of species in pots in a cold frame, as soon as ripe or in autumn.

C. CARPATICA 'Bressingham White'
Habit Clump-forming, herbaceous, perennial.
Flowers Solitary, upright, open bell-shaped, 3cm (1¼in) or more across, borne during summer. White.
Leaves Rounded and heart-shaped. Bright green.
• HEIGHT 15cm (6in).
• SPREAD 30cm (12in).

C. carpatica 'Bressingham White'

☼ ◊ ✤✤✤

C. POSCHARSKYANA
Habit Vigorous, spreading, evergreen, perennial.
Flowers Star-shaped, to 2.5cm (1in) across, borne in clusters from summer to autumn. Pale lavender.
Leaves Rounded to oval and toothed. Mid-green.
• HEIGHT 15cm (6in).
• SPREAD to 60cm (24in).

C. poscharskyana

☼ ◊ ✤✤✤

C. 'G.F. Wilson'
Habit Compact, mound-forming, herbaceous, perennial, with slender runners.
Flowers Solitary, nodding to semi-erect, cup-shaped, 2.5cm (1in) across, borne in mid- to late summer. Deep violet.
Leaves Toothed and oval. Pale yellow-green.
• HEIGHT 10cm (4in).
• SPREAD 20cm (8in).

C. 'G.F. Wilson'

☼ ◊ ✤✤✤ ♛

C. 'Birch Hybrid'
Habit Vigorous, prostrate, evergreen, perennial, with runners.
Flowers Open bell-shaped, 2cm (¾in) across, prolific, borne in clusters in summer. Mauve-blue.
Leaves Oval to heart-shaped and toothed. Bright green.
• HEIGHT 10cm (4in).
• SPREAD 50cm (20in) or more.

C. 'Birch Hybrid'

☼ ◊ ✿ ✿ ✿   ♈

C. COCHLEARIIFOLIA
Habit Tufted, patch-forming, rhizomatous, herbaceous, perennial.
Flowers Drooping, bell-shaped, 15mm (⅝in) long, borne in summer. White, lavender, or slate-blue.
Leaves Rounded to heart-shaped, toothed, in rosettes. Bright green
• OTHER NAMES
C. bellardii, C. pusilla.
• HEIGHT 8cm (3in)
• SPREAD 30cm (12in).

C. cohleariifolia
Fairies' thimbles

☼ ◊ ✿ ✿ ✿   ♈

C. PORTENSCHLAGIANA
Habit Mound-forming, evergreen, perennial.
Flowers Long bell-shaped, 2cm (¾in) across, borne in spreading sprays from mid- through to late summer. Deep purple.
Leaves Kidney- to heart-shaped. Mid-green.
• OTHER NAME
C. muralis.
• HEIGHT 15cm (6in).
• SPREAD 50cm (20in).

C. portenschlagiana
Dalmatian bellflower

☼ ◊ ✿ ✿ ✿   ♈

C. RAINERI
Habit Spreading perennial.
Flowers Solitary, upright, open bell-shaped, to 4cm (1½in) across, borne in summer. Pale lavender.
Leaves Oval, toothed. and hairy. Grey-green.
• CULTIVATION Protect from winter wet and provide sharp drainage.
• HEIGHT 8cm (3in)
• SPREAD 20cm (8in).

C. raineri

◐ ◊ ✿ ✿ ✿   ♈

C. BARBATA
Habit Short-lived, rosette-forming, perennial or biennial.
Flowers Drooping, bearded, bell-shaped, to 3cm (1¼in) long, borne in one-sided spikes on upright stems, in early summer. Lavender-blue.
Leaves Narrowly lance-shaped. Pale to mid-green.
• HEIGHT 30cm (12in)
• SPREAD 20cm (8in).

C. barbata
Bearded bellflower

☼ ◊ ✿ ✿ ✿

C. CARPATICA var. TURBINATA 'Jewel'
Habit Compact, clump-forming, herbaceous, perennial.
Flowers Solitary, upright, open bell-shaped, 3cm (1¼in) or more across, during summer. Bright blue-purple.
Leaves Rounded and heart-shaped. Emerald.
• HEIGHT 10cm (4in).
• SPREAD 30cm (12in).

C. carpatica var.
turbinata 'Jewel'

☼ ◊ ✿ ✿ ✿

C. ZOYSII

Habit Tufted, semi-evergreen, perennial.
Flowers Horizontal to ascending, tubular, to 2cm (¾in) long, borne in mid-summer. Clear to pale lavender-blue.
Leaves Small, toothed, oval, glossy. Mid-green.
• CULTIVATION Needs sharply drained, alkaline soil. Dislikes winter wet.
• HEIGHT 5cm (2in).
• SPREAD 10cm (4in).

C. zoysii
Crimped bellflower

☼ ◊ ❄❄❄

C. ARVATICA

Habit Carpet-forming, perennial, with runners.
Flowers Solitary, upright, shallowly funnel-shaped, 2–4cm (¾–1½in) long, borne in summer. Pale blue or white.
Leaves Oval to heart-shaped and toothed. Mid-green.
• OTHER NAME
C. acutangula.
• HEIGHT 10cm (4in).
• SPREAD 20cm (8in).

C. arvatica

☼ ◊ ❄❄❄   ♈

C. GARGANICA
'Blue Diamond'

Habit Spreading, evergreen, perennial.
Flowers Star-shaped, upright, to 2cm (3in) across, borne profusely in sprays in summer. Grey-blue, with dark blue centre.
Leaves Kidney- or heart-shaped to oval and toothed. Grey-green.
• HEIGHT 5cm (2in).
• SPREAD 30cm (12in).

C. garganica
'Blue Diamond'

☼ ◊ ❄❄❄

Scrophulariaceae	POUCH FLOWER, SLIPPER FLOWER

CALCEOLARIA TENELLA

Habit Vigorous, creeping, mat-forming, evergreen, perennial. **Flowers** Pouched, slipper-like, 7–9mm (⅓–⅜in) across, usually borne singly, in summer. Bright yellow, marked red. **Leaves** Broadly oval, finely-toothed. Pale yellow-green.
• NATIVE HABITAT Alpine regions, Chile.
• CULTIVATION Needs peat-rich, gritty, moist but well-drained, neutral to acid soil. Shade from the hottest mid-day sun, and protect from winter wet.
• PROPAGATION By seed in autumn or early spring, in containers in a cold frame. Divide in spring.

HEIGHT
5cm (2in)

SPREAD
to 30cm (12in)

Cruciferae/ Brassicaceae	

ALYSSUM WULFENIANUM

Habit Tufted, upright or prostrate, evergreen, perennial. **Flowers** Cross-shaped, to 6mm (¼in) across, borne in loose, rounded clusters in early summer. Yellow. **Leaves** Small, oblong to oval, hairy, forming rosettes. Grey-green.
• NATIVE HABITAT Southeast Alps.
• CULTIVATION Needs well-drained, moderately fertile, gritty soil. Trim lightly after flowering.
• PROPAGATION By softwood cuttings in late spring, or by seed in autumn or early spring, in containers in a cold frame.

HEIGHT
10–15cm (4–6in)

SPREAD
to 50cm (20in)

Rosaceae	MOUNTAIN AVENS

GEUM MONTANUM

Habit Clumping, rhizomatous, semi-evergreen, perennial. **Flowers** Solitary, cup-shaped, to 4cm (1½in) across, borne in spring and early summer. Deep yellow. **Leaves** Divided, with a large, kidney-shaped or rounded lobe. Dark green.
• NATIVE HABITAT Mountain pastures, central and southern Europe.
• CULTIVATION Grow in a site with fertile, well-drained, preferably gritty soil.
• PROPAGATION By division or by seed in pots in a cold frame, both in autumn or spring.

HEIGHT
15cm (6in)

SPREAD
40cm (16in)

Guttiferae/Clusiaceae	

HYPERICUM REPTANS

Habit Mat-forming, stem-rooting, deciduous, sub-shrub. **Flowers** Solitary, cup-shaped, to 3cm (1¼in) across, borne in summer. Golden-yellow, opening from crimson buds. **Leaves** Oval and leathery, Mid-green, turning red and yellow in autumn.
• NATIVE HABITAT Himalaya, southwest China.
• CULTIVATION Suitable for growing in a rock garden or on a sunny, retaining wall. Needs moist but sharply drained soil.
• PROPAGATION Separate rooted stems in spring. Sow seed in autumn in containers in a cold frame.

HEIGHT
5cm (2in)

SPREAD
20cm (8in)

| Leguminosae/Papilionaceae | WINGED BROOM |

GENISTA SAGITTALIS

Habit Prostrate, mat-forming, deciduous, shrub.
Flowers Pea, 1cm (⅜in) long, borne in dense,
terminal spikes, to 4cm (1⅜in) long. Bright yellow.
Leaves Few, small, lance-shaped, borne on
upright, broadly winged green stems, giving
the shrub an evergreen appearance. Mid-green.
• NATIVE HABITAT Meadows, rocky areas, open
woodlands, and by roadsides, in the hills and
mountains of central and southern Europe.
• CULTIVATION Suitable for growing in a rock
garden or on top of a retaining wall, or for clothing
a sunny bank. Grow in poor or moderately
fertile, light, well-drained soil. Resents being
transplanted, so set young plants out directly
from their containers into their permanent
flowering site as soon as possible.
• PROPAGATION By seed in autumn or spring,
in containers in a cold frame, or by semi-ripe
cuttings in summer.
• OTHER NAME *Chamaespartium sagittale*.

HEIGHT
15cm (6in)

SPREAD
to 1m (3ft)
or more

Leguminosae/ Papilionaceae	

CYTISUS ARDOINOI

Habit Deciduous, semi-prostrate, hummock-forming, shrub. **Flowers** Pea, 1cm (⅜in) long, borne in lateral clusters on arching stems, in late spring and summer. Bright yellow. **Leaves** Tiny, 3-lobed, divided, and hairy. Greyish-green.
• NATIVE HABITAT Maritime Alps.
• CULTIVATION Suitable for a rock garden or raised bed. Grow in poor, or moderately fertile, light, well-drained, acid or slightly alkaline soil.
• PROPAGATION By seed in autumn or spring, in a cold frame, or by semi-ripe cuttings in summer.

☀ ◊
❄ ❄ ❄

HEIGHT
20–60cm
(8–24in)

SPREAD
20–60cm
(8–24in)

Rosaceae	

POTENTILLA AUREA

Habit Mat-forming, semi-evergreen, perennial. **Flowers** Saucer-shaped, 2cm (⅜in) across, borne in clusters from late spring to summer. Deep yellow. **Leaves** Rounded, with finger-like segments, sharply toothed, glossy, with silver-haired margins. Deep green.
• NATIVE HABITAT Pyrenees and Alps.
• CULTIVATION Suitable for growing in a rock garden in gritty, well-drained soil.
• PROPAGATION By division, or by seed in containers in a cold frame, in autumn or spring.

☀ ◊
❄ ❄ ❄

HEIGHT
10cm (4in)

SPREAD
20cm (8in)

Primulaceae	GOLDEN CREEPING JENNY

LYSIMACHIA NUMMULARIA 'Aurea'

Habit Very vigorous, stem-rooting, prostrate, evergreen, perennial. **Flowers** Cup-shaped, to 2cm (⅜in) across, borne in summer. Golden-yellow. **Leaves** Paired, broadly oval to rounded, with a heart-shaped base. Golden-yellow.
• NATIVE HABITAT Garden selection.
• CULTIVATION Grow in moist but well-drained soil in partial shade. Needs full sun for best leaf colour. Rampant, so site away from choice alpines.
• PROPAGATION Separate rooted stems in spring or autumn.

☀ ◊
❄ ❄ ❄

HEIGHT
to 5cm
(2in)

SPREAD
indefinite

Leguminosae/ Papilionaceae	HORSESHOE VETCH

HIPPOCREPIS COMOSA

Habit Creeping, woody-based, semi-evergreen, perennial. **Flowers** Pea, 1cm (⅜in) across, borne in clusters in spring and late summer. Lemon-yellow. **Leaves** Divided, oval. Mid-green.
• NATIVE HABITAT Central and southern Europe.
• CULTIVATION Suitable for growing in rock crevices, retaining walls, or paving. Grow in poor, alkaline, well-drained soil in full sun.
• PROPAGATION Sow scarified seed in autumn or spring, in containers in a cold frame. Will self-sow freely. Take stem-tip cuttings in summer.

☀ ◊
❄ ❄ ❄

HEIGHT
to 40cm
(16in)

SPREAD
to 40cm
(16in)

Guttiferae/Clusiaceae	

HYPERICUM EMPETRIFOLIUM subsp. *OLIGANTHUM*

Habit Prostrate, evergreen, shrub. *Flowers* Star-shaped, to 2cm (⅜in) across, borne in clusters of 4–7 in summer. Deep yellow. *Leaves* Whorled, linear, with inrolled margins. Dark green.
• NATIVE HABITAT Maquis, Greece.
• CULTIVATION Suitable for growing on a sharp-drained rock garden. Dislikes excessive winter wet.
• PROPAGATION Separate rooted stems in spring, or sow seed in autumn in containers in a cold frame.
• OTHER NAME *H. empetrifolium* var. *prostratum*.

☀ ◌
❄ ❄

HEIGHT
5cm (2in)

SPREAD
to 30cm or more (12in)

Compositae/Asteraceae	GOLDEN YARROW, WOOLLY SUNFLOWER

ERIOPHYLLUM LANATUM

Habit Vigorous, clump-forming, semi-evergreen, perennial. *Flowers* Daisy, 2–4cm (¾–1⅝in) across, borne in succession from late spring to summer. Bright mid-yellow. *Leaves* Spoon- to lance-shaped, lobed at stem. Woolly-white to silver-grey.
• NATIVE HABITAT Western N. America.
• CULTIVATION Suits the front of a flower border, dry retaining wall, or paving crevices. Tolerates poor, sharply drained, even dry soil.
• PROPAGATION Divide in spring or after flowering. Sow seed in autumn, in containers in a cold frame.

☀ ◌
❄ ❄ ❄

HEIGHT
20–50cm
(8–20in)

SPREAD
20–60cm
(8–24in)

Scrophulariaceae	

CALCEOLARIA 'Walter Shrimpton'

Habit Clumping, evergreen, perennial. *Flowers* Slipper-like, 2.5cm (1in) long, borne in clusters of 2–5 in summer. Bronze-yellow, with brown spots and a white band. *Leaves* Spoon- to diamond-shaped. glossy, hairy, in rosettes. Dark green.
• NATIVE HABITAT Garden origin.
• CULTIVATION Needs fertile, gritty, neutral to acid soil. Shade from hot mid-day sun and protect from winter wet. In an alpine house, grow in equal parts loam, leaf-mould, and sharp sand.
• PROPAGATION Root rosettes in early summer.

☀ ◐
❄ ❄ ❄

HEIGHT
10cm (4in)

SPREAD
23cm (9in)

Papaveraceae	WELSH POPPY

MECONOPSIS CAMBRICA

Habit Tap-rooted, semi-evergreen, tufted, perennial. *Flowers* Solitary, shallowly cup-shaped, 5–6cm (2–2¾in) across, borne on wiry stems from spring to autumn. Lemon-yellow to orange. *Leaves* Finely divided or irregularly lobed, in basal tufts. Pale to blue-green.
• NATIVE HABITAT Woods, western Europe.
• CULTIVATION Grow in any moist but well-drained soil, in sun or part-shade. Self-sows freely.
• PROPAGATION Sow seed when ripe or in early spring, either *in situ* or in pots in a cold frame.

☀ ◐
❄ ❄ ❄

HEIGHT
45cm (18in)

SPREAD
to 25cm
(10in)

Polygonaceae	

PERSICARIA VACCINIIFOLIA ♇

Habit Mat-forming, trailing, semi-evergreen, perennial. *Flowers* Tiny, bell-shaped, borne in upright spikes to 8cm (3in) long, in late summer and autumn. Deep pink. *Leaves* Oval and glossy. Mid-green, turning red in autumn.
• NATIVE HABITAT Himalaya.
• CULTIVATION Grows best when allowed to tumble over large rocks. Needs moist soil.
• PROPAGATION Divide in early spring or autumn, or sow seed in spring, in containers in a cold frame.
• OTHER NAME *Polygonum vacciniifolium.*

☼ ◊
❄ ❄ ❄

HEIGHT
20cm (8in)

SPREAD
50cm (20in)
or more

Ericaceae	CHECKERBERRY, WINTERGREEN

GAULTHERIA PROCUMBENS ♇

Habit Creeping, rhizomatous, evergreen, shrub. *Flowers* Urn-shaped, borne in clusters 1–2.5cm (⅜–1in) long, in summer. White or pale pink. *Fruits* Rounded. Red. *Leaves* Oval, pointed, leathery. Aromatic when crushed. Dark green.
• NATIVE HABITAT Woods, eastern N. America.
• CULTIVATION Suits a woodland or peat garden. Prefers a site in partial or dappled shade with moist, leaf-rich soil that is acid to neutral.
• PROPAGATION Separate rooted stems in spring, or sow seed in pots in a cold frame in autumn.

☼ ◊ pH
❄ ❄ ❄

HEIGHT
15cm (6in)

SPREAD
1m (3ft) or
more

Papaveraceae	

PAPAVER ATLANTICUM

Habit Short-lived, clump-forming, evergreen, perennial. *Flowers* Solitary, saucer-shaped, to 5cm (2in) across, borne in summer. Soft orange. *Leaves* Oblong to lance-shaped, coarsely toothed, and very hairy. Mid-green.
• NATIVE HABITAT Morocco.
• CULTIVATION Suitable for growing on a rock or scree garden. Needs sharply drained, moderately fertile soil in partial shade.
• PROPAGATION By seed in spring, in pots in a cold frame. Self-seeds freely.

☼ ◊
❄ ❄ ❄

HEIGHT
30cm (12in)

SPREAD
15cm (6in)

VIOLA

The genus *Viola* comprises about 500 species of popular annuals, biennials, and perennials, some of which are evergreen or semi-evergreen. Violets and pansies have a long flowering season and are valued for their often sweetly scented or showy blooms. Several compact species are suitable for the rock garden. Some, like *Viola pedata*, dislike excessive winter wet and so are best grown in pots in an alpine house. Shade-loving species, like *V. odorata* and *V. riviniana* 'Purpurea', which self-seed freely, are ideal for naturalizing in a woodland garden or shady border but will spread and often become a nuisance in a rock garden. Drifts of self-sown seedlings can look very attractive in scree plantings.

Grow in poor to moderately fertile, moist but well-drained soil in sun or partial shade. Generally, violets need dappled shade, while pansies prefer sun. Dead-head frequently to prolong flowering, and trim back vigorous species and cultivars after flowering to maintain compactness. The smaller alpine species need sharp drainage in gritty, moderately fertile soil, except for *V. calcarata*, which grows best in more fertile soils. In an alpine house, use a mix of loam, leaf-mould and grit or tufa chippings. Pot-grown specimens are best re-potted annually in late summer or early autumn.

Propagate species by sowing seed as soon as ripe or in spring, in containers in a cold frame. Divide *V. biflora*, *V. cornuta*, and *V. odorata* in spring or autumn. *V.* 'Huntercombe Purple' and other cultivars should be divided about every three years to maintain vigour. Take softwood cuttings of cultivars, such as *V.* 'Jackanapes', in spring or late summer. Many *Viola* species and cultivars tend to be short-lived, so propagate regularly to maintain stocks.

V. 'Nellie Britton'
Habit Clump-forming, evergreen, perennial.
Flowers Solitary, pansy, 2.5cm (1in) wide, borne in profusion in summer. Pinkish-mauve.
Leaves Oval, toothed, and glossy. Mid-green.
• TIPS Needs well-drained but not dry soil.
• OTHER NAME *V.* 'Haslemere'.
• HEIGHT 15cm (6in).
• SPREAD 30cm (12in).

V. 'Nellie Britton'

☼ ◊ ❀ ❀ ❀   ♛

V. 'Huntercombe Purple'
Habit Spreading, clumping, evergreen, perennial.
Flowers Solitary, pansy, 2.5cm (1in) wide, borne in summer. Deep violet-purple.
Leaves Oval, toothed, and glossy. Mid-green.
• TIPS Best divided every 3 years.
• HEIGHT 15cm (6in).
• SPREAD 30cm (12in).

V. 'Huntercombe Purple'

☼ ◊ ❀ ❀ ❀   ♛

V. PEDATA
Habit Stemless, clump-forming, herbaceous, perennial.
Flowers Violet, short-spurred, 3cm (1¼in) across, borne in late spring and summer. Pale violet with yellow centre.
Leaves Finely divided. Mid-green.
• TIPS Best grown in an alpine house.
• HEIGHT 5cm (2in).
• SPREAD 10cm (4in).

V. pedata
Birdsfoot violet, Crowfoot violet

◐ ◊ ❀ ❀ ❀

V. CALCARATA
Habit Clump-forming, perennial.
Flowers Pansy, slender-spurred, to 4cm (1⅝in) across, borne in late spring and summer. White-lavender.
Leaves Oval or lance-shaped. Mid-green.
• TIPS Prefers a site with deep, rich soil.
• HEIGHT 10–15cm (4–6in).
• SPREAD 20cm (8in).

V. calcarata
Long-spurred pansy

☼ ◐ ❀ ❀ ❀

V. ODORATA

Habit Stoloniferous, mat-forming, semi-evergreen, perennial.
Flowers Solitary, violet, sweet-scented, 2cm (¾in) across, with short spurs, borne in late winter and spring. Violet or white.
Leaves Heart-shaped. Bright green.
• TIPS Self-seeds freely. Good for naturalizing.
• HEIGHT 20cm (8in).
• SPREAD 30cm (12in).

V. odorata
English violet,
Sweet violet

☼ ◊ ❋ ❋ ❋ ⚱

V. 'Jackanapes'

Habit Clump-forming, short-lived, evergreen, perennial.
Flowers Pansy, spurred, 2cm (¾in) across, borne in spring and summer. Deep brownish-purple, with yellow lower petals.
Leaves Oval and toothed. Bright green.
• TIPS Short-lived, so take cuttings regularly.
• HEIGHT 12cm (5in).
• SPREAD 30cm (12in).

V. 'Jackanapes'

☼ ◊ ❋ ❋ ❋ ⚱

V. RIVINIANA
'Purpurea'

Habit Tufted, evergreen, perennial.
Flowers Solitary, violet, to 2cm (¾in) across, borne in late spring and early summer. Violet, with white or pale purple spur.
Leaves Oval, toothed. Dark purplish-green.
• TIPS Suitable for naturalizing.
• HEIGHT 10cm (4in).
• SPREAD 20cm (8in).

V. riviniana 'Purpurea'
Common dog violet,
Wood violet

☼ ◊ ❋ ❋ ❋

V. BIFLORA

Habit Compact, rhizomatous, herbaceous, perennial.
Flowers Solitary or paired, violet, 15mm (⅝in) across, borne in late spring and early summer. Lemon-yellow, veined brown on lower petal.
Leaves Heart-shaped and toothed. Pale green.
• TIPS Suits naturalizing.
• HEIGHT 8cm (3in).
• SPREAD 20cm (8in).

V. biflora
Twin-flowered violet

☼ ◊ ❋ ❋ ❋

V. CORNUTA

Habit Rhizomatous, evergreen, clump-forming, perennial.
Flowers Solitary, pansy, slender-spurred, to 3.5cm (1⅜in) wide, borne from spring to summer. Pale to deep lilac-blue, or white.
Leaves Oval and toothed. Mid-green.
• TIPS Thrives in a sunny or shaded site.
• HEIGHT 15cm (6in).
• SPREAD 40cm (16in).

V. cornuta
Horned violet,
Pyrenean pansy

☼ ◊ ❋ ❋ ❋ ⚱

V. AETOLICA

Habit Clump-forming, evergreen, perennial.
Flowers Solitary, pansy, scented, 2cm (¾in) across, borne in late spring and summer. Yellow, with darker lower petals.
Leaves Oval to lance-shaped, scalloped. Mid-green.
• TIPS Suits a rock garden or raised bed
• HEIGHT 8cm (3in).
• SPREAD 15cm (6in).

V. aetolica

☼ ◊ ❋ ❋ ❋

GENTIANA

The genus *Gentiana*, commonly known as gentians, comprises about 400 species of annuals, biennials, and evergreen and herbaceous perennials. The autumn-flowering gentians are classified as semi-evergreen. Those described here are alpine species suitable for rock gardens, peat beds, or troughs. Most of them prefer cool, damp climates.

Cultivation requirements for the genus are grouped as follows:

Group 1 Need sunny site and neutral to alkaline soil.

Group 2 Need cool, moist, acid to neutral soil and good light. Dislike dry conditions.

Sow seed of species as soon as ripe in containers in a cold frame. Separate offsets or divide in early spring.

G. SAXOSA
Habit Rosette-forming, short-lived, evergreen, perennial.
Flowers Upright, bell-shaped, 2cm (¾in) long, borne in summer and early autumn. White, with faint green veins.
Leaves Narrow spoon-shaped and leathery. Dark green.
• CULTIVATION 1.
• HEIGHT 7cm (3in).
• SPREAD 10cm (4in).

G. saxosa
New Zealand gentian

G. TERNIFOLIA
Habit Trailing, semi-evergreen, perennial.
Flowers Solitary, bell- to trumpet-shaped, 4cm (1⅝in) long, borne in autumn. Sky-blue, with darker blue stripes.
Leaves Narrowly lance-shaped. Greyish-green.
• CULTIVATION 2.
• HEIGHT 8cm (3in).
• SPREAD 30cm (12in).

G. ternifolia

G. × *MACAULEYI*
'Well's Variety'
Habit Clump-forming.
Flowers Solitary, trumpet-shaped, borne during mid- and late summer. Deep blue.
Leaves Linear, pointed, and paired. Mid-green.
• CULTIVATION 2.
• OTHER NAME
G. 'Wellsii'.
• HEIGHT 8cm (3in).
• SPREAD 30cm (12in).

G. × *macauleyi*
'Well's Variety'

G. SINO-ORNATA
Habit Semi-evergreen, perennial, with prostrate shoots.
Flowers Solitary, trumpet-shaped, 6cm (2½in) long, borne in autumn. Bright deep blue, with white stripes.
Leaves Linear to lance-shaped, paired, and pointed. Mid-green.
• CULTIVATION 2.
• HEIGHT 7cm (3in).
• SPREAD 30cm (12in).

G. sino-ornata
Autumn gentian

G. 'Kingfisher'
Habit Semi-evergreen, perennial, with prostrate stems.
Flowers Solitary, trumpet-shaped, to 4cm (1⅝in) long, borne in autumn. Vivid blue.
Leaves Linear to lance-shaped and pointed. Dark green.
• CULTIVATION 2.
• HEIGHT 5cm (2in).
• SPREAD to 30cm (12in).

G. 'Kingfisher'

G. PARADOXA
Habit Tufted, herbaceous, perennial.
Flowers Solitary, broad trumpet-shaped, to 4–5cm (1½–2in) long, borne in late summer. Rich blue, white throat.
Leaves Linear, in whorls of 3–4. Yellow-green.
• CULTIVATION 1.
• HEIGHT 10–20cm (4–8in).
• SPREAD 10–20cm (4–8in).

G. paradoxa

G. × STEVENAGENSIS
Habit Semi-evergreen,
perennial, with
branching,
prostrate stems.
Flowers Terminal,
trumpet-shaped, 6.5cm
(2¾in) long, borne in
autumn. Purple-blue,
with yellow-green stripes.
Leaves Paired, linear,
thick. Mid- to dark green.
• CULTIVATION 2.
• HEIGHT 5cm (2in).
• SPREAD 30cm (12in).

G. × *stevenagensis*

G. SEPTEMFIDA
Habit Spreading to
upright, clump-forming,
herbaceous, perennial.
Flowers Narrowly bell-
shaped, 3.5cm (1½in)
long, borne in clusters in
late summer. Bright blue,
dark stripes, white throat.
Leaves Oval, pointed,
paired. Mid-green.
• CULTIVATION 1.
• HEIGHT 15–20cm
(6–8in).
• SPREAD 30cm (12in).

G. *septemfida*

G. 'Inverleith'
Habit Vigorous,
semi-evergreen,
perennial.
Flowers Solitary,
trumpet-shaped,
to 6cm (2½in) long,
borne during autumn.
Pale blue, with darker
stripes outside.
Leaves Lance-shaped,
recurved. Mid-green.
• CULTIVATION 2.
• HEIGHT 10cm (4in).
• SPREAD 30cm (12in).

G. 'Inverleith'

G. VEITCHIORUM
Habit Semi-evergreen,
perennial with trailing,
prostrate stems.
Flowers Solitary,
narrowly trumpet-
shaped, 5cm (2in) long,
borne in autumn. Dark
blue, with greenish-
yellow stripes outside.
Leaves Linear to oblong,
paired. Mid-green.
• CULTIVATION 2.
• HEIGHT 5cm (2in).
• SPREAD to 20cm (8in).

G. *veitchiorum*

G. VERNA subsp. BALCANICA
Habit Clump-forming,
evergreen, perennial.
Flowers Solitary,
salver-shaped, 2.5cm
(1in) across, borne in
spring. Deep sky-blue,
with white centre.
Leaves Small, oval to
lance-shaped, in basal
rosettes, paired at stems.
Dark to mid-green.
• CULTIVATION 1.
• OTHER NAME
G. verna 'Angulosa'.
• HEIGHT 6cm (2½in).
• SPREAD to 15cm (6in).

G. verna
subsp. *balcanica*

G. VERNA
Habit Mat-forming,
evergreen perennial.
Flowers Solitary, salver-
shaped, 2.5cm (1in)
across, borne in spring.
Pure sky-blue, with
white centre.
Leaves Oval to lance-
shaped, in basal rosettes,
paired on the stems.
Dark to mid-green.
• CULTIVATION 1.
• HEIGHT 4cm (1½in).
• SPREAD to 10cm (4in).

G. *verna*
Spring gentian,
Star gentian

G. ACAULIS
Habit Mat-forming,
evergreen, perennial.
Flowers Solitary,
trumpet-shaped, 5cm
(2in) long, borne in
spring. Vivid, deep blue.
Leaves Oval to lance-
shaped, pointed, glossy,
and rosetted. Dark green.
• CULTIVATION 1.
• OTHER NAMES
G. excisa, G. kochiana.
• HEIGHT 8cm (3in).
• SPREAD 30cm (12in).

G. *acaulis*
Trumpet gentian

Cruciferae/ Brassicaceae	

ARABIS PROCURRENS 'Variegata'

Habit Prostrate, mat-forming, evergreen or semi-evergreen, perennial. **Flowers** Cross-shaped, 8–10mm (⅓–⅜in) across, borne in loose clusters in late spring. White. **Leaves** Narrowly oblong to lance-shaped, glossy. Mid-green, with cream or pink margins.
• NATIVE HABITAT Garden origin.
• CULTIVATION Tolerates any well-drained soil in sun. Remove all-green shoots to keep variegation.
• PROPAGATION By softwood cuttings in summer.
• OTHER NAME *A. ferdinandi-coburgii* 'Variegata'.

☼ ◊
❄ ❄ ❄

HEIGHT
5–8cm
(2–3in)

SPREAD
30–40cm
(12–16in)

Crassulaceae	COMMON HOUSELEEK

SEMPERVIVUM TECTORUM

Habit Vigorous, clump-forming, fleshy, evergreen, perennial. **Flowers** Small, star-shaped, borne in hairy-stemmed dense clusters, 5–10cm (2–4in) across, in summer. Red-purple. **Leaves** Thick, oval to narrowly oblong, bristle-tipped, in large rosettes. Blue-green, suffused red-purple.
• NATIVE HABITAT Mountains, southern. Europe.
• CULTIVATION Good for growing on old roof tiles, in gritty, sharply drained, moderately fertile soil.
• PROPAGATION By seed in spring, or by offsets in spring or early summer.

☼ ◊
❄ ❄ ❄

HEIGHT
15cm (6in)

SPREAD
to 50cm
(20in)

Ericaceae	COMMON BEARBERRY, KINNIKINNICK

ARCTOSTAPHYLOS UVA-URSI

Habit Low-growing, evergreen, shrub.
Flowers Tiny, urn-shaped, borne in sprays 2–3cm (⅘–1⅕in) long, in summer. White, tinted pink. **Leaves** Small, oval, and leathery. Dark green. **Fruits** Rounded berries. Scarlet.
• NATIVE HABITAT Moors, heaths, open woodland in northern Eurasia and N. America.
• CULTIVATION Grow in a rock or woodland garden, or peat bed, in moist, acid, leaf-rich soil.
• PROPAGATION By semi-ripe cuttings in summer, or layer or separate rooted stems in autumn.

◑ ◊ pH
❄ ❄ ❄

HEIGHT
to 10cm
(4in(

SPREAD
to 50cm or
more (20in)

Crassulaceae	

JOVIBARBA HIRTA

Habit Clumping, stoloniferous, fleshy, evergreen, perennial. **Flowers** Bell-shaped, borne in branched clusters, to 8cm (3in) across, in summer. Yellow-brown. **Leaves** Lance-shaped, hairy-margined, fleshy, in rosettes. Green, flushed red.
• NATIVE HABITAT Central and southeast Europe.
• CULTIVATION Grow in troughs or on the top of retaining walls, in poor, gritty, sharply drained soil.
• PROPAGATION By offsets in spring or summer.
• OTHER NAMES *J. globifera* subsp. *hirta*, *Sempervivum hirtum*.

☼ ◊
❄ ❄ ❄

HEIGHT
15cm (6in)

SPREAD
30cm (12in)

Crassulaceae	COBWEB HOUSELEEK

SEMPERVIVUM ARACHNOIDEUM

Habit Clump-forming, evergreen, perennial.
Flowers Small, star-shaped, borne in flat heads,
to 2.5cm (1in) across, in summer. Red-pink.
Leaves Oval, fleshy, in tight, crowded rosettes,
and cobwebbed with white hairs. Mid-green to red.
• NATIVE HABITAT Mountain rocks in Europe
• CULTIVATION Suitable for growing in a scree
bed or trough, with gritty, sharply drained,
moderately fertile soil.
• PROPAGATION By seed in spring in pots in a cold
frame, or by offsets in spring or early summer.

☼ ◊
❄ ❄ ❄

HEIGHT
8cm (3in)

SPREAD
to 30cm
(12in)

Compositae/Asteraceae	

RAOULIA HOOKERI var. ALBO-SERICEA

Habit Mat-forming, evergreen, perennial. **Flowers**
Insignificant, borne in heads to 7mm (¼in) wide,
in summer. Pale green or straw-coloured. **Leaves**
Oval to spoon-shaped, intensely silky-haired,
closely overlapping along stems. Grey-silver.
• NATIVE HABITAT Gravel and scree, New Zealand.
• CULTIVATION Needs gritty, fertile, moisture
retentive, sharply drained soil. Shade from the
hottest sun and protect from winter wet.
• PROPAGATION Divide in spring.
• OTHER NAME *R. lutescens.*

☼ ◊
❄ ❄

HEIGHT
1cm (1/2in)

SPREAD
to 20cm or
more (8in)

Compositae/Asteraceae	NEW ZEALAND EDELWEISS

LEUCOGENES GRANDICEPS

Habit Mat-forming, evergreen, perennial. **Flowers**
Small, daisy, flat, 9–15mm (⅜–⅝in) across, with a
collar of densely white-woolly bracts, borne in early
summer. Yellow. **Leaves** Oval to wedge-shaped,
downy, closely overlapping on stems. Silver-white.
• NATIVE HABITAT Mountain screes, New Zealand.
• CULTIVATION Needs gritty, fertile, moist but
sharply drained soil. Protect from winter wet.
• PROPAGATION Take stem tip cuttings in late
summer, or sow seed as soon as ripe in containers
in a cold frame.

☼ ◊
❄ ❄

HEIGHT
10–15cm
(4–6in)

SPREAD
10–15cm
(4–6in)

Compositae/Asteraceae	

ARTEMISIA SCHMIDTIANA 'Nana'

Habit Rhizomatous, tufted, evergreen, perennial.
Flowers Tiny, borne in clusters, to 10cm (4in)
long, in summer. Yellow. **Leaves** Linear, finely
cut, silky-haired, lobed. Silver-white.
• NATIVE HABITAT Garden selection. The species
is found in the mountains of Japan.
• CULTIVATION Suitable for growing in rock
gardens and raised beds. Needs gritty, well-
drained, moderately fertile soil.
• PROPAGATION By heeled, side-shoot cuttings
in summer.

☼ ◊
❄ ❄ ❄

HEIGHT
8cm (3in)

SPREAD
30cm (12in)

Crassulaceae	CILIATE HOUSELEEK

SEMPERVIVUM CILIOSUM

Habit Clump-forming, evergreen, perennial.
Flowers Small, star-shaped, borne in compact,
flat clusters 2.5cm (1in) across, in summer.
Greenish-yellow. **Leaves** Thick, fleshy,
lance-shaped, incurved, white-hairy, forming
dense rosettes. Grey-green.
• NATIVE HABITAT Rocks and screes, in the
mountains of Bulgaria, former Yugoslavia,
and northwest Greece.
• CULTIVATION Best in an alpine house in areas
prone to damp winters. Even though it is very cold

hardy, it dislikes winter wet. Grow in pans in a
mix of equal parts loam-based potting compost
and sharp grit. The rosettes die after flowering,
but are rapidly replaced by daughter rosettes
which emerge from the base of the rosettes on
lateral stolons. Sempervivums tolerate poor soils
and dry conditions, but will not thrive in warm,
humid climates.
• PROPAGATION By seed in spring in containers
in a cold frame. Separate offsets in spring
or early summer.

HEIGHT
8cm (3in)

SPREAD
to 30cm
(12in)

Compositae/Asteraceae	

RAOULIA AUSTRALIS

Habit Mat-forming, evergreen, perennial.
Flowers Insignificant, borne in heads to 5mm
(⅕in) wide, in summer. Pale yellow. **Leaves**
Minute, spoon-shaped, intensely hairy, closely
overlapping along the rooting stems. Silver-grey.
• NATIVE HABITAT Gravel and scree, New Zealand.
• CULTIVATION Needs gritty, fertile, moisture-
retentive, but sharply drained soil, and some shade
from the hottest sun. Protect from winter wet.
• PROPAGATION Divide carefully in spring.
• OTHER NAME *R. lutescens.*

HEIGHT
1cm (½in)

SPREAD
30cm (12in)
or more

Crassulaceae	

SEMPERVIVUM GIUSEPPII

Habit Vigorous, clump-forming, evergreen,
perennial. **Flowers** Small, star-shaped, borne in
terminal heads, 3.5cm (1⅜in) across, in summer.
Dark red. **Leaves** Oval, fleshy, hairy when young,
in tight rosettes. Pea-green, with dark tips.
• NATIVE HABITAT Mountain rocks, Spain.
• CULTIVATION Good as a pot plant in an alpine
house. Outdoors, suits a scree bed or trough, with
gritty, sharply drained, moderately fertile soil.
• PROPAGATION By seed in spring, or by offsets
in spring or early summer.

HEIGHT
8cm (3in)

SPREAD
30cm (12in)

Umbelliferae/Apiaceae	

AZORELLA TRIFURCATA

Habit Cushion-forming, evergreen, perennial.
Flowers Tiny, borne in small clusters in summer.
Creamy-white. **Leaves** Triangular, with sharp-
tipped lobes, in dense rosettes. Glossy, dark green.
• NATIVE HABITAT Open, rocky places, Chile
and Argentina.
• CULTIVATION Suits a scree or raised bed in poor
or moderately fertile, gritty, sharply drained soil.
• PROPAGATION By seed in autumn, in containers
in a cold frame. Root rosettes as cuttings in spring.
• OTHER NAME *A. nivalis.*

HEIGHT
10cm (4in)
or more

SPREAD
20cm (8in)

Crassulaceae	MOUNTAIN HOUSELEEK

SEMPERVIVUM MONTANUM

Habit Vigorous, mat-forming, evergreen,
perennial. **Flowers** Small, star-shaped, borne
in loose clusters to 6cm (2½in) across, in summer.
Red-purple. **Leaves** Broadly lance-shaped, sharp-
pointed, fleshy, finely-haired, rosetted. Dull green.
• NATIVE HABITAT Mountains, central Europe.
• CULTIVATION Suits a scree bed or trough, with
gritty, sharply drained, moderately fertile soil.
• PROPAGATION By seed in spring, or by offsets
in spring or early summer.
• OTHER NAME *S. helveticum.*

HEIGHT
10cm (4in)

SPREAD
30cm (12in)

Caryophyllaceae	

SAGINA BOYDII

Habit Very slow-growing, compact, cushion-forming, evergreen, perennial. **Flowers** Tiny, usually petalless, borne in summer. Mid-green. **Leaves** Rigid, linear to narrowly wedge-shaped, recurved, densely packed in crowded rosettes. Glossy, dark green.

• NATIVE HABITAT Mountains of Scotland.

• CULTIVATION Valued for its neat, symmetrical, compact rosettes of foliage. Best grown in an alpine house in order to maintain its compact form. Grow in a mix of 3 parts grit or sharp sand, with 1 part peat or leaf-mould. Provide bright, filtered light, and maintain a cool, moist, buoyant atmosphere as it dislikes hot, dry conditions. Very susceptible to red spider mite, under glass. Outdoors, it is ideal for growing in a trough, in very low-fertility, very sharply drained soil, in good light but with shade from hot sun.

• PROPAGATION Root individual rosettes as cuttings in early summer.

HEIGHT
2.5cm (1in)

SPREAD
8cm (3in)

Umbelliferae/Apiaceae	

BOLAX GUMMIFERA

Habit Slow-growing, cushion-forming, evergreen, perennial. **Flowers** Tiny, seldom produced, borne in clusters of 3–20, in summer. Greenish-white. **Leaves** Deeply lobed, leathery, forming dense rosettes. Dark blue-green.
• NATIVE HABITAT Southern Chile, southern Argentina, and the Falkland Islands.
• CULTIVATION Needs poor, gritty, sharply drained soil, in a scree or raised bed. May be grown in tufa.
• PROPAGATION Root rosettes as cuttings in spring.
• OTHER NAMES *B. glebaria, Azorella glebaria.*

HEIGHT
5cm (2in)

SPREAD
15cm (6in)

Plantaginaceae	

PLANTAGO NIVALIS

Habit Rosette-forming, evergreen, perennial. **Flowers** Tiny, tubular, borne in spikes to 1cm (½in) across, on long stalks in summer. Green. **Leaves** Lance-shaped, silky-haired. Silver-green.
• NATIVE HABITAT Mountains, southern Spain.
• CULTIVATION In an alpine house, use a mix of 4 parts peat or leaf-mould to 1 part grit or sharp sand. Outdoors, grow in a trough in low-fertility, sharply drained soil. Protect from winter wet.
• PROPAGATION Sow seed in autumn, or divide in spring.

HEIGHT
2.5cm (1in)

SPREAD
8cm (3in)

Caryophyllaceae/ Illecebraceae	

PARONYCHIA KAPELA subsp. *SERPYLLIFOLIA*

Habit Mat-forming, evergreen, perennial. **Flowers** Tiny, borne in heads, to 2cm (¾in) across, in summer. Greenish-white, with silvery-white papery bracts. **Leaves** Oval to lance-shaped. Silvery blue-green.
• NATIVE HABITAT Hot, dry sites, Mediterranean.
• CULTIVATION Grow in poor, sharply drained soil. Suitable for growing in a trough, raised bed, or tufa.
• PROPAGATION Sow seed in winter, divide in spring, or take stem-tip cuttings in early summer.

HEIGHT
5cm (2in)

SPREAD
20cm (8in)

SEDUM

The genus *Sedum*, commonly known as stonecrops, comprises about 400 species of succulent annuals and evergreen, semi-evergreen, and deciduous perennials. Some of the larger perennials, along with a few shrubs and sub-shrubs, are sometimes included in the genus *Hylotelephium*. Stonecrops are valued for their neat and attractive, often beautifully coloured or bloomed, foliage. The star-shaped flowers, although usually individually small, are grouped in showy clusters or sprays. Most of them originate in the mountains of the northern hemisphere, and a few are found in arid areas of South America and Africa.

The stonecrops described here are ideal for growing in rock gardens or for cultivation in an alpine house. They can be used to great effect if planted as a genus collection in a trough or raised bed,

and will provide very attractive contrasts of colour, texture, and form. The more robust types may also be grown at the front of a sunny, well-drained herbaceous or mixed border.

Grow in moderately fertile, well-drained, gritty soils in full sun. *Sedum spathulifolium*, *S. kamschaticum* 'Variegatum', and other vigorous species tolerate light shade. Trim back spreading species after they have flowered to maintain the shape of the plant and prevent encroachment on other, less-vigorous, neighbours.

Propagate species by seed sown in autumn, in pots in a cold frame. Divide during spring and mid-summer. Take stem cuttings of non-flowering shoots or root individual rosette cuttings, in early or mid-summer. Handle stonecrops carefully, as all parts can cause stomach upsets if ingested and contact with the sap may irritate the skin.

S. CAUTICOLA
Habit Trailing, stoloniferous, semi-evergreen, perennial.
Flowers Star-shaped, borne in rounded, terminal clusters, to 10cm (4in) wide, in autumn. Rose-purple ageing to carmine-red.
Leaves Rounded to spoon-shaped or oval, borne on purple-tinted stems. Grey-green.
• HEIGHT 8cm (3in).
• SPREAD 30cm (12in).

S. cauticola

☀ ◊ ❁❁❁   ♗

S. LYDIUM
Habit Mat-forming, stem-rooting, evergreen, perennial.
Flowers Star-shaped, borne in flat-topped, terminal clusters 2.5cm (1in) across, during summer. White.
Leaves Cylindrical, fleshy, tightly rosetted. Bright green, with red tips.
• HEIGHT 5cm (2in).
• SPREAD 20cm (8in).

S. lydium

☀ ◊ ❁❁❁

S. SPATHULIFOLIUM
'Purpureum'
Habit Mat-forming, evergreen, perennial.
Flowers Star-shaped, borne in flat clusters, 15mm (⅝in) across, in summer. Yellow.
Leaves Spoon-shaped and fleshy. Silvery-green, suffused red-purple.
• HEIGHT 10cm (4in).
• SPREAD 60cm (24in).

S. spathulifolium
'Purpureum'

☀ ◊ ❁❁❁   ♗

S. OBTUSATUM
Habit Cushion-forming, evergreen, perennial.
Flowers Star-shaped, to 1cm (⅜in) across, borne in flat, terminal clusters, 10cm (4in) wide, in summer. Bright yellow.
Leaves Spoon-shaped and fleshy. Blue-green, suffused crimson.
• OTHER NAME
S. rubroglaucum.
• HEIGHT 5cm (2in).
• SPREAD 20cm (8in).

S. obtusatum

☼ ◊ ❀ ❀ ❀

S. ACRE 'Aureum'
Habit Mat-forming, evergreen, perennial.
Flowers Star-shaped, borne in flat-topped clusters, to 4cm (1½in) across, in summer. Yellow-green.
Leaves Triangular and overlapping. Bright yellow.
• HEIGHT 5cm (2in).
• SPREAD 60cm (24in).

S. acre 'Aureum'

☼ ◊ ❀ ❀ ❀   ♈

S. KAMSCHATICUM 'Variegatum'
Habit Clump-forming, rhizomatous, semi-evergreen, perennial.
Flowers Star-shaped, 15mm (⅝in) across, borne in flat-topped clusters, 5cm (2in) wide, in late summer. Golden-yellow.
Leaves Lance- to spoon-shaped. Green, tinted pink, cream-margined.
• HEIGHT 10cm (4in).
• SPREAD 25cm (10in).

S. kamschaticum 'Variegatum'

☼ ◊ ❀ ❀ ❀   ♈

S. SPATHULIFOLIUM 'Cape Blanco'
Habit Mat-forming, evergreen, perennial.
Flowers Star-shaped, 15mm (⅝in) across, borne in summer. Yellow.
Leaves Spoon-shaped, fleshy, rosetted. Silvery-green, with white bloom.
• OTHER NAME
S. spathulifolium 'Cappa Blanca'.
• HEIGHT 10cm (4in).
• SPREAD 60cm (24in).

S. spathulifolium 'Cape Blanco'

☼ ◊ ❀ ❀ ❀   ♈

S. ACRE
Habit Mat-forming, evergreen, perennial.
Flowers Star-shaped, borne in flat-topped clusters, to 4cm (1½in) across, in summer. Bright yellow.
Leaves Triangular, overlapping, borne on trailing or upright stems. Pale green.
• HEIGHT 5cm (2in).
• SPREAD 60cm (24in).

S. acre
Biting stonecrop, Wallpepper

☼ ◊ ❀ ❀ ❀

S. RUPESTRE
Habit Vigorous, mat-forming, evergreen, perennial.
Flowers Star-shaped, 15mm (⅝in) across, borne in terminal clusters 6cm (2½in) wide, on upright, woody stems, in summer. Yellow.
Leaves Pointed, fleshy, cylindrical. Grey-green.
• OTHER NAME
S. reflexum.
• HEIGHT 10cm (4in).
• SPREAD 60cm (24in).

S. rupestre
Stone orpine

☼ ◊ ❀ ❀ ❀

SOIL PREPARATION AND PLANTING

The rock garden is perhaps the best-known place for growing rock plants and alpines. However, if space is restricted, raised beds, troughs, sinks, and other containers with free drainage can provide very attractive alternatives. Together with the use of different composts, they also extend the range of plants that can be grown in a garden.

Selecting and buying plants

A well-planned rock garden can provide colour throughout the year, more so than other plant groups in the garden. Where early-flowering alpines are grown, it is important to consider their characters, such as form and habit, and the colour offered by fruit, foliage, and stems, to ensure year-round interest. Before buying, research the range of plants that are likely to thrive in the soil type, aspect, and climate of the garden, by consulting standard texts and visiting established rock gardens.

Garden centres and other non-specialist outlets offer a wide range of rock plants, and these are likely to be the more robust and easily grown. Bear in mind that some may be vigorous species that will overwhelm smaller, more choice alpines, if not sited with due attention to their size, vigour, and propensity for self-seeding.

Specialist nurseries are likely to provide a wider range of unusual plants and can offer guidance on the suitability of plants for a given situation and on their cultural needs. Beware of making expensive purchases of rarities unless confident that their specific needs can be met.

Choose plants that have healthy foliage, with no sign of pests, diseases, root restriction, or water deprivation. Look for a weed-free compost surface and, before planting, discard the top layer of compost to avoid introducing weed seeds to the rock garden. The

SELECTING ALPINE PLANTS

SAXIFRAGA

GOOD EXAMPLE

POOR EXAMPLES

Healthy-looking, compact growth

Unbalanced, weak growth

Weeds in compost

Weed-free compost

Roots curled around inside of pot

invasion of mat- or cushion-forming alpines by pernicious seeders like pearlworts and bittercress, will prove tediously difficult to eradicate if they are allowed to establish.

Siting a rock garden

Most alpines need high levels of light and excellent drainage, and so prefer an open sunny site, away from shade cast by buildings or trees. Although some alpines grow well beneath them, trees can present several problems. For example, dripping water can spoil foliage and set up a site for fungal infection, while fallen leaves can smother small plants in autumn. Moreover, tree roots may compete for water and nutrients, and can even undermine rock work.

Avoid frost pockets and sites exposed to searing winds. A sloping site is ideal in that drainage is likely to be good and the potential for integrating rocks in a naturalistic manner is far greater than on a flat site. Natural and aesthetically pleasing effects are achieved if the rock garden is set in informally planted surroundings. If the style of the garden is predominantly formal, it may be better to consider rectangular raised beds, which are more easily integrated and unified with a strong geometric layout.

Choosing stone

Using locally available stone is the cheapest option, and will almost certainly harmonize more naturally with the general surroundings. This may not be possible in areas where supplies are limited or where geological formations are unsuitable. For example, shales and chalk weather too quickly, and igneous rocks, like granite or basalt, or hard rocks with no clear strata, are difficult to arrange in a natural layout and can take many years to achieve a weathered appearance. Slates can be useful and attractive, but are often difficult to blend in, except in areas where they occur naturally. Avoid buying rock that has been taken from ecologically precious limestone pavements.

TYPES OF STONE

Sandstone
This is one of the most suitable rocks to use in a rock garden. Its natural strata lines are clearly visible and allow the rock to be split easily.

Tufa
Scarce and expensive, tufa is lightweight and limy and its air pockets provide perfect drainage. Niches for cushion plants can easily be drilled or excavated.

Limestone
A good choice, either obtained second-hand or from working quarries. For conservation reasons, avoid rock that has been pillaged from limestone pavements.

How to Prepare the Site

1 Place a 15cm (6in) layer of coarse rubble, broken bricks, ballast, or gravel over the base of the site to form a mound and guarantee good drainage at the base.

2 Cover the mound with inverted turves or a punctured polypropylene sheet to prevent compost from percolating through to the rubble, thus clogging drainage.

3 Cover the turves with a 23–30cm (9–12in) layer of mixed compost. Using string and pegs, mark the outlines of "keystones" and rock outcrops.

4 Dig out receiving hollows for large rocks, with a spade. Manoeuvre stones into place with a crowbar. Tip them back slightly and wedge with smaller rocks for stability.

5 Infill around the rocks with carefully mixed compost (see pp.160–1). Check regularly for stability. Firm the soil gently around the stones to eliminate air pockets.

6 Fill around the stones with compost, burying them to one-third of their depth. Top with a final layer of equal parts loam, leaf-mould or garden compost, and grit.

Preparation and construction

Perennial weeds can be very difficult to eradicate from established rock gardens, especially if they seed into dense mat- or cushion-forming plants. It is best to begin a programme of weed eradication several months before construction starts, using a systemic herbicide to ensure that deep roots are killed completely. Any subsequent seedling regrowth can be readily removed by hand

Make sure that the site, particularly if level, is well-drained and install a soakaway or other drainage system, if necessary. This is most important on heavy clay soils. Sloping sites are usually free-draining, but may need a drainage ditch or soakaway at the lowest point. If the underlying drainage is good, simply dig over the soil and remove any weed regrowth. Consolidate the surface by gentle treading to avoid subsequent soil settlement, then fork over lightly to maintain the soil structure. Never attempt to construct the rock garden when the soil is wet, as the weight of heavy rocks will damage soil structure and cause compaction. This, in turn, will interfere with free drainage, making establishment and healthy root growth difficult.

Wear stout gloves and protective footwear throughout construction. Use rollers to move large rocks, and arrange for the consignment to be delivered as close as possible to the construction site. It may be necessary to use a block-and-tackle and crowbar to manoeuvre large rocks into place. Set the rocks tipped backwards slightly, so that rainwater runs into the bed rather than on to the plants beneath. Bury about one-third of the rock to ensure stability, checking for any movement as work proceeds.

The largest stones act as "keystones" (the dominant rock of the outcrop), and must be set in place first. Position the remaining rocks with their strata aligned, so that they flow naturally from the keystone to form outcrops in the required direction. Secondary keystones

PLANTING DURING CONSTRUCTION

1 *Set plants against a firmed rock with the roots against its face. Place battens on either side so that a second rock can be placed without crushing the plants.*

2 *When the second stone is set firmly in place, remove the battens. Using a mixed compost (see pp. 160–1), infill around the rocks and at the plant's roots. Firm the plant in gently.*

3 *Add a 2.5cm (1in) layer of stone chippings, gravel, or grit as a top-dressing to ensure sharp drainage at the vulnerable neck of the plants, and to create an attractive and natural finish.*

can be used to extend the outcrops. Make regular visual checks and arrange rocks so that they are positioned to provide the widest possible variety of planting niches. Butting up rocks face-to-face will ensure sites for crevice dwellers, while terraces between successive tiers provide suitable conditions for mat-forming alpines. Plants that need a cool, moist root run beneath the rocks can be set in place during construction. Position them between two successive layers of rock, and protect them from crushing with battens or fragments of rocks.

Soils for rock gardens and scree beds

In the wild, many alpines grow in a substrate made up largely of rock fragments, interspersed with detritus that is often rich in organic matter and retains moisture. This substrate is very sharply drained and often low in nutrients. These two factors should be taken into account when creating a mix in which plants will thrive and still retain their natural, compact character. A special compost that suits most rock garden plants can be made up of equal parts garden soil or loam, peat or leaf-mould, and sharp grit or sharp, salt-free

PLANTING A ROCK GARDEN

1 *Water plants and allow them to drain. Arrange them on the surface of the soil according to the planting plan.*

2 *Remove each plant from its pot and loosen the root ball gently. Dispose of the top layer of compost, plus weeds and their seeds*

3 *With a trowel, make a planting hole large enough to accommodate the root ball. Ease the plant into the hole and label.*

4 *Infill with compost and firm gently. Top-dress with a layer of grit or rock chippings, easing a little grit beneath the plant necks.*

5 *When the entire rock garden is fully planted, fill in any gaps in the top-dressing with grit, and water the plants in well.*

sand. This should be used to form a top layer of at least 20mm (⅜in). Scree plants need a very well-drained, low-fertility compost made up of one part of loam and one part of peat or leaf-mould, with 3 parts or more of grit or stone chippings. In very dry areas, it is wise to use a more moisture-retentive mix of 2 parts each loam and leaf-mould, with 1 part coarse sand, and 2 parts stone chips (or less in dry areas). For acid-loving plants use a mix of 4 parts lime-free leaf-mould, composted, granulated bark or bracken litter, and one part lime-free grit or coarse sand. On naturally alkaline soils, pocket plantings of this mix are best regarded as short-term, as lime eventually percolates into the mix often causing the plants to perish.

Planting a rock garden

Alpines and rock plants are nearly always pot-grown. Most can be planted at any time of the year, if given conscientious after-care, especially with regard to watering and weeding. Like other plant groups, however, they should not be planted when the soil is wet or frozen, or when the weather is warm and dry. Plants with grey or soft foliage and many cushion-forming alpines are best set out in spring or early summer. Water all plants thoroughly before planting and allow them to drain. Dig a hole that will accommodate the roots without crowding. Slide them gently from their pots and tease out the root ball very carefully. Position the plant in the hole and fill in with compost, firming gently. Set the plant with its collar slightly proud of the compost surface, then top-dress with grit or rock chippings, easing it in gently around the plant neck with the fingers. Water thoroughly after planting and continue until the plant begins to make new growth. If the weather is dry after planting, water at weekly intervals, if necessary. Check first by feeling the soil beneath the top-dressing, taking care to avoid disturbing the roots. Once they are established, plants seldom need additional watering

PLANTING IN A VERTICAL CREVICE

1 *Remove compost with a spoon or widger. Wedge a small stone firmly at the base of the crevice, using a hammer if necessary.*

2 *Add a 2.5cm (1in) layer of compost, then gently ease in the small rootball of of a young plant (here,* Campanula).

3 *Cover with compost, and wedge in place with a small stone. Add more plants, at least 10cm (4in) apart. Water in carefully.*

HOW TO PLANT IN A DRY-STONE RETAINING WALL

1 *Check that there is sufficient compost in the planting crevice. Set a small rooted cutting on the flat of the stone. Ease in the roots with a widger.*

2 *Bed the plant into the compost and pack more compost into the crevice to hold the plant in place. This is easiest with small plants and slightly moist compost. Firm in with your fingers.*

3 *For larger plants, scoop out some compost from the crevice. Ease in the rootball and trickle in more compost while holding the plant in place. Water in from the wall top or with a mist sprayer.*

except in prolonged periods of drought. Netting should be used to protect plants, especially woolly-leaved species, as birds may tweak out or damage rosette-forming plants, or shred woolly leaves for nest material. Check plants regularly, refirming soil as necessary.

Planting in a scree bed

Key to a successful scree bed are care during planting and conscientious watering until the plants are well-established. It can be more difficult to grow plants in a scree bed because the surface layer of sharply drained compost dries out before the plants can develop a root system that is able to reach moisture at deeper levels. At the same time, care must be taken not to overwater the site.

When planting, shake off most of the compost from the root ball and keep the bare roots moist. Set the plant in a planting hole, spreading the roots out, and then infill carefully with scree mixture. Top-dress with a layer of chippings and water each plant immediately and thoroughly. Keep watering regularly until new leaves or shoot growth are evident.

Top-dressing

When planting is complete, it is best to top-dress any bare soil with grit or chippings that will blend with the rocks. As well as being aesthetically satisfying, this maintains a perfectly drained layer around the neck of plants, conserves soil moisture, and prevents compaction by heavy rain or watering. It also prevents light from reaching weed seeds at the soil surface. Top-dressing needs to be at least 2.5cm (1in) deep to be effective, preferably twice that, and on scree beds it can be up to 15cm (6in) deep.

Troughs, sinks, and other containers

Almost any perfectly drained, frost-proof container can be used for growing alpines. The advantage of container plantings is that they can be filled with a specific compost to suit a given group of plants. Traditional stone troughs are now scarce and expensive, but glazed stone sinks make attractive alternatives when coated with hypertufa. This is a mix of 1–2 parts sphagnum peat or sifted peat substitute, 1 part coarse sand or grit, and 1 part cement, mixed with just enough water to form a stiffish paste. Clean glazed sinks thoroughly and score the outer surface with a wire brush or glass cutter. Adhesion will be more secure if the surface is first coated with an epoxy bonding agent. Using gloved hands, apply the fresh hypertufa mix to a thickness of 2cm (¾in), from below the inside rim to just below the expected compost level. Roughen the surface to

resemble stone. After one week, scrub with a stiff wire brush, then wash with a suspension of manure to encourage rapid colonization by algae, mosses, and lichens to create an attractive weathered appearance. The hypertufa mix can be adjusted, with an increased proportion of sand and grit to 3 parts, to make a stiffer mix that is sufficiently rigid and durable for an entire trough. Use 2 stout boxes as a mould, one inside the other, with a cavity of 5–7cm (2–3in) between them.

Place troughs in their final position before filling and planting up, especially if rocks are used. They will be heavy, even when empty, and may prove impossible to move when full. Choose

How to Make a Hypertufa Trough

1 Coat the surfaces of the inner and outer boxes with oil to prevent sticking. Place a 2.5cm (1in) layer of hypertufa in the outer box.

2 Put wire netting on the hypertufa to reinforce it and push stout pieces of dowel into the bottom to make drainage holes.

3 Reinforce the sides with vertical netting. Place the inner box centrally. Fill the cavity with more hypertufa and tamp down.

4 Cover the top of the hypertufa with plastic sheeting until the mix has set (usually about a week). Keep frost-free.

5 When the hypertufa has set, remove the outer box. If hypertufa has stuck to the box, separate gently with a hammer and chisel.

6 Remove the inner box, again with a hammer and chisel if necessary. Paint with liquid manure to encourage algal growth.

an open site, with at least part-day sun, preferably on a hard, level surface with easy access to water. Raise containers off the ground, so as not to hinder drainage, by placing them on sturdy stable pillars of stone or brick. Ensure that there is no danger of them tipping over.

Many rock plants will thrive in a proprietary potting compost mixed with about one-third by volume of sharp grit to improve drainage, and bonemeal. Acid-loving plants need a lime-free compost with granitic or acid sandstone chippings. Cover drainage holes with crocks or wire gauze and fill the bottom third or quarter of the trough with stone chips. Top with a thin, inverted layer of turf (or peat substitute) and fill to within

5cm (2in) of the rim with compost (see pp. 160–1). If rocks or tufa are used, set them in the compost to form suitable crevices and niches for the proposed plantings. Water thoroughly to settle in the compost and let them drain before planting.

Choose compact, slow-growing plants that will neither dominate the site nor exhaust compost nutrients too quickly. Arrange container-grown plants on the compost and, when they are in final position, plant as described for planting in the rock garden. Top-dress with a layer of rock chippings and water throughly. In hot weather, provide shade for the plant until it is well established.

HOW TO PLANT UP AN ALPINE TROUGH

1 If planting in tufa, drill holes about 2.5cm (1in) wide, 7cm (3in) deep, and 10cm (4in) apart. Immerse tufa in water overnight.

2 Lay fine-mesh netting over the trough base, cover the holes with crocks, and add 7–10cm (3–4in) of coarse grit.

3 Partly fill the trough with a gritty, moist compost, firming in stages. Set the tufa in place, buried by at least ⅓–½ its depth.

4 Fill the trough with compost to within 5cm (2in) of the rim. Trickle a little compost into the tufa cavities.

5 Wash the roots of plants to go in the tufa; ease into the planting holes. Dribble in compost, firm in, wedge with small stones.

6 Arrange plants in their pots to check the arrangement and spacing. Then plant, firm them in, and water well.

ROUTINE CARE

As with any other group of plants, alpines and rock plants need regular care and maintenance if they are to continue to give their best. In most routine maintenance, perhaps the primary difference is that of scale.

Weeding

Thorough site preparation and the use of sterilized compost when planting helps to minimize weed problems, at least for the first few years. It is vital, however, to remove any seedling weeds as soon as they emerge, and to remove all weeds before they seed. Once weeds have rooted into dense mats or compact cushions they are very difficult to extract without resorting to the use of snub-nosed tweezers. It is possible to treat perennial weeds by painting with a systemic weed killer, but bear in mind that these are so effective that they will also kill any alpine plant that they come into contact with. For weeding around alpine plants, use a 3-pronged cultivator, which helps to loosen and aerate the surrounding soil.

Feeding

If the original compost has been prepared properly, newly planted areas will not need feeding for several years. Eventually, however, the soil will be depleted of nutrients and growth, and flowering may begin to deteriorate. Although an annual dressing in spring of slow-release fertilizer and bonemeal can be given, slow-release fertilizers tends to cause uneven growth in alpines. A better method, therefore, is to carefully remove the top-dressing and the top 1cm (½in) of compost, and replace it with fresh compost and a further top-dressing of grit. The top-dressing on the surface of the rock garden is likely

WEEDING

Before
Use a 3-pronged cultivator to weed around young plants. This also loosens and aerates the soil. Remove top-dressing first, and replace it after weeding.

REMOVING DEAD GROWTH

Before
When danger of frost has passed in spring, remove any dieback, by cutting back to healthy growth with sharp scissors or secateurs.

RENEWING TOP-DRESSING

1 *Remove the old top-dressing as well as the top layer, to about 1cm (⅜in), of compost. Fill in around the plants with fresh compost.*

2 *Top-dress the bed with a fresh layer of coarse grit or rock chippings, lifting cushions gently, if necessary, to renew top-dressing around the plant collar.*

REMOVING DEAD ROSETTES

1 *Dead rosettes may cause rot if not removed. Cut out carefully with a sharp knife or scissors without disturbing the rest of the plant.*

2 *Top-dress any exposed soil. This prevents weed from becoming established in the gaps before the plant produces new growth to fill the space.*

to need topping up occasionally, especially on slopes. Recover any bare patches of soil, paying particular attention in autumn, to ensure good soil coverage during winter. Top-up again, as required, in spring, applying a slow-release fertilizer at the same time, if needed.

Watering
Once rock plants are well-established, they root deeply and seldom need more water than is provided by rainfall. In prolonged drought, however, they should be soaked thoroughly in the early morning or evening, but not during the heat of the day. If the soil is dry to a depth of about 5cm (2in), soak until water has penetrated to the full depth of the roots. Containers used for alpines need more attention as they dry out quickly in hot weather, and the plants have a confined volume of soil from which to extract moisture. Overhead irrigation for troughs is best done in the early morning or evening.

Trimming and pruning
The routine pruning of shrubs, sub-shrubs, and evergreen perennials in a rock garden is limited, for the most part, to the removal of dead, diseased,

or damage wood to keep them healthy. They are usually so slow-growing that they seldom need pruning to restrict size, but when this does become necessary it is very important to maintain the natural form and habit of the plant. A few species, notably *Helianthemum*, *Arabis*, *Aubrieta*, and *Aurinia*, benefit from hard annual clipping after flowering, to keep them dense and compact.

Where over-vigorous plants threaten to encroach upon their neighbours, they can be cut back in spring. It may be sufficient to pull out excess growth by hand from the margins of vigorous mat-forming species, and refirm any rooted stems that have been lifted by mistake. On other plants, excess growth may need to be lifted with a hand fork. Clear sufficient space to allow for regrowth of the pruned plant without further impeding the growth of the surrounding plants. Plants that are hard-pruned will benefit from an application of balanced fertilizer to promote new growth.

It is more important with alpines than with other plants to remove dead leaves and flowers, especially tree leaves, towards autumn. If left in place, these may cause rotting in winter. Carefully cut out dead rosettes from plants such as saxifrages, using sharp scissors, but do not pull them out as this is likely to dislodge healthy rosettes at the same time. Dead material from the smallest alpines should be picked out carefully by hand, or by using tweezers if necessary. Routine dead-heading of alpines is also important, especially with plants that are known to self-seed freely, like *Campanula cochlearifolia* or violas.

Pests and diseases

Good garden hygiene and cultural practices are the primary approach when controlling pests and diseases in the rock garden. Aphids may need to be controlled, but are most likely to be a problem where plants are grown in over-fertile soils. Rich soils produce soft growth that is not only more prone to

RENOVATING AN ALPINE BED

1 *Vigorously spreading plants may encroach on smaller neighbours. Dig out, pull up, or trim back in spring, to give nearby plants space to grow.*

2 *Once the bed has been cleared of unwanted growth, add a dressing of balanced fertilizer before replacing a fresh layer of grit or gravel on the surface of the compost around the plants.*

attack by sap-sucking insects, but also less tolerant of winter cold. A sharp surface of top-dressing goes some way to deterring slugs and snails, but some luscious plants like *Campanula zoysii* are still likely to need additional protection.

Insects such as ants can also cause damage, by undermining roots when they build nests beneath cushion-forming plants. It is important to control these nests before extensive colonies become established.

Protection from birds in the form of netting is important for new plantings. Nesting birds in spring are particularly determined to uproot rosettes.

PROPAGATION

Most species of alpine and rock plant can be raised from seed but a few, like the celmisias, may produce infertile seed in cultivation. Some cultivars come true from seed, but most need to be increased vegetatively.

Seed collection

As many alpines flower early in the year, seed is often ripe by mid-summer and may be sown immediately. It usually germinates rapidly, producing strong seedlings before winter. Any autumn-sown seed that germinates immediately should be overwintered in a cold frame.

Collect the ripe seed, taking off the seedhead and its stem. Place in a paper bag to dry and label immediately to avoid confusion. Separate the seeds from their dry capsules by shaking or rubbing them between the fingers. Sieve the seeds clean of debris and seal them in labelled, paper envelopes. Put them in an airtight container and store in a cool place until sowing.

Seed treatments and germination

Scarify hard-coated seeds by chipping or abrading with fine emery paper, or soak in water for 12–24 hours. Most

---

SOWING SEED

1 Fill a pot with a mix of equal parts seed compost and perlite or sharp sand. Firm gently to level and remove air pocket.

2 Using a clean piece of paper folded in half, tap the seed (here, Lewisia) thinly and evenly onto the surface.

3 Cover with a fine layer of sieved seed compost. Top-dress with 5–10mm (¼–½in) layer of grit. Label and water thoroughly.

4 Prick out seedlings when they have 2 true leaves (see inset). Lift gently with a widger, handling only by the leaves.

5 Pot seedlings up singly into pots of equal parts loam-based potting compost and grit. Firm in gently with a dibber.

6 Top-dress seedlings with grit and water, and place in light shade. Pot on or plant out seedlings when the roots fill the pot.

alpine seed needs exposure to cold before it will germinate. The easiest way to effect this is to sow fresh seed in autumn, then plunge the pots in a cold frame in a cool, sheltered site for overwintering. Alternatively, seal the pots in a plastic bag, place in the bottom of a refrigerator for about 3 weeks, then plunge in sand outdoors until germination. A few seeds, such as *Trillium*, need alternating periods of cold and warmth under glass to germinate successfully, while those of primulas and anemones are best sown as soon as ripe and will often germinate within 3–4 weeks.

The speed of germination varies with the age, type, and species of seed, and the time of sowing. Autumn or early spring sowings usually germinate in spring. If they appear before severe weather has passed, move them to a cold frame or cold greenhouse for overwintering. A few seeds, like those of *Ranunculus*, may take several years to germinate, and the slow germinators often do so erratically. In these cases, prick out seedlings as they appear, and keep the pots until more develop.

Softwood and greenwood cuttings

Most rock plants can be raised from these types of cutting. Softwood ones are taken from the tips of non-flowering (vegetative), leafy shoots during active growth or in summer, following shearing back after flowering. Greenwood cuttings are taken in early summer and are slightly riper than softwood ones, but can be treated in the same way.

Cuttings are best taken early in the morning, when shoots are fully turgid. For softwood cuttings, select strong, healthy shoots that are soft and pliable, whereas those just starting to harden at the base suit greenwood cuttings. Cut with a sharp knife and place directly into a plastic bag to conserve moisture and prevent wilting. Prepare and insert cuttings as soon as possible as they will not root well, or at all, if allowed to wilt. Ready-prepared pots

TREATING CUTTINGS

1 *Remove lower leaves and soft tips (here,* Gypsophila repens*). Dip in hormone rooting powder, then insert in a prepared pot of moist cutting compost.*

2 *Water with fungicide, then drain and label. Put pot in a sealed plastic bag and place in good light out of hot sun. root in a propagator with gentle bottom Reat, or in a mist propagation unit.*

3 *When well rooted, water and allow to drain. Separate and pot up singly; hold only by the leaves. Top-dress, water in, and label. Return to the propagator. Harden off when new growth appears.*

BASAL CUTTINGS

*Primula
marginata*

Taking basal cuttings
*In spring, take cuttings 5–7cm (2–3in)
long, with new leaves and a short
stem. Trim the base, remove lower
leaves, and insert to the depth
indicated (see inset).*

Basal cuttings

Some plants, such as *Primula marginata*
and its cultivars, can be propagated by
basal cuttings. These are taken from
young shoots at or just above soil level.
Basal cuttings are usually taken in
spring. If taken in summer or early
autumn, they must be well-rooted in
time for overwintering. Fill pots with
a mix of equal parts proprietary cutting
compost and fine grit. Take 5–7 cm
(2–3in) cuttings (or 2–3cm (⅘–1⅛in) ones
on small alpines), trim the base cleanly
below a node, and remove the lower
leaves. Dip the base in hormone rooting
powder and insert one-half to one-third
of the stem (as shown). Keep the leaves
clear of the soil and of the leaves of
neighbouring cuttings. Water in and root
in a cool, shaded propagator or frame.
When rooted, after about 3–6 weeks,
pot up singly, or line out in a cold frame
or nursery bed to grow on.

Semi-ripe and ripewood cuttings

Plants such as *Cassiope* suit semi-ripe
cuttings, which are taken from non-
flowering shoots of the current year's
growth, just as it begins to harden at
the base. The shoots should offer slight
resistance to pressure when bent gently
between fingers and thumb. Semi-ripe
material is generally ready for taking
between mid- and late summer.
Ripewood cuttings are taken from
evergreen plants, such as *Salix*, during
late summer and autumn when the
current season's growth is fully ripened.

Taking cuttings

Depending on the plant concerned and
available material, cuttings will be about
1–4cm (⅖–1⅗in) long. Cut them from
the parent plant using a sharp knife or
secateurs. Make a clean cut just below a
node and remove soft tips and the lower
leaves before dipping the cutting base in
hormone rooting powder. Alternatively
take the cutting with a heel of older
tissue at the base, and trim it up cleanly
with a sharp knife. Insert small cuttings,
to one-third or one-half of their length,

of 1 part by volume of loam, grit, and
peat help to reduce their exposure time
to open air. Trim to 2.5–7cm (1–3in)
long, cutting just below a node.
Remove lower leaves and any soft tips,
especially if they show signs of wilting.
Using a dibber, make a hole in the
compost and insert cuttings to a depth
of up to half their length, with the lower
leaves just above the surface. Root with
gentle heat from below, in good light,
but out of direct sun to avoid
overheating.

Inspect daily and remove dead or
diseased cuttings with tweezers, since
they will infect healthy ones. Watering
is seldom required until after rooting.
When plants produce new growth,
check for rooting by pulling gently.
When well-rooted, pot up into a mix of
equal parts potting compost and grit.

SELECTING CUTTING MATERIAL

1 Semi-ripe (Phlox)
In mid- to late summer, select non-flowering shoots that are just hardening, but not woody at the base. Remove 3cm (1⅛in) lengths, trimming to about 1cm (⅜in). Insert to the depth indicated (inset left).

2 Ripewood (Dryas)
In late summer and autumn, select the current season's shoots and take cuttings about 2.5cm (1in) long. Trim to about 1cm (⅜in) long, below the base of the leaves. Insert to the depth shown (inset left).

3 Rosette (Saxifraga)
Individual rosettes may be inserted as cuttings during early and mid-summer. With a sharp knife, cut the rosette off at the base, about 1cm (⅜in) below the leaves. Trim cleanly across the base, and insert to the depth shown.

4 Leaf (Sedum)
Throughout the growing season, select young but fully developed leaves that are healthy and undamaged. Cut off and trim cleanly across the base, inserting at an angle of 45 degrees, as shown (insert left).

into dibbled holes in pots of cutting compost topped with a 1cm (⅜in) layer of fine sand. Label each pot, water with fungicide, and root in a propagator in a cool greenhouse. Alternatively, if large numbers of cuttings are taken, they can be rooted in a prepared cold frame with sharp drainage of rubble or gravel at its base. Dig over the soil at the base of the frame, top with a mix of equal parts peat or proprietary cutting compost and grit, and finish with a 2.5cm (1in) layer of sharp sand. After inserting the cuttings, close the frame. Ventilate in warm weather, shade from hot sun, and insulate in periods of frosty weather. Check frequently for disease, and remove diseased material and fallen leaves regularly. Water sparingly, keeping the compost just moist.

As growth begins, apply a half-strength, balanced liquid fertilizer. The cuttings, whether in a cold frame or propagator, should be well rooted by the following spring. Pot up singly into a mix of equal parts potting compost and grit or, when danger of frost has passed, harden off and transfer to a nursery bed. Grow on, keeping the rooted cuttings

moist, shaded from hot sun, and apply a balanced liquid fertilizer occasionally during the growing season. Transfer the new plants to their permanent positions in autumn, or the following spring.

Leaf cuttings
Several plants with fleshy leaves, such as *Haberlea*, *Lewisia*, *Ramonda*, or *Sedum* species, are suitable for leaf cuttings. Cut mature young leaves from the parent stem or rosette at their base with a sharp knife. Root the cuttings in pots filled with a mix of equal parts standard cutting compost and sharp sand. Trim the leaf base cleanly and insert at an angle of 45°, just sufficiently deep to be held in place in the compost. Enclose in a plastic bag. When the new plantlet appears from the leaf base at soil level, pot it up singly and grow on.

Irishman's cuttings
Dianthus and species, and other stem-rooting or creeping species, frequently produce ready-rooted sideshoots. These can be removed from the parent clump and potted up, or transferred to a nursery bed for growing on.

"Irishmans" Cuttings

1 *Lift the rooted shoots at the margins of the mat, close to the base of the plant (here,* Veronica*) and remove them with a sharp knife. Trim off any sideshoots and straggly roots (see inset).*

2 *Pot up the cuttings individually into a small pot of gritty compost. Firm gently, water and top-dress with grit. Grow on in a cold frame and plant out when the root system is well established.*

Division

Many alpines can be propagated by division. The technique is essentially the same as that used for herbaceous border perennials, but on a much smaller scale. The most suitable species are those that are mat-forming with fibrous roots, and clump-forming species that produce clusters of shoots that are easily separated. Division is also used to rejuvenate clump-forming species when they lose vigour or die out at the centre.

When to divide

Most plants are best divided in early spring, as new growth begins. Many can also be divided in autumn, and will form a new root system while the soil is still warm. In areas with very cold winters, however, it may be safer to divide in spring immediately after flowering. Do not divide plants in cold, wet conditions, or in freezing weather. A few plants, like primulas and *Meconopsis*, are divided after flowering when they begin a period of strong vegetative growth.

How to divide

Lift plants, shaking loose soil from the roots. Large clumps can be divided using back-to-back forks or, for smaller scale plants, back-to-back handforks. Lever the plant into two halves, making sure that each division has a healthy clump of roots and growth buds, then tease out by hand into smaller pieces. For best results, re-plant immediately into holes that are large enough to accommodate the rootball without restriction. Firm in and water well. Keep the soil moist until the plants are well established.

With small or precious plants, pot up smaller divisions to grow on in a cold frame in shade until they are well established. A mix of loam-based potting compost and grit is best for this method, or use an ericaceous mix for lime-hating plants.

If immediate re-planting is not possible, wrap the divisions in moist sacking or plastic to prevent them from drying out until they can be dealt with.

PROPAGATING BY DIVISION

1 *Fibrous-rooted plants, (here, Gentiana acaulis) can be divided to produce new plants. Lift a clump of the parent plant and shake off loose soil.*

2 *Tease the clump apart using back-to-back handforks, then separate into smaller pieces by hand. If necessary, cut through tough roots with a sharp knife.*

3 *Re-plant pieces with a good root system and growth buds, setting directly into their permanent site. Make a hole big enough to accommodate the roots. Firm and water in with a fine rose.*

Root cuttings

A limited number of rock plants and alpines, including *Anchusa caespitosa* and *Pulsatilla* species, can be increased by root cuttings. These should be taken when the plants are dormant in late autumn or winter. Select a strong healthy parent and lift it from the soil. Choosing the plumpest healthy roots, cut them off from the parent plant and section them into pieces about 5cm (2in) long. Make a straight cut at the top end (that is, the end nearest the parent crown) and a slanting cut at the bottom end to ensure that they are inserted the right way up. Wash the cuttings in tepid water. Re-plant the parent. Insert the cuttings in pots at least 10cm (4in) deep. Place a layer of crocks in the bottom of the pot, topped with a 2.5cm (1in) layer of loam-based potting compost, then fill with washed sand and firm. Insert the roots, right way up, into dibbled holes around the edge of the pot, aligning the straight-cut edge with the sand surface. Plants with slender or wiry roots should be laid flat on the sand surface. Top-dress with grit, label, and water the cutting in. Place in a cold frame on a layer of grit or gravel, or in a propagator. Keep well-ventilated, but close the frames in periods of cold weather. Do not water again until new shoots appear.

When new shoots are showing strong growth, check that they have rooted fully by sliding them very gently out of their pots. If well-rooted, pot them up singly in a mix of loam-based potting

HOW TO PROPAGATE BY ROOT CUTTINGS

1 *In late autumn or early winter, use a hand fork to lift a plant with a well-developed root system (here, Primula denticulata).*

2 *Wash soil from the roots then select the thickest healthy roots for cuttings. Cut off with a sharp knife close to the crown of the parent plant.*

3 *Cut into 5cm (2in) sections, with a straight cut at the end closest to the parent plant and a sloping cut at the lower end.*

4 *Over a layer of crocks and compost, fill the pot with sharp sand. Insert cuttings with the straight end level with the surface.*

5 *Cover with a 1cm (⅜in) layer of grit, water thoroughly, allow to drain, then place the pot in a propagator.*

compost and sharp sand. Top-dress the pots with a layer of grit and water well. Set the pots in a sheltered place outdoors, with shade from direct sun, or in an open frame. Grow on until they are well established and the roots fill the pots, then plant out into their permanent flowering site. If they are not ready for planting by late summer, leave them in pots until the following spring.

Scooping rosettes

Robust and rapid-growing species of rosette-forming plants, like *Primula denticulata*, can be propagated by scooping their rosettes in mid-winter. This is essentially a modification of root cuttings that is practiced on plants *in situ*. Some growers consider this technique to be rather risky, since plants *in situ* are exposed to the worst of the weather as well as soil-borne fungi and other pests. Nevertheless, it is a suitable method for increasing robust, hardy species like *P. denticulata*, and is a useful technique for producing a particularly good colour form that has appeared in a group of seed-raised plants.

The rosettes are scooped out with a sharp knife to expose the top of the rootstock, thereby stimulating the production of multiple rosettes at their apex. Select strong-growing rosettes and brush the cut top of the root with fungicidal powder to prevent grey mould (*Botrytis*). Cover the cut tops with a thin layer of sharp horticultural sand.

Shoots should soon appear on each root apex. When they reach about 2.5–5cm (1–2in) tall, lift the whole clump and and tease it apart into individual plantlets, with each bearing vigorous, healthy roots and shoots. Use a sharp knife for separating the clump, if necessary, rather than risk damaging the plantlets.

Pot up the young plants into a mix of equal parts potting compost and sharp sand. Water thoroughly, and grow on in a sheltered site outdoors, shaded from direct sun. Keep moist and plant out when the roots have filled the pots.

HOW TO SCOOP ROSETTES

1 *Scoop out the live crowns of a robust rosette-forming plant, (here,* Primula denticulata*) with a sharp knife, so that the tops of the roots are visible (see inset).*

2 *Dust the cut surfaces with fungicide to discourage mould and fungal infections. Then cover the exposed surfaces with a thin layer of sharp horticultural sand.*

3 *When new shoots reach 2.5–5cm (1–2in) high, carefully lift the whole clump with a handfork or trowel Separate into individual plants and pot up to grow on.*

ALPINE HOUSES AND FRAMES

For gardeners wishing to grow alpine plants that are unable to withstand the variable conditions of low-altitude, temperate climates, an alpine house provides the ideal solution.

Using the alpine house and frames
An alpine house is an unheated, well-ventilated greenhouse used for growing and displaying alpines and small bulbs. The alpine house is not designed to keep plants warm and must always have maximum ventilation. Vents need be closed only during prolonged freezing or foggy, humid conditions in winter.

To reduce temperatures in the hottest months, an alpine house should have a hard floor for damping down and the facility for shading in summer. Electric fans can also help by ensuring good air flow. When used in conjunction with nearby frames (which can be used as an "overspill" area for plants that are not in flower), the alpine house offer cool fresh air and low temperatures in summer, without the rapid rise in temperatures experienced under glass.

Plants are usually grown in pots plunged in a sand bed on a raised bench to reduce changes in temperature and to keep the roots cool and moist. A plunge bench also allows easy irrigation of plants that dislike overhead watering. Growing alpines in pots ensures that special watering, compost or feeding requirements can be provided for individual plants. Plastic pots can be used, although clay ones stay cool in sand and are more attractive for display.

Composts
All alpines need freely drained compost and benefit from a layer of crocks in the bottom of clay pots, or grit in plastic ones. Many will thrive in a mix of equal parts loam-based potting compost and grit; or a mix of equal parts sterilized loam, leaf-mould, and grit. High-growing alpines need a less fertile compost and prefer a mix of equal parts loam and leaf-mould, with 2–3 parts grit or stone chips. For acid-loving plants, provide a mix made up of 4 parts lime-free leaf-mould, and 1 part each of lime-free loam and sharp sand. Top-dress pots with a layer of grit, or limestone chips for lime-loving plants, and acid, granitic grit on sandstone, or granulated bark for lime-hating plants. Some of the very moisture-sensitive cushion-formers can be propped up with an additional layer of small stones.

CARE OF ALPINES AFTER FLOWERING

Alpines indoors
After flowering, alpines (here, Dionysia*) needing careful watering should be plunged under cover.*

Alpines outdoors
Alpines tolerant of variable summer weather can be plunged in an open frame outdoors after flowering.

Protecting alpines in frames
Alpines grown in frames can be displayed in full flower in the alpine house.

REPOTTING A SAXIFRAGE

1 When a plant has become pot-bound, transfer it to a larger pot with minimum disturbance to the rootball.

2 Choose a pot that is one size larger than the existing pot. Use crocks and grit at the base to provide drainage.

3 Cover the drainage hole with crocks, then cover the crocks with gravel. This will also prevent compost. from blocking the hole.

4 Remove the plant from its pot by tapping gently on the base to loosen the root ball. Tease out the roots carefully.

5 Cover crocks with a little compost, position the plant with its neck at the same level as in the original pot. Top up with compost.

6 Spread grit or rock chippings over the surface and tuck it under the collar of the plant to keep it moisture-free.

7 Place the pot up to its neck in a bowl of water and leave it until the surface of the compost and gravel appears damp.

8 Remove the pot and place it on a layer of sand in an open frame, where excess moisture can drain away easily.

9 The repotted plant can then be plunged in sand in a plunge frame or bed in the alpine house to re-establish and grow on.

GLOSSARY OF TERMS

Italicized words have their own entry.

ACID [of soil] With a *pH* value of less than 7; see also *alkaline* and *neutral*.

ALKALINE [of soil] With a *pH* value of more than 7; some plants will not tolerate alkaline soils and must be grown in soil that is *neutral* or *acid*.

ALPINE HOUSE An unheated greenhouse, used for the cultivation of mainly alpine plants. An alpine house provides greater ventilation and usually more light than a conventional greenhouse.

ALTERNATE [of leaves] Borne singly at each node, on either side of a *stem*.

AXIL The angle between a leaf and *stem* where an axillary bud develops.

BLOOM 1. A flower or blossom. 2. A fine, waxy, whitish or bluish-white coating found on *stems*, leaves, or fruits.

BRACT A modified leaf at the base of a *flower* or flower cluster. Bracts may resemble normal leaves or can be reduced and scale-like in appearance; they are often large and brightly coloured.

BUD A rudimentary or condensed *shoot* containing embryonic leaves or *flowers*.

CALYX (pl. calyces) The outer part of a *flower*, usually small and green but sometimes showy and brightly coloured, that encloses the *petals* in *bud* and is formed from the sepals.

CAPSULE A dry fruit that splits open when ripe to release its *seeds*.

COROLLA 1. Collective name for *petals*. 2. Inner *whorl* of *perianth segments* in some monocotyledons.

COTYLEDON A seed leaf; the first leaf or leaves to emerge from the seed after germination.

CROWN The part of the plant at or just below the soil surface from which new shoots are produced and to which they die back in autumn.

CUTTING A section of a plant that is removed and used for propagation. For the various methods, see pp. 168–175.

CULTIVAR (CV) A contraction of "cultivated variety"; a group (or one among such a group) comprising cultivated plants that are clearly distinguished by one or more characteristics which are retained when propagation is performed.

DEAD-HEAD To remove spent *flower heads* so as to promote further growth or flowering, prevent seeding, or improve appearance.

DECIDUOUS Losing its leaves annually at the end of the growing season.

DIE-BACK Death of the tips of shoots due to frost or disease.

DISC FLORET, DISC FLOWER A small and often individually inconspicuous, usually tubular *flower*, often making the central portion of a composite *flower head*, such as a daisy.

DIVISION A method of propagation by which a clump is divided into several parts during *dormancy*.

DORMANCY The state of temporary cessation of growth and slowing down of other activities in whole plants, usually during winter.

ELLIPTIC [of leaves] Broadening in the centre and narrowing towards each end.

ENTIRE [of leaves] With untoothed margins.

EVERGREEN Retaining its leaves at the end of the growing season, but losing some older leaves during the year. **Semi-evergreen** plants retain some leaves or lose older ones only when the new growth is produced.

EYE The centre of a *flower*, of particular note if different in colour from the *petals*.

FLORET A single *flower* in a head of many flowers.

FLOWER The part of the plant containing the reproductive organs usally surrounded by sepals and *petals*.

FLOWER HEAD A mass of small *flowers* or *florets* that, together, appear to form a single flower.

GENUS (pl. genera) A category in plant classification, consisting of a group of related *species*.

HABIT The characteristic growth or general appearance of a plant.

HARDY Able to withstand year-round climatic conditions without protection.

HERBACEOUS Dying down at the end of the growing season.

HYBRID The offspring of genetically different parents, usually produced accidentally or artificially in cultivation, but occasionally arising in the wild.

LAYERING A propagation method whereby a *stem* is induced to root by being pegged down in the soil while still attached to the parent plant.

LEAF-MOULD Fibrous, flaky material derived from decomposed leaves, used as a soil improver.

LIME Compounds of calcium, the amount of lime in the soil determines whether it is *acid*, *neutral*, or *alkaline*.

LINEAR [of leaves] Very narrow with parallel sides.

LOAM Well-structured, fertile soil that is moisture-retentive but free-draining.

MULCH A layer of organic matter applied to the soil over or around a plant to conserve moisture, protect the *roots* from frost, reduce the growth of weeds, and enrich the soil.

NATURALIZE To establish and grow as if in the wild.

NEUTRAL [of soil] With a *pH* value of 7, the point at which soil is neither *acid* nor *alkaline*.

PERENNIAL Living for at least 3 seasons. A woody-based perennial dies down only partially, leaving a woody stem at the base.

PERIANTH The outer part of the *flower* comprising the calyx and the corolla. Often used when the *calyx* and the *corolla* are very similar in form.

PERIANTH SEGMENT One portion of the *perianth*, resembling a *petal* and sometimes known as a tepal.

PETAL One portion of the usually showy and coloured part of the *corolla*.

PETIOLE The stalk of a leaf.

pH The scale by which the acidity or alkalinity of soil is measured. See also *acid*, *alkaline*, and *neutral*.

PROSTRATE With *stems* growing along the ground.

RAY PETAL The *petal* or fused petals, often showy, of a *ray flower*.

RECURVED Applied to *petals* of *flowers* and florets that curve backwards.

REFLEXED Applied to *petals* that are bent backwards at an angle of more than 90°. Also referred to as fully reflexed.

ROOT The part of a plant, normally underground, that functions as anchorage and through which water and nutrients are absorbed.

ROSETTE A group of leaves that radiate from about the same point, often borne at ground level at the base of a very short *stem*.

RUNNER A horizontally spreading, usually slender *stem*, that forms *roots* at each *node*, often confused with *stolon*.

SCALE A reduced or modified leaf.

SEED The ripened, fertilized ovule containing a dormant embryo capable of developing into an adult plant.

SEEDHEAD Any usually dry fruit that contains ripe seeds.

SEEDLING A young plant that has developed from a *seed*.

SELF-SEED To produce *seedlings* around the parent plant.

SEPAL Part of a *calyx*, usually insignificant, but sometimes showy and *petal*-like.

SHOOT The aerial part of a plant which bears leaves.

SIMPLE [of leaves] Not divided into leaflets.

SINGLE A flower with the normal number of petals or tepals for the species, arranged in a single whorl. Also applied to (composite) flowerheads that have a single row of outer ray florets with the centre filled with disc-florets.

SOLITARY Flower borne singly rather than in an inflorescence.

SPATHE One, or sometimes two, large *bracts* that surround a flower cluster or individual *bud*.

SPECIES A category in plant classification, the rank below *genus*, containing closely related, very similar individual plants.

SPRAY A group of *flowers* or *flower heads* on a single, branching stem.

SPUR A hollow projection from a *petal*, that often produces nectar.

STAMEN The male reproductive organ in a plant, comprising the *anther* and usually its *filament* or *stalk*.

STEM The main axis of a plant, usually above ground and supporting leaves, *flowers*, and fruits. Sometimes referred to as a stalk.

STERILE Infertile, not bearing spores, pollen, or *seeds*.

STIGMA The part of the female portion of the *flower*, borne at the tip of the *style*, that receives pollen.

STOLON A horizontally spreading or arching *stem*, usually above ground, which roots at its tip to produce a new plant.

STYLE The part of the *flower* on which the *stigma* is borne.

SUB-SHRUB A plant that is woody at the base although the terminal shoots die back in winter.

TOOTH A small, marginal, often pointed lobe on a *leaf*, *calyx*, or *corolla*.

TENDER Of a plant that is vulnerable to frost damage.

TRUE [of seedlings] Retaining the distinctive characteristics of the parent when raised from *seed*.

UPRIGHT [of habit] With vertical or semi-vertical main branches.

WHORL The arrangement of 3 or more organs arising from one point.

INDEX

Each genus name is shown in **bold** type, followed by a brief description. Species, varieties and subspecies are given in *italics;* cultivars are in roman type with single quotes. Common names appear in brackets.

A

Acantholimon
Fully hardy, evergreen perennials, grown for their flowers and tight cushions of spiny leaves.
glumaceum 114

Aethionema
Fully hardy, short-lived shrubs, sub-shrubs, and perennials, grown for their prolific, often fragrant, flowers.
armenum 114
grandiflorum
(Persian stone cress) 36
pulchellum see
A. grandiflorum
'Warley Rose' 112

Alchemilla
(Lady's mantle)
Fully hardy perennials, bearing sprays of tiny flowers in summer.
alpina (Alpine lady's mantle) 56

Alpine bells see
Cortusa matthioli
Alpine clematis see
Clematis alpina
Alpine catchfly see
Lychnis alpina
Alpine columbine see
Aquilega alpina
Alpine fleabane see
Erigeron alpinus
Alpine lady's mantle see
Alchemilla alpina
Alpine pasque flower see
Pulsatilla alpina
Alpine poppy see
Papaver alpina

Alyssum
Fully hardy perennials, grown for their small, yellow flowers in early summer.
montanum (Mountain alison) 58
saxatile 'Citrina' see
Aurinia saxatilis 'Citrina'
'Dudley Nevill' see *Aurinia saxatilis* 'Dudley Nevill'
wulfenianum 139

Anacyclus
Frost-hardy, summer-flowering, prostrate perennials, bearing daisy-like flowers in summer.
depressus see
A. pyrethrum var. *depressus*
pyrethrum var. *depressus* 102

Anagallis (Pimpernel)
Fully to frost-hardy annuals and creeping perennials, grown for their bell- to open saucer-shaped flowers.
tenella 'Studland' 77

Anchusa
Fully to frost-hardy annuals, biennials and perennials, with usually blue flowers.
caespitosa see A. cespitosa
cespitosa 89

Andromeda
(Bog rosemary)
Fully hardy, evergreen shrubs, grown for their small, urn-shaped flowers in spring and early summer
polifolia 'Alba' 18
'Compacta' 23
'Compacta Alba' see
A. polifolia 'Alba'

Androsace
(Rock jasmine)
Fully to frost-hardy annuals and perennials, grown for their cushions of small, hairy leaves and tubular-based flowers.
carnea (Pink rock jasmine) 79
subsp. *laggeri* 79
jacquemontii see
A. villosa var. *jacquemontii*

Androsace continued
laggeri see
A. carnea subsp. *laggeri*
lanuginosa 79
sarmentosa 79
villosa 79
var. *jacquemontii* 79

Anemone (Windflower)
Fully to frost-hardy perennials, with shallowly cup-shaped flowers in spring.
apennina 135
blanda [blue form] 135
'Atrocaerulea' 135
'Radar' 134
'White Splendour' 134
hepatica see *Hepatica nobilis*
hortensis 135
x *lipsiensis* 134
magellanica see *A. multifida*
multifida 134
nemorosa 'Bracteata Pleniflora' 134
'Robinsoniana' 135
pavonina 134
ranunculoides 135
'Flore Pleno' see 'Pleniflora'
'Pleniflora' 135
x *seemannii* see *A.* x *lipsiensis*
trullifolia 135

Anemonella
Fully hardy, tuberous perennial, grown for its fragile flowers in spring and early summer.
thalictroides (Rue anemone) 72

Antennaria
Fully hardy, evergreen or semi-evergreen perennials, grown for their "everlasting" flower heads and woolly leaves.
dioica 'Rosea' (Cat's ears, Pussy-toes) 78

Anthyllis
Frost-hardy, rounded, bushy perennials, grown for their flowers and divided leaves.
montana 37

Aquilegia (Columbine)
Fully to frost-hardy perennials, grown for their spurred flowers borne in spring and summer.

B

ACKNOWLEDGMENTS

Key: t=top; b=bottom; r=right; l=left; c=centre; cra=centre right above;
cla=centre left above; crb=centre right below; clb=centre left below

The publishers would like to thank the following for their
kind permission to reproduce the photographs:

Alpine Garden Society 29, 52tr, 99br, 117tl, 139bl, 147cr;
A-Z Botanical Collection 32br, 44l, 83t, 100br, 138tr,/
Derek Gould 135crb/**Jiri Loun** 113l, **J Malcolm Smith** 51bl;
Gillian Beckett 25tr, 84tl, 94tr, 97b, 98cr, 102tr & bl, 124cl, 126bl, 127br, 132tl;
Kenneth A Beckett 76bl, 84bl; **Deni Bown** 46br; **Neil Campbell-Sharpe** 2;
Eric Crichton 10, 4ltl, 54br, 56br, 87tl, 103bl, 127tr, 128tl, 143tr;
Geoff Dann 15tr; **Garden Matters** 81bl; **Garden Picture Library** 14, /
Brian Carter 120cr,/**David England** 7,/**Vaughan Fleming** 74tl,/
Jerry Pavia 123br; **John Glover** 88, 135tr, 147tl; **Derek Gould** 22tl, 141tr;
Chris Grey-Wilson 50tl, 53, 95br, 100tl, 146br; **Jerry Harpur** 13;
Muriel Hodgman 131bl; **Mike Ireland** 77r, 145br;
Andrew Lawson 28l, 30tl, 72bl, 104tl, 135bl, 145tl;
Photos Horticultural 27, 33tr, 47cr, 56bl, 58bl, 59l, 68bl, 91, 128tr, 154bl;
Howard Rice 47br; **Eric Sawford** 144br; **Harry Smith Collection** 28tr, 30tr,
33bl, 38tl & r, 49bl, 51r, 54tl, 61bl, 63tl, 65tl, 67bl, 74bl & br, 85bl, 87br, 90tl & br,
92bl, 94tl, 95tr, 105tr, 110bl, 118cr, 119cr, 123cr, 124t & bl, 125tr, 127tl, 128bl,
135tl, 141br, 147cl, 148bl, 153r; **Elizabeth Whiting & Associates** 11.

Special photography Howard Rice

In addition to the above, the publishers would also like to thank
the staff of the Royal Horticultural Society Publications.

Abbreviations

C	centigrade	in	inch, inches
cm	centimetre	m	metre
cv.	cultivar	mm	millimetre
F	Fahrenheit	oz	ounce
f.	forma	sp.	species
ft	foot, feet	subsp.	subspecies
g	gramme	var.	variant